I0176255

TRAIN YOUR BRAIN
FOR
SUCCESS

What others are saying...

What a noble book. Coach Sharon is dedicated to helping the reader lead a happier and more fulfilling life. She starts with the wisdom of ages that points the way. Then she creates a beautiful recipe for changing your life and getting you there. It is a delicious, readily consumed dish combining psychology, neuroscience, and philosophy with proven techniques of motivation. And your digestion is smooth and easy thanks to her methods. When you finish this banquet, you'll be a happier person. All you need is the desire to indulge.
~Billionaire Businessman

It's so easy for one day to become a week, a month, a couple of years—a regret. Through *Train Your Brain for Success*, Coach Sharon gives the tools to reset your objectives and act on them in a purposeful, productive and easy to follow manner.
~Chris W., People Magazine "50 Most Beautiful People," Dalai Lama's Unsung Hero of Compassion, Skiing Magazine "25 Greatest Skiers in North America," Thirteen Paralympic Medals, Paralympic Hall of Fame, US Ski and Snowboard Hall of Fame, Founder of One Revolution Foundation

The principles Coach Sharon shares in *Train Your Brain for Success* will help the reader learn the most important issues of mind mastery: taking false thoughts captive, and replacing them with the truth. As a man thinketh in his heart, so is he, Proverbs tells us. For the reader who reads this book repeatedly, and is not just a hearer but a practitioner of the principles, nothing will be impossible for them through the magic of mental training.
~Richard R., Hollywood Movie Producer, Radio Host, Author, Actor, Musician, California

Coach Sharon has created through *Train Your Brain for Success* an invaluable tool for coaches and counselors alike who are looking for a structured, step-by-step approach to motivating clients while helping them to develop a meaningful and achievable life plan. Accessible, timely, and fun—this is a must have for any professional who is in the business of helping clients realize purposeful change and fulfillment.
~Angela P., M.A., Clinical Mental Health Counselor, Utah

I am so pleased with all that Coach Sharon has tied together: organization, visualization, gratitude, emotional intelligence, spirituality, SMART goals. I have read about and worked with many of these aspects of life and work, and she synthesized them so well. Coach Sharon's caring attitude lines every page of the book. Anyone reading *Train Your Brain for Success* would feel how much she wants them to succeed.
~Elizabeth P., Educational Speaker and Trainer, Massachusetts

Being a small business owner is rewarding, exciting, and a little terrifying! Setting goals and using a positive mental attitude has been crucial to dispel my fears and has greatly contributed to my personal and professional development. Coach Sharon helps guide you through effective goal setting and ultimately laying a strong foundation from which you can build the life you love. Whether you are looking for personal or professional growth, *Train your Brain for Success* will help you get started and guide you through a journey of EMPOWERMENT! I'm confident that you will see remarkable change in your life and will create a life you love by following this workbook!
~Jennifer B., Small Business Owner, Washington

Train Your Brain for Success is a detailed guide for creating abundance in your life. This brain boot camp will teach how changing your thoughts will help you achieve your goals. Coach Sharon has an enthusiasm and genuine love for life that is contagious! The push to set goals, and truly envision them coming true has been invaluable. Follow the daily activities and watch your dreams come true—if you can visualize it, it is possible!
~Keri G., Health and Fitness Coach, California

WOW! This *Train Your Brain for Success* workbook is very much inspired and inspiring! I wish I had this when I was a young mother. I believe many will be blessed and freed by completing this 30-day boot camp. Principles of a fulfilling life!
~Zee B., Virginia

What I love most about *Train Your Brain for Success* is that it is not just your typical self-help book or a book that you read and quickly forget about. It is a literal tool—a workbook, an interactive training program—that requires you to think through the patterns of your life right there and then, instead of doing what we so often do: put it off until "tomorrow." This workbook will propel you forward, driving you to start making the change today. It literally has the power to change the course of your life. As I read through each segment of the book, I found myself challenged and eagerly wanting to change the rhythm of my life. The relevant and applicable tools in this book are so profound in helping you focus your life in a world filled with distractions. If you dare to do more than just read this book, if you dare to work through it, I am confident that you will have a different life after 30 days.
~Miriam F., NYC, New York

If you're ready for positive change in your life, this *Train Your Brain for Success* boot camp is for you! I was surprised how easily Coach Sharon helped me to realize my deepest goals and how to create realistic steps to achieve them. It is truly astounding how simple steps made such a profound difference in my life—even after just one week! I am beyond thrilled at the changes I've seen in my life!
~Laura R., Virginia

There are so many reasons I love this *Train Your Brain for Success* workbook. To start with, it really works! This is an excellent manual that teaches you about the most important lesson in life: that it is never too late to make your dreams come true. It empowers you with strength, optimism, curiosity and initiative. It is very easy to read and simple to understand, entertaining, realistic and charming. I truly believe if you read it once, or twice, or as many times as you need, and start living these principles, your life will change for the better!
~Gabriella K., New Hampshire

Train Your Brain for Success was literally the catapult to my regrouping after facing overwhelm and post-partum depression from two small children and sandwich generation care-giving realizations, all with a career and a husband who works shift work. I was precisely at my wits end and knew that I needed to rethink things and change my approach. I was full of self-doubt and was dangerously seeking help in the wrong ways. This workbook literally changed my life, and I am so thankful to God for His divine timing. Once you pick up this book, you really cannot put it down. If you stick to it, the positive change is unavoidable. It has already helped me to prepare, organize and launch a dream I have struggled with for years! I am so full of joy and so ready to take on my future while leaving plenty of time to live present in the now!
~Dawn K., Maryland

Train Your Brain for Success contains the perfect mix of goal work and reward to motivate me to success. This program is worth reviewing and repeating as new goals and situations arise in my life. With Coach Sharon's method, reaching goals is obtainable for even the busiest person.
 ~**Kendra T., Virginia**

The principles of *Train Your Brain for Success* are the foundation to finding true success in your own life. If you are ready to be set free from your self-limiting mindsets and beliefs and to step into the world of personal potential, let Coach Sharon teach you and push you to do more, to be more and to have more.
~**Lance K., Boston, Massachusetts**

The greatest gift anyone could ever give you is a new mindset—one that allows you to live out your potential and be who you were created to be. Through *Train Your Brain for Success*, Coach Sharon teaches you how to literally reprogram your mind toward positivity, happiness and abundance so that success can't help but come to you!
~**Anna B., Florida**

Both insightful and informative, *Train Your Brain for Success* programs your life for success through practical and systematic steps that not only help you to choose your path for success in life but to actually make it happen. In our world today with so many broken homes and its negative effects on children, it is critical that we be intentional on training ourselves and the next generation for happiness and success!
~**Jennifer R., Virginia**

Let Coach Sharon literally retrain your brain to realize and unleash the success that you are designed to be. You will be glad, and your loved ones will be glad too."
 ~**Josh C., Washington D.C.**

Train Your Brain for Success is a BRILLANT book that offers proven tactics to help re-wire the way you think with a lot of encouragement along the way to help you stay on track.
~**Stephanie G., New Hampshire**

Mindset is everything. I've owned successful franchises as well as been in the home-based business industry for over a decade. And here's one thing I know for sure—having the right "tool" (business plan, product, marketing, etc.), but the wrong mindset will take you somewhere, but it won't be in the direction you want to go. Mindset IS your greatest tool. It's why Napoleon Hill's book cover says, "THINK and Grow Rich." It's why the Bible says, "As a man thinks, so is he," and so on. Let averages be for stats, not your state of being. Your mindset IS your state of being. If you want to break out of "average" and reach higher levels of success, *Train Your Brain for Success* has golden nuggets that will help you begin to shift your momentum in the direction you want, need and deserve to take your life.
~**Lukeus C., North Carolina**

Train Your Brain for Success is an amazing tool to go forward in the dreams and vision that God has placed in your heart. I think of the scripture verse Romans 12:2 "And be not conformed to this world: but be ye transformed by the renewing of your mind, that you may prove what is good and acceptable and perfect will of God." This coaching book will give you the techniques through charts, setting goals, tasks, and many other valuable tools to change your thinking process to successfully do and become who you were created to be.
~**Maria L., Virginia**

TRAIN YOUR BRAIN

FOR

SUCCESS

WORKBOOK FORMAT

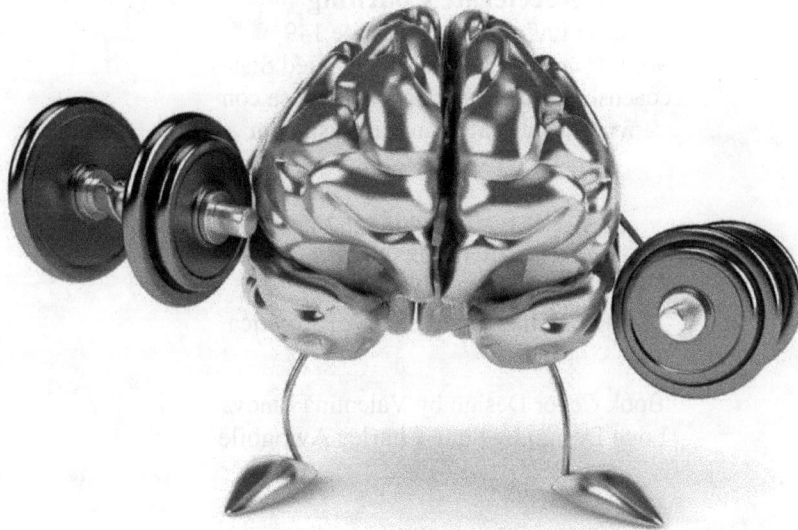

A 30-DAY BOOT CAMP
TO TRAIN YOUR CONSCIOUS AND SUBCONSCIOUS MIND FOR
HAPPINESS, ABUNDANCE, AND SUCCESS

Life and Career Coach
Sharon Minard, M.A.

Copyright © 2017 by Sharon Minard

All rights reserved. No part of this publication may be reproduced, distributed, or transmitted in any form or by any means, including photocopying, recording, or other electronic or mechanical methods, without the prior written permission of the publisher, except in the case of brief quotations embodied in critical reviews and certain other noncommercial uses permitted by copyright law. By honoring copyright laws, you support the hard work of writers around the world.

Counselors, Coaches, Teachers and Pastors may use exercises in this book with clients, students and church members as long as credit is given to the author, book and cited research.

Ordering Information:
Special discounts are available on bulk purchases by corporations, associations, churches, educational institutions and others. For details, contact the publisher at the address or web address below.

Accelerate Coaching
45 Lafayette Road, Suite 149
North Hampton, NH, 03862, United States
coachsharon@acceleratecoachingusa.com
www.acceleratecoaching-usa.com

ISBN-13: 978-0-9985867-0-0
ISBN-10: 0-9985867-0-6

Printed in the United States of America

Book Cover Design by Valentina Pinova
Logo Design by Shay Charles Awogbile

While the author has made best efforts to determine the source of all quotes contained herein, when a quote is commonly attributed to two or more people, the author has not included a definitive source.

This publication is designed to provide accurate and authoritative information in regard to the subject matter covered. However, neither the author nor the publisher assumes responsibility for any errors or omissions. The author and publisher specifically disclaim any liability resulting from the use or application of the information contained in this book. This publication is sold with the understanding that the author and publisher are not engaged in rendering legal, financial, accounting, medical or psychiatric services. If you require legal advice or other expert services, please seek the services of a competent professional.

About the Author

Sharon Minard is a certified professional Life and Career Coach and founder of Accelerate Coaching which is based out of the greater Boston area. She specializes in personal and professional growth with a goal of helping individuals to achieve their God-given potential.

Formerly, Sharon served as Director of Career Services for Liberty University, the largest non-profit university in the United States. As Career Director, she helped thousands of students realize their natural abilities, talents, skills, interests and personality type; and then directed them into appropriate and fulfilling careers. Sharon communicated through individual counseling sessions as well as large audience presentations on such topics as: choosing a major, personality and skills evaluations, resume and cover letter writing, interview preparation, and success in the workplace. She also worked with alumni who were in career transition. She loved seeing lives changed by taking simple but deliberate steps.

Sharon has now broadened her focus to professional Life Coaching in order to cultivate change in individuals at a much deeper level. She has a Master's degree in Counseling and Life Coaching. She was also trained and certified at the Fowler International Academy of Professional Coaching. In addition, Sharon has received Leadership and Healthcare Coach Training through the Institute of Coaching at Harvard Medical School. Sharon also routinely attends life coaching conferences and studies cutting-edge research to improve her knowledge and techniques.

As a collaborative, holistic, solution-focused Life and Career Coach, Sharon looks at your life as an interconnected whole, not just bits and pieces. Using proven techniques from psychology, neuroscience and life coaching, she will help you to literally rewire your mind for success so that you can create a more positive, productive and happier you. Her program took years of research and client application to refine and make it as effective possible. Stick with her program, and you will find the success you desire as you create a life you LOVE!

Certified Professional Life & Career Coach
M.A. Counseling & Life Coaching, Liberty University
B.A. Education & Theatre Performance, Lynchburg College
Leadership & Healthcare Coach Training, Institute of Coaching at Harvard Medical School
Happy Wife & Mom of Four

DISCLAIMER:

Sharon Minard is not a licensed medical physician, legal advisor, financial consultant or psychiatrist. If you suffer from severe mental, emotional or physical trauma, please seek professional help from a mental health provider before beginning this program. If you require legal advice or other expert services, please seek the services of a competent professional.
No results are guaranteed from this program.

Some days I literally want to pinch myself!

I just can't believe how happy I am. I can't believe the life I now have. I am so incredibly blessed! I absolutely LOVE MY LIFE!

These are thoughts that cross my mind daily.

Do I have a perfect life? Do I have a perfect marriage, perfect kids and a perfect house? Do I have a perfect body, personality and intelligence level? Do I never make mistakes or face obstacles or hard times?

ABSOLUTELY NOT!

So why am I the happiest I've ever been in my entire life?

It is because I have trained my brain to think this way, and my life has transformed in the process. Follow me on a journey where you will learn the true secrets of happiness, abundance and success.
The Best is Yet to Come!

Love, Peace & Joy,

Coach Sharon

Contents

Introduction

Congratulations! You have come to the right place if you feel like you are...

- ✓ **STUCK** in life as you can't seem to reach the next level of success.
- ✓ Going in **CIRCLES** as you keep repeating the same circumstances.
- ✓ Unable to fully tap into your **PURPOSE** and God-given **POTENTIAL**.
- ✓ Frequently finding yourself **UNFOCUSED, UNMOTIVATED** or **UNHAPPY**.
- ✓ Repeatedly attracting the **WRONG KINDS OF PEOPLE** or **CLIENTS** into your life.
- ✓ Regularly facing **OBSTACLES** that leave you **DISCOURAGED** and **DEFEATED**.
- ✓ Never able to obtain and hold onto to the true **SUCCESS, WEALTH, ABUNDANCE** and **HAPPINESS** that you desire and deserve.

AND I have even better news! This brain boot camp is not only going to improve your life—it is going to completely **TRANSFORM** your life!

This is Coach Sharon of Accelerate Coaching, and I am thrilled you have made the decision to change your life for the better by committing to this revolutionary, brain-training boot camp. Over the next 30 days, you will learn how to literally **REWIRE** your brain for success. Using proven techniques from the fields of psychology, neuroscience and life coaching, you will create a more positive, focused, productive, satisfied, successful, and most importantly, HAPPIER you! Stick with this program, and you will find the success you seek as you create a life you LOVE!

Did you know that by committing to this program you are way ahead of 99% of the population? Did you know that there is only one main difference between the highly successful 1% of the population and the other 99%? You see, the highly successful literally think (and, therefore, act) differently than the rest of us. They have programmed their minds to overcome self-limiting subconscious beliefs—the same beliefs that currently hold you in an invisible cage and limit how far you can go in life. Because of this different thinking process, the highly successful are able to continually set goals, design action plans, overcome obstacles, achieve their dreams and dramatically propel their lives forward.

Did you catch that?

The only thing that separates you from the most successful people in the world is HOW YOU THINK.

By simply changing **HOW** you think, you can completely transform your life! Therefore, I will teach you how to think (and act) like the highly successful by rewiring your mind, especially your subconscious mind, for success. Just imagine how incredible your life would be if you developed the thinking patterns, belief systems and habits of the highly successful! Your dreams of success, happiness and abundance are more attainable than you ever thought possible!

Through this Train Your Brain for Success Boot Camp, you will learn step-by-step how to:

➢ **THINK like the HIGHLY SUCCESSFUL** as you will literally grow new neural connections in your brain.

➢ **OVERCOME SELF-LIMITING SUBCONSCIOUS BELIEFS** and break free from your self-created cage that has been holding you back from your true potential.

➢ Identify and **CONQUER YOUR FEARS and OBSTACLES,** thus removing what's standing in the way of your desired success, happiness and abundance.

➢ Activate the **LAW OF ATTRACTION toward ABUNDANCE, WEALTH and HAPPINESS,** instead of attracting what you don't want.

➢ Follow your passions, interests, talents and skills to **TAP INTO YOUR FULL POTENTIAL and PURPOSE** on this earth.

➢ Devise goals and focused action plans to **CREATE A LIFE YOU LOVE**.

➢ Create a more **BALANCED LIFE** where you live by your values—what's really important to you—instead of allowing life to dictate your time, energy and focus.

➢ Become **HAPPIER and MORE SUCCESSFUL** as you become the **DESIGNER OF YOUR LIFE!**

Isn't it time to stop making excuses, and start making your dreams a reality?

If so, you MUST learn how to make your conscious and subconscious mind come into agreement; otherwise, they will continually fight each other and hinder you from creating the life you desire and deserve.

If you wonder why change is so hard, it is because your conscious mind is only the tip of the iceberg in comparison to the powerful and dominating subconscious mind. In fact, it is estimated that your **subconscious mind is over 30,000 times more powerful** than your conscious mind, and it **DOES NOT LIKE CHANGE.** Your subconscious mind is your primitive, emotional brain, and it will fight hard to keep you stuck right where you are now.

This program or brain boot camp will literally reshape your brain!

However, over the next 30 days, I will teach you how to reprogram both your conscious and subconscious mind to accept change and embrace success. Think of your subconscious mind as the blueprint that determines the outcomes of how your life is built. I will teach you how to rewrite your blueprint so that it is set for success because until you do this—no matter how hard you try—you will not see the change you want in your life.

**When you finish this program,
you will not be the same person that you are today.**

I know this is true! I created this brain boot camp to help my clients, and instead it completely transformed my own mindset and life! I began to see that I had created the life I was living by my own thoughts and subconscious beliefs. My eyes were opened to a new level of awareness as I saw how my self-limiting beliefs and thought patterns had created a cycle that only allowed me to move but so far in life. I had no one else to blame but myself. Instead of taking control and living my life by design, I had been going through life on autopilot—allowing my habitual thinking patterns and subconscious self-limiting beliefs to RUN MY LIFE!

It's Time to Get Out of Autopilot, and Start Creating a NEW REALITY!

You see, your brain in its efforts to keep your life running "efficiently" locks you into thought patterns, habits and belief systems that can keep you going in circles as they define your self-image, your level of success and ultimately your perspective on life. It is your current perspective that defines your current reality. As a result, you live life locked in an invisible cage of your own doing.

Don't believe me? Let me explain. Imagine a bird confined to a small cage made of four walls that he can vaguely see through. In this small cage, the bird can barely flutter his wings, much less fly. This small living space is the bird's "reality." Now remove the walls of the cage, and suddenly the bird sees the expansive world around him. There are no limits to where the bird can fly or to the resources available to him. But most importantly, he can now spread his wings and do what he was created to do—FLY! The world is now his for the taking. He now has a new perspective and thus a new reality.

Isn't it time to kick down the walls around you and do what you were created to do—spread your wings and FLY?! The expansive world full of exciting opportunities and unlimited abundance awaits you!

IT'S YOUR TIME TO FLY!

The wonderful thing is that when you positively change your perspective, you are better able to allow good things to come into your life. Your life is whatever you ALLOW it to be. Therefore, I will show you how to give permission to allow love, happiness, joy, health, wealth, favor, intelligence, wisdom, creativity, success and ABUNDANCE to fill your life. Get ready to be transformed. You are now deciding to be the author of your destiny.

As you commit to follow each step of this program, you will train your conscious and subconscious mind to create thoughts and beliefs that will ALLOW you to move toward your dreams and goals. You will also become more focused, productive, satisfied, successful and most importantly, happier! You will literally grow new neural connections in your brain that will allow you to bring the success you desire into your life as you create a life you LOVE!

WARNING:

I must warn you that creating this new life (new perspective) will take consistent effort because you will have to disconnect your old thinking patterns, habits and beliefs and create new ones—this requires commitment as well as AWARENESS. My goal is to increase your level of awareness to your own thought life and current perspectives so that your eyes will be opened to the truth of success and living an abundant life.

When your eyes are opened, you will see the vast abundance that awaits you. You will see that there is always a solution. No matter how difficult things may get, you will see that things are always somehow going to work out for your good. Usually your answer is right in front of you, but you have to be "aware" enough to see it.

Therefore, each day, I will give you a lesson with an exercise to begin to reprogram your conscious and subconscious mind. As the program progresses, you will add in your own personal goals which will be broken down into small daily tasks. Most people (the 99%) try to change their lives by taking on enormous tasks and then feel discouraged and quit because change didn't happen overnight. Life is a marathon, not a sprint.

Remember, the tortoise wins the race.

Slow and steady are qualities of the most successful in the world. Daily, they do the small things that count and which add up to great accomplishments. Don't try to take the quick route, you will fizzle out and quit. Failure is okay, but quitting is not. We can learn and grow from failures, but quitting is not an option for the highly successful. Either you choose to conquer life, or you allow life to conquer you. Either you allow your life circumstances to make you or to break you.

Therefore, I offer no guarantee of results because you will get out of this program what you put into it. Some of you will give 110% and will see profound change and transformation. Others will only give 10% and will see little to no change. Change does not happen magically overnight, but requires time, effort and discipline. You can't expect to go to the gym once in a while and become a body builder or fitness model. You must put in the time and effort.

> "You'll never change your life until you change something you do daily. The secret to success is found in your daily routine."
>
> ~John C. Maxwell

Isn't your future worth a few minutes out of your day?

I highly challenge you to complete this program in 30 days for the quickest results in retraining your habits and thinking patterns. However, because everyone has different schedules and timetables, I have created this program with daily challenges but have also designed it so that you can work at your own pace. Sometimes life happens—unexpected occurrences, sickness, unusual busyness, vacations—and keeping up with the daily assignments can be challenging. However, getting behind does not mean quitting. Just pick up where you left off, and KEEP GOING.

ALWAYS remember to focus on what you CAN DO…not on what you can't.

Therefore, if you can't put seven days a week into this program, then what can you commit to? Five days a week? Three days? It may take you 60 or even 90 days to finish this program….but that's okay! Just don't quit!

Also, the assignments are based on the days of the week. However, if you get off schedule, that's okay; just keep going as your brain will still recognize the message that is being sent. So, even if it's Monday, and you are still on last Friday's assignment, go ahead and complete it on Monday. Don't wait until the following Friday to continue. In addition, the weekends are a great time to catch up on any assignments missed during the week.

> *This program is about training your brain to see solutions instead of just focusing on problems and obstacles.*

The goal is progress not perfection.

For all you perfectionists out there, please don't beat yourself up if you can't complete each day "perfectly." However, for those who want to just zip through the program as fast as possible, it would be more beneficial for you to take your time. This program is designed to build upon each day and week to create new mindsets and habits as your brain will literally rewire and reshape itself. Plus, each week, the information and assignments will get better and juicer as we dive deeper and deeper into uprooting what's holding you back and in creating new, incredible belief systems, thought patterns and success habits to dramatically propel your life forward. I purposely save the best for last, so no matter what, keep going!

Reprogramming your mind takes consistent effort and focus, but it will be worth it as the results will be **transformational**! However, transformation only occurs IF you apply the information in this book to your life. Without application, little will be produced in just skimming and skipping through the readings and assignments. You are welcome to do a quick read through of the entire book, just be sure to come back to Day 1 and complete each assignment. Studies show that learning without application is more or less useless. You must apply your learning. This is why this book is in a workbook format.

Think about it: how many times have you read an inspirational book or heard a great quote from someone highly successful, and how many times did the book or quote make you become highly successful? While the words may have inspired you, if they did not take root inside you and be properly nourished, then more than likely they just fell to the ground producing little to nothing. In my lifetime, I have read many inspiring books and heard numerous incredible quotes, and while they sounded great at the time, they never made a lasting difference in my life. WHY? Because:

1) I did not truly understand them (I was still living by old self-limiting mindsets).
2) I did not _apply_ them to my everyday life.

It is not until you apply what you learn that you will truly understand what is being taught. It takes application to reprogram your thinking patterns and mindsets. But once you do, just wait, those same books and quotes will take on a life of their own because you will finally "get it." You will begin seeing from a new perspective.

Therefore, understand that this book is not fairy dust to magically make you a big success. It is a manual to retrain and reshape your brain to think like the highly successful. As you go through the readings and exercises, take your time and think things through. With each assignment, dig deep and be honest with yourself. Go at your own pace, but just keep going!

Further, the brain always prefers the route of least resistance in order to conserve energy. Introspective thinking takes energy, so you will have to press through your urge to quit—your natural desire to conserve energy. Plus, your brain is like a muscle; the more you use it, the stronger and more developed it becomes. A strong brain can do more, both faster and easier.

This book is a literal boot camp for strengthening and reconditioning the brain!

In addition, it will also be tempting to not write down the answers to the daily assignments. However, to rewire your brain, writing down your answers on paper is crucial. The assignments of this book are based on proven techniques from psychology, neuroscience and life coaching and can be verified by studying the habits of the highly successful. With consistency, you will literally **grow new neural connections in your brain** that will allow you to bring success into your life.

So no matter what, keep going!

And remember, your subconscious mind does not like change—it will attempt to sabotage and stop your efforts toward change and transformation. Therefore, be consistent and committed with this program. Your brain needs consistency to develop these new positive neural pathways and networks. Working on this program once in a while will not create the necessary changes in your brain. I encourage you to set a time during the day to work on this program so that it becomes part of your daily schedule.

You will never have the time to do something unless you <u>MAKE</u> the time to do it.

This time allotment will now become your dedicated, daily, self-development time, and which I hope after 30 days will become a life-long daily habit of self-development. Once you've decided on a time of day that works best for you, put this time down on your schedule, calendar or mobile device. Also, send yourself reminders on your mobile devices and/or use post-it notes around your home to remind yourself to complete this program. Every morning, my daily tasks pop up on my mobile devices to remind me of what I need to do for the day.

> **WARNING!**
>
> **Your subconscious mind will fight you and try to convince you to QUIT!**

Most importantly, keep this program in sight—by your bed, on your desk, on your kitchen table or wherever you will daily work on it. Keep it in sight, or you will quickly forget about it…and your subconscious mind will make sure of it! Do whatever it takes to keep this program in the forefront of your mind so that can push through and finish it. Transforming your thinking will transform your life! Your future is worth the effort!

Excuses are the Ultimate Dream Killers!

Decide today to stop making excuses and start living the life you desire and deserve. Decide to stop waiting until "tomorrow" to begin moving your life forward because "tomorrow" will never come. Start living your life by design, not just by happenchance.

> "Insanity:
> doing the same thing over and over again and expecting different results."
>
> ~Albert Einstein

Start where you are at **NOW**. Don't say, "*IF I was only this, or IF I only had that...**THEN** I could do such and such.*" You can make excuses all day long, but they will not get you anywhere. Saying, "*If I was only smarter, prettier, more popular,*" or "*When I have more time, money, or friends…THEN I could live my dreams*" is believing a LIE. **"IF" and "WHEN" will NEVER come!** If you keep doing things as you've always done them and expect things to change, then you are living a life of insanity! This is the mentality of the 99% of the population.

Change Your Perspective and You Will Change Your Life

The majority of the population have what I call the "worm's perspective," while the highly successful have the "eagle's perspective." The eagle sees the big picture—the trees, plants, mountains, streams, rolling hills and rich, available resources. If the eagle doesn't see what he wants, he flies somewhere else to find it. In contrast, the earth worm sees mainly dirt and more dirt or the "same old, same old." Further, the worm is clueless to the grand world around him as his perspective is so small. He eats, sleeps and wiggles through dirt all day long. This small world is his reality. You know what else the worm eats? Animal dung! Ever feel like life throws tons of dung at you?! The majority of the population has a "dirt and dung" reality. Is this you?

I know this is true because if the majority of the population had the eagle's perspective, then they would already be living a life of success, happiness and abundance. My entire life I have had the worm's perspective. However, because of the principles in this book, I now feel like I have finally "awoken from my sleep" as my eyes have been opened to a new world of opportunities and possibilities. When you finally "wake up," you will see how you have been sleepwalking through life. You will perceive how you have been crawling blindly through the dirt and dust of the earth instead of spreading your wings and flying.

Are you going to have a worm's perspective (eating dirt and feeling small, insignificant and powerless) or will you choose to have an eagle's perspective (seeing the big picture, taking control and responsibility for your life, and being assertive in pursuing your dreams)? There is no limited view or lack mindset when you see things from a higher perspective.

ARE YOU READY TO FLY?!

Today is YOUR day! Your days of wishing and begging are behind you. You can have anything you want, BUT it begins with **YOU**! This means that you must stop seeing yourself as a victim of your circumstances. You may have had horrific and appallingly unfair things happen to you in the past (and there is NO justification for these wrong or unfair doings). HOWEVER, either you can allow the past to dictate your life, or you can take control and finally get in the driver's seat.

This is where true FREEDOM comes—
when you see the POWER you have over your now and your tomorrow.

BUT this means you must STOP blaming others and making excuses. You must stop blaming your past and using it as an excuse to not move forward into the purpose and potential you are capable of. You must stop blaming your parents, your siblings, your relatives, your spouse and your kids. No longer can you blame your boss, your co-workers and your company. You must stop blaming your school, friends, neighborhood, city and government. No more can you use your race, sex, ethnicity, nationality, ancestry or genetic makeup as an excuse. You must stop blaming God, the universe, bad luck, the economy, the stock market and your bank account.

You alone must decide to step up to the plate and be honest with yourself. Your current life is your own doing. It is what you have ALLOWED it to be. You have created your current life or reality according to your mindsets and perspectives. Like a cage around you, they have limited how far you can go in life.

BUT HAVE NO WORRIES!
You can CREATE your life to be <u>ANYTHING</u> YOU WANT!

You are the author of the pages of your life—the pen is in your hand. Everything you need is available to you right now. You just have to see it (become "aware"), and choose to reach out and take it. When you change your perspective, you change your reality, and this changes the course of your destiny. Isn't it time to stop making excuses, and start living your life by design? Isn't it time to spread your wings and fly?

ARE YOU READY TO FLY?!

This program is designed to enable you to create the life you desire and to push you to be what you are capable of being. But YOU must decide that today is YOUR day for change. You alone must decide that you will begin to make your dreams a reality and start living a life of abundance. You must choose to be a victor and no longer a victim by choosing to take control of your life. I cannot force you to start your race to victory, nor can I drag you over the finish line. This is your race, and you alone choose your results.

> "The only person you are destined to become is the person you decide to be."
>
> ~Ralph Waldo Emerson

Today is YOUR day!

Isn't it time to take the driver's seat and decide where your life is going instead of just running on autopilot? Isn't it time to start the journey toward the life you truly desire? If you don't start moving, you will never get there. Even a very slow pace is better than not moving at all. And it's never too late to start. It doesn't matter what is in your past—your past is the past. It's time to say goodbye to yesterday, and step into today, so you can create the tomorrow you desire.

So.......

IF you are up for the challenge,

IF you believe your future is worth the effort,

IF you no longer want to live a life of the status quo,

IF you want to embrace success and find out what you are truly capable of,

THEN CONGRATULATIONS, you have just made one of the best decisions of your life!

Never forget, the world NEEDS you to be the best possible you that you can be!

Don't you deserve to be the BEST YOU POSSIBLE?

Let's Start FLYING!

Now it's time to put that commitment in writing…(next page).

NOTE: I highly encourage you to complete this workbook with a partner, your spouse, or in a group setting. Otherwise, find someone who you know will keep you accountable. Your accountability partner should preferably be someone who will be objective and who will check in on your progress once a week. You can also use social media to your advantage to hold you accountable. You will be surprised at how much more you will accomplish with an accountability partner(s). This is why Life Coaching is so powerful—it's all about accountability!

WARNING: This program is for mentally and emotionally healthy individuals who want to improve their lives and begin to achieve their goals and dreams. If you suffer from severe emotional or physical trauma, depression, guilt, shame or helplessness, please seek professional assistance from a mental health provider. Return to this program when you feel mentally and emotionally healthy enough to move forward.

Declaration of Commitment to Live My Dreams

I, _____ (name), commit to complete this 30-Day Boot Camp to train my brain for success and a life of happiness and abundance. No matter how much I want to quit, I will fight for my future. This day, I choose to live my life with purpose knowing that I have incredible potential within me. From this day forward, I choose to live my life without regrets. I choose to be free which means taking control of my life and my destiny. This day, I choose a life of happiness, abundance and success. I choose to live my dreams and be who I was created to be! This day, I CHOOSE TO SPREAD MY WINGS AND FLY!

Signature_____   Date_____

Witness Signature _____   Date_____

Now read the above statement out loud as a declaration to living out your dreams.

(This declaration is also available to print at www.trainyourbrainworkbook.com and to cut out in the *"Declaration Cut Out"* section located in your Toolbox at the end of the book).

Never forget...

Today is ALWAYS a new day.

It is NEVER too late to live your dreams.

Your future starts NOW!

Live life to its fullest.

Live a life of no regrets!

Congratulations! You are now on the path to success! Let's start flying!

Tips to Completing this Program

Your subconscious mind does not want you to complete this program and will try to stop you by causing you to make excuses, distracting you, convincing you that change isn't worth the effort and that you should stay stuck right where you are. Decide today that you will no longer be a victim but a VICTOR in this life!

Therefore:

✓ Challenge yourself, but also go at your own pace.

✓ Don't worry if you get behind. Pick up where you left off, and keep going!

✓ Don't worry if you are not on the right day of the week. Just keep going!

✓ Don't worry if you can't complete each day perfectly. The goal is progress not perfection. Don't stress yourself out. Just keep going!

✓ Start where you can, and do what you can. Just try to be as consistent as possible. This is a life-transforming program, so just keep going!

✓ Keep the program in sight and/or send yourself reminders to complete it. Just keep going!

✓ Try to complete the program at the same time of day as it is easiest to form a new habit by doing it at the same time every day.

✓ Recognize that you will have days when you won't "feel" like doing your daily reading and assignments. When this happens to me, I tell myself, *"Just do five minutes of self-development today."* Suddenly, I don't feel stressed about it anymore. AND nine times out of ten, I end up enjoying the material and easily completing my goal of 30 minutes.

✓ Find a workout partner(s) to help you complete this workbook. Two or more people working together creates accountability which will better help you to conquer your subconscious mind's goal to make you quit!

✓ The weekends are a good time to make up anything missed during the week. Just keep going!

✓ Focus on what you can do, not on what you can't. Just keep going!

✓ Did I mention…**JUST KEEP GOING**??!!

Week 1: Establishing Your Foundation for Change

During this first week, you will work on better understanding yourself and will determine where you want to go in life—this is foundational for success. Therefore, you will need to set aside some time to complete these self-reflection exercises as they will require you to dig deep to "find yourself" and to determine what you really want in life. This may be the hardest week for you as these tough questions will begin to **wake up your brain out of autopilot** so that you can become self-aware and bring the change you desire.

Your subconscious mind will fight you tooth and nail to quit because the subconscious does not like change. You must decide to push through and obtain the life you desire. Without challenge, there is no change. Everything in your life is a reflection of the choices you have made. If you want different results, you must make different choices. Therefore, the choice is yours. I can't force you to start your race to victory, nor can I drag you over the finish line. This is your race.

Most people spend more time planning their vacation than they do planning their lives. I typically cover much of this week's assignments in my first one-on-one coaching session (which runs 90 minutes). Decide today whether your future is worth a few minutes of your time and attention each day. **The highly successful MAKE time for daily self-development** (30 minutes a day is a great goal). Will you make time or make excuses?

The goal of this program is progress not perfection. Therefore, do what you can, but try to be as consistent as possible. Creating the change you desire takes consistent effort. Lasting change doesn't magically happen overnight but is a result of *small, consistent efforts over time*. So, no matter what, just keep going! Plus, the lessons will progressively get better and better!

Decide today whether you will live your dreams and accomplish your goals or whether you will maintain the status quo as you continue to get stuck in repeating cycles. Stick with this program, and you will begin to create the life you desire—a life you will LOVE! I know you can do it!

Week Overview:

Day 1: Motivated Monday: Self-Assessment Test

Day 2: Thoughtful Tuesday: Self-Awareness, Life Goals

Day 3: What and Why Wednesday: Wheel of Life, 12 Month Goals

Day 4: Thankful Thursday: Key Goal, SMART Goals, Goal Tasks

Day 5: Fearless Friday: Overcoming Fears and Obstacles

Day 6: Celebrate Saturday: Celebrating Your Achievements, Pathways Thinking

Day 7: See It Sunday: Power of Visualization

Now is the time to create the life you desire! I believe in you! You can do it!

Day 1: Motivated Monday

It's time to get motivated and get moving! We will start by talking about YOU! There is only one you, and only YOU can do what you were put on this earth to do. To accomplish your purpose, you must understand yourself—what makes you "tick." Understanding your personality is key to your success as you must identify your strengths, weaknesses, relationship styles and best suited careers. Therefore, today you will complete a free online personality assessment. Within the assessment, you will fall into one of 16 categories. However, within each category, there are millions of slight variations; this is what makes you special and uniquely you!

Assignment:

Please take the FREE personality assessment at **www.trainyourbrainworkbook.com.** It should take you around 10 minutes to complete. Think VERY carefully before answering the questions. This is about being completely honest with yourself concerning who you truly are. People often answer the way they want to be seen versus how they really are and can end up with the wrong results. For example, your job may force you to be more extraverted (social), but in reality you are actually an introvert (prefer to work alone).

Next, read over your four-letter personality type description. It should describe your personality 80% correctly. Again, there are millions of slight variations within each personality type as no two people are exactly alike. If you do not match the description by 80%, I encourage you to take the test again. (Note: the most problematic letters are the "N" and "S." Therefore, if you have an "N" in your four-letter description, please also read the description with an "S." For example, if your four-letter type says E_N_FJ, please also read E_S_FJ to see which description is a better fit.)

Finally, read over the sections (on the side of the test page) concerning your strengths, weaknesses, relationship styles, ideal careers, etc. Each section is very revealing and helpful in better understanding yourself. You may also find it helpful to Google your four-letter personality type for even more diverse descriptions available on the web. I highly recommend you bookmark the test link, or print out your results to refer back to.

Please go to www.trainyourbrainworkbook.com, and complete Day 1: *Personality Assessment.*

My Four-Letter Personality Type:

Something new or interesting I learned about myself today:

Great job! Understanding yourself is KEY to success.
Also, if you want to better understand those around you (spouse, family and friends), have them take the test and then you read their descriptions!
Create better and more understanding relationships today!

Day 2: Thoughtful Tuesday

Today is about self-awareness, and this assignment will require a bit of thought and self-reflection. It is one of the most difficult challenges of this program as it requires you to dig deep and find yourself and what you truly want in life. This program is designed to enable you to create the life you desire and to push you to be what you are capable of being.

You see, right now you are living most of your life on autopilot. Your brain in its efforts to be efficient keeps you locked into your current patterns of thinking and perspectives and thus keeps you, more or less, going in circles. Therefore, until you learn to become self-aware, can you begin to think BIGGER. Thinking bigger starts with understanding yourself, your thoughts and your feelings. It's about becoming aware of where you are now and where you want to go in life. It's also about becoming aware of your habits, your fears, and what's really holding you back (your inner beliefs). This deep thinking gets you out of autopilot and stimulates the brain to expand the limits of your imagination. You now begin to see yourself and your life in a new light or new perspective. In this new perspective, you become aware of the power that you have over your reality. Your reality is what you have created it to be. If you don't like it, you can easily change it.

You possess the creative power to shape your life any way you want!

Living out your purpose and destiny in this earth is about being the best YOU that you can possibly be. It's about using the strengths, talents, gifts, abilities, learned skills, life experiences, insights, wisdom, knowledge, interests and passions within you to make this world a better place. It's about living out the big dreams in your heart.

This may surprise you, but your purpose is already within you. Think about this: a seed has within it the DNA to become a tree. The seed doesn't need to be told its purpose; it is already programed that way. However, the seed must be properly nourished to sprout, grow into a tender plant, and ultimately become its full potential—a strong, fully-grown, beautiful tree. Nevertheless, this never changes the fact that <u>full potential</u> (a big, beautiful, flourishing tree) is the seed's <u>ultimate destiny</u>. You have within you a powerhouse of potential to do something great with your life and to make a positive difference in this world. AND how you will use that potential is totally up to you!

It's time to dig deep and begin to find your purpose—what YOU are capable of, your full potential. You probably already know it or have a "sense" about it. Think back to when you were a child—when your future held limitless potential. What were your BIG dreams? I bet you saw yourself as something great—doing BIG things! I bet you envisioned yourself making a positive difference in this world. All of your potential is already within you; you just have to recognize it, nourish it, and let it come forth. How exciting!

YOU ARE THE AUTHOR OF YOUR DESTINY!

> "Your talent is God's gift to you. What you do with it is your gift back to God [and the world]."
>
> ~Leo Buscaglia

Assignment:

The following assignment has seven parts and is foundational to the rest of the program. Take your time, and think things through as you focus on being truly honest with yourself. (However, if you become overly "stuck" on a particular question, just go with your "gut" feeling or initial thought/answer.) Please write your answers below or in a journal/notebook of your choosing.

---

1) My three Greatest Strengths: (What are you really good at? What is naturally easy for you? What talents do you have? What are you able to do that makes you stand out from others? Why do people like you? Refer to your personality description from yesterday if needed).

    1.

    2.

    3.

---

2) My heart's Passion: (*"If I could do anything, I would…."* Remove all limits. What is it that you MUST do in your lifetime to feel like you are truly LIVING? Or what would you LOVE to do, day after day, even if you never got paid for it? If you still feel unclear, ask yourself, *"I am happiest when I…."* What you are passionate about will help reveal your purpose.)

---

3) My three Lifelong Goals: (These are your greatest life ambitions. Dream as big as possible. Push yourself outside your comfort zone. In your BIG dreams is where you will find your passions and your purpose. Your big dreams make you feel ALIVE. If you knew you couldn't fail, what would you do?)

    1.

    2.

    3.

4) My personal definition of Success: (Success is different to each person because success is about living out the dream in YOUR heart. Success can be anything from being a school teacher to being a multi-zillionaire, but it's all success because success comes from the heart.)

5) Where I want to be in five, 10 and 20 years (career, family, finances...): (If you feel very unclear about your future, you may skip this question for now. However, it may help to think about how you want your future to be different than it is today. What do you want to change? Even a very vague description will begin to give your mind direction.)

      In five years, I want to be...

      In 10 years, I want to be...

      In 20 years, I want to be...

6) My three Legacies I want to be remembered for: (Legacies are what you want to leave behind. When you die, what are the three most important things you want others to remember about you? These will reveal your core values. Your legacies could range from being a good friend, spouse or parent to building a successful business empire to helping the poor to being devout in your spiritual beliefs. If only three things could be said of you at your death, what would you be proud to have spoken?)

      1.

      2.

      3.

Now that you have a good grasp on what is important to you, what you are passionate about, what you are naturally good at (strengths), and what direction you want your life to go, it is time to create your Mission Statement. You were created to contribute to this world in your own special way and which will usually involve one or more of the following: serving, helping, creating, designing, building, teaching, training, equipping, inspiring, impacting, leading, giving, protecting, enabling, empowering, honoring, advising, assisting, solving, pursuing and so on. (If needed, look again at your personality description as well as the strengths section.)

Therefore, a **Mission Statement** is about defining your purpose as well as your overall contribution to the world. It is a one-sentence statement that in essence says:

"I want to be/do_____ through/by doing/resulting in _____".

Sample Mission Statements:

Here's My Mission Statement: "My mission on this earth is **to empower** others to become all they are created to be **by educating** them through coaching and ministry settings."

Oprah Winfrey: "**To be** a teacher. And to be known for **inspiring** my students to be more than they thought they could be."

Amanda Steinberg: "**To use** my gifts of intelligence, charisma, and serial optimism **to cultivate** the self-worth and net-worth of women around the world."

A Top Executive: "**To be** a role-model, leader and person of integrity who **draws out** the best in others (my company, colleagues, clients, family) so they can reach new heights of excellence."

A Health Professional: "**To serve** others **through** my medical expertise, compassion, and overall positivity so that everyone I work with will be blessed by my actions."

An Entrepreneur: "**To use** my creative abilities **to inspire** others through my business endeavors and philanthropic causes."

A Mom and Wife: "**To be** the best mother and wife I can possibly be, to live the model of a healthy and balanced life so that I **can help and teach** others to do the same."

An Entertainer: "**To enable** others to feel positive **through** my writing and entertainment venues."

---

7) My Mission Statement: (Life is short; what will you do with the time you have on this earth? Take a moment, and think this through. This is your <u>ROUGH DRAFT</u>, so don't worry if it's not perfect or if you still feel unclear about what you really want in life. You will finalize this statement later in the program.)

REMEMBER, these are really tough questions that challenge you to dig deep and think about life and what you really want—which most people have never truly done. I cover this assignment in my first coaching session. Some people can come up with answers right away while others need time to think these through. Take your time (even a day or two if needed) to answer these very challenging life questions. <u>This is about digging deep and finding yourself.</u>

However, if you still feel unclear about your greater purpose, don't worry. As you begin to move forward, it will become clearer with time. When I went to college to become a teacher, I had no idea I would end up becoming a university career services director, move to the Boston area, become a life coach, take courses through Harvard Medical School and author a book on the neurobiology of success! However, each step I took opened a new door of opportunity and a new world of possibilities.

BUT, if you don't take a step forward, you will never know what you are capable of. There are talents, skills and abilities locked up inside of you that you won't even know about until you begin to step out!

Plus, what you naturally gravitate toward will reveal your interests and passions.

It is interesting to note that I can now look back and see a pattern in my life as I wrote my undergraduate thesis paper on learning modalities of the right and left brain hemispheres. In career counseling and life coaching, I have worked with personality assessments (based on brain processing). And I used hypno-birthing (visualization exercises that tap into the subconscious mind) with three of my four child deliveries. I can also see an ongoing pattern of wanting to help others to become better (through my desire for teaching, career counseling, life coaching and ministry).

Therefore, begin to see the patterns in your life to reveal your interests and passions. Also, remember, no one can completely plan out his or her life because many exciting and unexpected things can happen along the way (and it's good to stay FLEXIBLE!).

However, you most certainly can map out your <u>NEXT STEP</u>!

So, don't worry if you don't see the big picture now, just move forward with what you have, and new doors will open for you. Choose to live your life with purpose, not regrets. Use your strengths, abilities and passions to make a positive difference in the world. The world is counting on you to live your mission. The world is counting on you to be who you were created to be! So go ahead, and take that first step!

> "Faith is taking the first step even when you
> don't see the whole staircase."
>
> **~Martin Luther King, Jr.**

Phew! You really dug deep today and pushed yourself to think BIGGER.
It's time to come "alive," and become the person you are capable of!
Congrats! You took another step up the staircase of success! Way to go!

Day 3: What and Why Wednesday

Today you are looking at the "WHATs" and "WHYs" of your life, and you will determine whether your life is in proper balance. You will do this through an exercise called the Wheel of Life.[i] This exercise provides a powerful visual of your current life situation. <u>Please read the following pages in order to complete the Wheel of Life and questions below.</u> (This exercise is also available in **video/audio** and **printable** format at www.trainyourbrainworkbook.com.)

Wheel of Life sections:
Leisure/Fun, Health/Fitness, Environment/Surroundings, Community, Spiritual, Friends/Family, Learning/Self-Development, Significant Other, Finances, Career/Work

WHEEL OF LIFE

If this wheel represented your life, what kind of ride would you have? _____

My Key Goal _____

My Intrinsic Goal _____

Wheel of Life Exercise
(Also available in audio format at www.trainyourbrainworkbook.com)

It is important to remember that your life is not a bunch of non-related pieces. Each piece or part fits together to make an interconnected whole. Typically, we focus on a few pieces of our life and forget that neglecting other parts can cause imbalance and thus unhappiness. To create the balance we want and need in our lives, we must first evaluate our lives. Therefore, today you will be looking at the ten main areas of your life, as seen on the Wheel of Life picture, and then rating each area on a scale of "1" to "10." "10" meaning you are completely happy and satisfied in this particular area, a "5" meaning you are partially satisfied and a "1" meaning you are completely dissatisfied with this life area.

Health and Fitness—Please rate your overall health and fitness level on a scale of "1" to "10." Think about your diet, exercise, sleep, water intake, and any ailments or weight issues you might have. If you feel this area is in good shape, but you still have a little room from improvement, you would give this area maybe an "8" or "9." If you feel this area is okay but has a lot of room to grow, you would rate it at maybe a "4," "5" or "6." And if your health and fitness are completely lacking, you would give this section a rating of "1" or "2." (*Please write your rating number in the section of the Wheel of Life labeled health/fitness on the previous page*).

Community—Rate from "1" to "10" your happiness with your overall social sphere or network. This includes your neighborhood, church, societies and organizations you may be involved with. Are you happy in your community? What is your overall feeling about your current community as well as your contribution to your community? (*Please write your rating for community on the Wheel of Life.*)

Friends and Family—Rate your immediate social sphere, your close relationships. Here you are thinking about communication styles and boundaries. Do you have healthy boundaries, or do you have relationships that are completely draining you? Is the give-and-take of the relationships balanced? Or is this an area that's out of balance, and it's taking away from other areas? What relationships could use some work? Overall, are you happy in your relationships with friends and family? (*Please write your rating number for friends/family on the Wheel of Life.*)

Significant Other—Rate your intimate relationship with your spouse, partner, or boyfriend or girlfriend. Think about the relationship—are you happy? How is the communication between you? How do you react to each other? We often want to change the other person; however, the only person we can change is ourselves. But by changing the way we communicate, the way that we react, and the way we approach situations; over time, it will begin to change the way others react and communicate to us. (*Write your rating number for significant other on the Wheel of Life.*)

Career/Work—Rate your job, your career. Are you happy in your career field? Have you chosen the right career field—does it fit your personality, your values and your work ethic? Do you like what you actually do at work? Do you feel satisfied in your work? Do you do just enough to get by, or do you truly live each day as a way to tap into your potential and your purpose? Some of you may have ended up in career fields that are completely inappropriate to your personality. Others may desire to start your own businesses. Some of you may be stay-at-home moms who have temporarily set aside career. Others may be students who haven't figured out what you want to do with your life. You may even be an executive in mid-life crisis who is trying to figure out what career path best suits you and your family in this phase of your life. Others may find that you are not happy in your job, but it may actually have more to do with who you work with or the work load than the actual job itself. I will teach you how to better handle these external influences so you will feel more happiness at work. Let me make an important note here. In both career counseling and life coaching, one of the biggest issue I have found with unhappiness in a person's career is not the job, but the person's own attitude toward the job. Many people who thought they were in the wrong career field, take the personality assessment and realize that their current career is a perfect fit. Once they have this revelation, their entire perspective and attitude changes. Suddenly, they begin to take ownership and initiative to take their career to a whole new level, and they do! Please take a minute to think about and rate your overall satisfaction with your job at this point in time. *(Please write your rating on the Wheel.)*

Finances—Rate your finances. Do you make the amount of money you want to make? How much debt do you have? Do you follow a budget? Do you know where your money goes? Do you spend aimlessly, or do you hold onto every penny in fear of poverty? How much do you save? Do you have a three to six month emergency fund? Are you investing now toward retirement? Here you are thinking about not only how much money you have or want, but also how responsible you are with your finances for the present and future. Financial issues are the number one cause of divorce in America. Ignoring your finances is just asking for trouble. Finances don't fix themselves. But good news! There are many great resources for getting your finances back on track such as programs through financial experts like Robert Kiyosaki, Dave Ramsey, Gary Keesee, Dani Johnson and so on. *(Please write your rating number for finances on the Wheel of Life.)*

Learning/Self-Development—Rate your level of self-development. Do you take time to learn, to develop your skills and knowledge, or do you prefer to be a couch potato, watching hours upon hours of television? (By the way, the highly successful watch little to no television, instead they are voracious readers). There are endless self-development books and free online videos (i.e.YouTube) available that could literally make self-development a full-time job! Further, through ITunesU, you have access to thousands of online university courses (i.e. Harvard and Princeton) for FREE! There is so much free information at your fingertips, so take a minute to think about how you can improve your skills. If you are in sales, marketing or leadership, are you learning how to develop and improve these skills to give you the edge? If you like to cook, are you developing your cooking skills? Maybe you're into fitness or you're athletic; are you keeping up with the latest research to give you the best results? The more you can increase your skills and knowledge, the more you will increase your value and marketability in the market place. Don't underestimate the power of self-development as it is a major key to success. *(Write your rating number for learning/self-development on the Wheel.)*

Spiritual—Rate your overall feelings about your spiritual life. Do you feel happy in your beliefs? Even if you are an atheist, you still have beliefs about life, death, happiness, love and so on. Do you feel that your life and actions support and coincide with your beliefs and faith? Do you feel like there is room for growth in this area? Do you have a lot of questions that you need to find answers to? Do you feel like this area is underdeveloped as it usually gets ignored? Keep in mind that each area of your life is interconnected; each area affects the others. *(Please write your rating on the Wheel.)*

Environment/Surroundings—Rate your environment. This is your home and your office. Is it orderly and organized? Is it aesthetically pleasing? Or do you feel unhappy when you are in your environment? Does it take you ten minutes to find anything? Is it always a complete mess? One of the many great resources for organizing your living spaces is flylady.com, where the "Fly Lady" gives great tips for daily breaking down tasks to keep your home and/or office organized and decluttered.

Every day you take a few minutes to do a few cleaning tasks instead of taking a big chunk of your weekend to clean when you should be relaxing and having fun with your family or friends. (*Please write your rating number on the Wheel of Life.*)

Leisure/Fun—Rate your leisure and fun level. Leisure and fun are an area that can easily be overlooked but are critical for not only our physical health but also for our mental and emotional health. We need down time to rest and recoup, and we need to have fun and participate in enjoyable activities that help to energize our souls. We have to make time for ourselves. We have to make time for fun with friends and family. While some of you may put too much emphasis on leisure and fun that you don't get vital tasks done, others may be total workaholics who need to make it a priority to add into your life some healthy leisure and fun and not feel guilty about it. Balance is the key here. (*Please write your rating number for leisure/fun on the Wheel of Life.*)

All of the areas of your life are interconnected—each area is not in isolation but affects the others. The more you can strengthen each area, the more balance you will find in your life. Through this program, I will help you bring change in each of these areas so that you can have greater happiness, satisfaction and overall life balance.

Filling in your Wheel[ii]: Starting at the center point of the wheel, fill in each section according to the rating number. A rating of "1" would just fill in the very bottom of that section. A rating of "5" would fill in half of the section. A rating of "10" would fill in the entire section. Now look at your wheel. If this wheel represented your life, what kind of ride would you have? If all your sections are filled in to "10," then you would have a nice, smooth ride. My guess is your sections have varying numbers which could give you a pretty bumpy ride. I have yet to meet someone with all sections rated at level "10" as we all have room for growth. Typically, some sections may be strong while some underdeveloped; this makes for a bumpy ride as all the sections are interconnected.

Now let's look at your wheel and determine your **Key and Intrinsic Goals**. Your **Key Goal** is the area of your wheel (life) that you want to focus on as a PRIORITY and is the area that if corrected will also help many other areas of your life. Focusing on this area is a *KEY* to moving your life forward. For example, your work/career could be causing you financial stress, relationship stress, health issues, and lack of time for self-development, spirituality and leisure/fun. By making it a *priority* to change this area for the better, many other areas of your life would also be improved. (*Write your Key Goal in the section under the Wheel labeled Key Goal.*)

Next, your **Intrinsic Goal** is one you *naturally give attention to* and excel in. Intrinsic goals are great because you are already self-motivated to achieve them. However, they become problematic when given too much focus. For example, maybe you are a fitness nut and work out constantly (obsessively). Typically, you won't need any more focus on this area. This is an area that often *can be given too much time, energy and focus and can take away from the other areas*. Our ultimate goal is to bring into balance all areas of your life. (*Write goal under Wheel.*)

Congratulations!
You have completed the Wheel of Life Exercise. It's now time to take action. Are you ready?

Setting Goals is a Major Key to Your SUCCESS!

Please now look at your wheel of life, mission statement, and your list of strengths and weaknesses (refer to your personality assessment if needed) and begin thinking about your top 10 goals for the next 12 months. What would you like to accomplish in the next 12 months? Where do you want to be 12 months from now? How do you want your life to be different?

Studies[iii] have found that goal setting dramatically increases a person's physical and mental effort toward that goal. Goals are energizing as they increase performance, achievement, and ultimately, well-being[iv]. Research[v] also shows that goals with the most success must be clear, be challenging (but not extreme), have meaning to you (not pushed on you by someone else) and have a deadline. Here is one of my past goals list as an example.

My Top Ten Goals for the next 12 months:

1. Career/Finances: Create five new business contracts that will increase my income by 50% by the end of the year.

2. Self-Development: Read at least two books a month on personal development.

3. Health: Lose 10 pounds of fat and gain five pounds of muscle over the next four months.

4. Significant Other: Create a better relationship with my husband by complimenting and thanking him at least once a day.

5. Family: Take each of my children on a special "date" once a month.

6. Community: Volunteer one to two hours a week at my children's school.

7. Self-Development: Improve my photography skills through weekly practice, classes and online study (i.e. watching YouTube videos and reading photography blogs).

8. Spiritual: Develop a closer relationship with God through reading a daily devotional.

9. Recreation: Create two or three inexpensive family mini-vacations per year.

10. Environment: Organize and label boxes in attic and basement.

Writing these dreams and goals on paper is essential.

The highly successful of the population always put their dreams and goals on paper. Writing down goals is almost a magical process. When you write a goal down on paper, you take it out of the realm of dreams and ideas and bring it into the now of reality. You give your brain something tangible with which to work.

Now it's your turn. On the next page (or in a journal/notebook), quickly jot down goals that come to mind, and then put them in order of importance. This is your **rough draft**.

My Top Ten Goals for the Next 12 Months:

1.

2.

3.

4.

5.

6.

7.

8.

9.

10.

(Note: There is a printable version of this goals list at www.trainyourbrainworkbook.com.)

I know this is a REALLY tough week! I have probably given you harder assignments than you expected. I know you want to quit right now! I know your subconscious mind is fighting you tooth and nail to convince you that change isn't worth the effort. **BUT**…I also know that you have a dream in your heart that's worth fighting for, that you have untapped potential that could change the world, and that you were created to be more, do more and have more. AND I fully believe that you are capable of pressing through to your finish line!

> *"At the moment of commitment, the entire universe conspires to assist you."*
>
> *~Johann Wolfgang von Goethe*

Positive change requires commitment.

If positive change was easy, *everyone would already be doing it*. Positive change is never an easy, quick fix, but requires you to look hard at yourself and ask the tough questions. To create change, you must evaluate your current life and determine where you want to go in life. You must choose a destination and consistently work toward it. The good news is that with time, change will become easier (even effortless). However, at the beginning, you must commit and choose to press through…then just watch what happens!

Also, success is not success if your life is out of balance. You are an interconnected whole, not just bits and pieces. Each area of your life affects the other areas. Use the Wheel of Life exercise at least every six months to evaluate your life to promote optimal balance. Plus, you will be encouraged as you can see and measure your progress!

Having a balanced life is a key to happiness and fulfillment.

If you were tempted to skip the Wheel of Life activity, you have missed a very important step in creating a happy, healthy and balanced life. Refuse to allow your subconscious mind to sabotage your life and future anymore. Your life is of great value, and you deserve to live a happy, healthy, productive and successful life! Work at these assignments at your own pace. Don't rush! Don't skip! Be honest with yourself, and you will succeed! I believe in you!

> "The secret of getting ahead is getting started."
>
> **~Mark Twain**

Congratulations!
You are on your way to becoming like the highly successful!
Keep up the good work!

Day 4: Thankful Thursday

Thursdays will normally be our day to learn thankfulness. However, today we are going to determine your Key Goal as well as your goal tasks, so we could say this is Task Thursday. Yesterday we talked about your Key Goal on the Wheel of Life exercise. Your Key Goal is your *top priority* or *most urgent goal*. Your Key Goal should also help improve many other areas of your life as well as help your other goals to be completed faster. It is a KEY to moving your life forward. This Key Goal will be your main focus at this time.

Key Goal Examples:

Weight Loss: If I lose weight, I will feel better about myself, have more energy, and feel more confident at work, in relationships and in recreational and community activities.

Career: If I can improve my skills to grow my business, then I will bring in more income for my family to relieve financial stress, to fund the recreational activities and vacations I desire, to invest more into my financial future/retirement and to give more to good causes.

In creating your Key Goal, it needs to be a SMART Goal (specific, measurable, attainable, realistic and time-bound). You want your Key Goal to be as clear and specific as possible so that your mind will accept it as a realistic destination. (You will write your SMART goal at the end of today's lesson.)

A **SMART** Goal is:

Specific	Goal is clear and concise.
Measurable	You can measure your progress. You will know when you have obtained your goal.
Attainable	You are able to actually accomplish the goal. The goal must be both challenging and realistic. You are to push yourself but also keep within reality. (Don't expect to lose 50 pounds in a month).
Relevant	Goal must stem from your heart (versus someone else). Goal needs to have meaning and value to YOU.
Time-bound	There is a set date or deadline for accomplishing the goal.

Amazing things happen when you set a goal. Studies[vi] show that setting a goal begins to attract to you what you need because you are now consciously and subconsciously **AWARE** of the goal. Becoming aware of the goal allows you to then become aware of what you need to accomplish the goal, as well as aware of how you will do it. You also become aware of opportunities and connections that will help make the goal happen. For example, have you ever looked to buy a car and suddenly noticed car dealerships on every corner? Maybe you began to notice ads on cars and began to research the best car to buy for your price point. Quickly, you became very AWARE of your options.

All successful businesses know that setting a very clear and specific goal and then brainstorming and defining how the goal will be accomplished creates clear action steps to make the goal a reality. Goal setting is really an act of faith as you see the goal as yours and begin to find ways to move toward it.

Also, you **MUST SET A DATE** or **DEADLINE** for when the goal is to be completed. Without a deadline, there is no motivation to keep going. Without a clear and timed outcome, there will be no end point for the mind to focus on and move toward. You must give the mind something concrete to grasp onto. Without a deadline, there will be no sense of urgency to motivate you to take that first step in the right direction.

You may have heard the saying, *"If you don't know where you're going, any road will get you there."* Would you start off to an unknown destination without a map? Not if you want to get there by a specific time. And if you want to reach your destination by a specified time, wouldn't you research and figure out the most efficient path and means to get there? Deadlines encourage motivation and efficiency.

So where are you going, and when do you want to get there?

I must add that goals and deadlines must be realistic for YOU. Just because your best friend lost 30 pounds in one month's time doesn't mean that you should set your goal to match him/her. Don't stress yourself out and set yourself up for failure by being unrealistic and constantly competing with others' success. Let others motivate you to do more, but always be true to yourself.

Let me also quickly clarify that your goal cannot be contingent on others, meaning it has to be completely in your control. You cannot guarantee you will be the top salesperson of your company as it is contingent on others' success. However, you can set the goal to sell a specific number of products or reach a specific dollar amount in sales.

Which goal is in your control?

____ I will get a promotion.
____ I will learn and implement the top five ways people in my company get promoted.

____ I will have more loving relationships with my family members.
____ I will implement three practical ways to show my family how much I love them.

____ I will have a better marriage.
____ I will say an encouraging word or compliment to my spouse at least three times a day.

Did you notice how the first goals are vague while the second goals are more specific and in your control? Again, an effective goal is a **SMART** goal:

✓ **S**pecific in defining exactly what you want.
✓ **M**easurable in that you will know when you have obtained it.
✓ **A**ttainable in that it is realistic for you to achieve.
✓ **R**elevant in that it is meaningful to you or stems from your heart (versus someone else).
✓ **T**ime-bound as defined as having a deadline.

SMART Goals are a BIG KEY to SUCCESS!

Writing SMART goals takes time and effort, but it will be well worth the effort in the long run. What highly successful business doesn't have clearly defined goals and action plans? So too, you must clearly define what you want in order to create a clear path to get there.

Here are a few SMART goal examples:

Work Goal:

My goal is to break my company's sales record of $250K by selling $265K **(relevant and measurable)** this month **(time-bound)** through increasing my customer base by 7% **(specific and attainable).** I will do this through calling no less than 50 new companies **(specific)** and setting up no less than 20 new face-to-face consultations **(specific).**

Note: The goal should challenge you, but if it is not **attainable** or realistic, then the numbers or time period should be changed. You can always increase your goals with time. For example, your first month's goal could be to increase your customer base by 3%, month two by 5%, month three by 7%. You may have deadlines set by others that push you to extremes–going above and beyond. However, for your own personal goals, set them high, but do not set yourself up for burn-out, especially as you are just beginning. Slow and steady is better than exhaustion and quitting. You know your personality. **Make your goals work for you, not against you.**

Family/Relationship Goal:

My goal is over the next two months **(time-bound)** to implement three practical ways **(specific and attainable)** to promote more loving relationships with my family members **(relevant)** as measured by 50% less fights **(measurable).** This will include 1) one-on-one activities with each of my children once a month, 2) a romantic date night with my spouse once a month (with no electronic devices) and 3) making it a priority to be home for family dinner at least four nights a week.

Note: After this new goal is well established, the person could then focus on something new such as creating better communication with his/her family by learning effective listening techniques and applying them in these situations over the next three months.

Weight Loss Goal:

By December (four months) **(time-bound,)** I will have lost 10 pounds of fat and gained five pounds of muscle (measured by a fitness caliber instrument) **(specific, measureable)** through a life style of an all-natural diet **(specific)**, drinking 10-12 glasses of water a day **(specific)**, getting eight hours of sleep a night **(specific)** and doing high intensity interval training three to four times a week for 30 minute sessions **(specific, attainable**—challenging but still realistic**).**

Note: If the goals become unrealistic, they need to be re-written so that they are achievable. Challenging but realistic is key to goal achievement.

I encourage you to write all your top ten goals as SMART goals, but at the very least, write your most important and pressing goal (Key Goal) as a clearly defined SMART goal.

It is very important to note that:

- **Without clarity, your mind is confused as to what you want.**
- **Without a deadline, there is no urgency or accountability.**
- **Without being realistic or relevant, there is no purpose behind it.**

Remember, if you don't meet your deadlines, don't give up! Just reset your timeline, pick up and keep going! It's about progress, not perfection. You will get there…if you don't give up!

Now it's time to write your Key Goal as a SMART goal and then add action steps (tasks) that will make the goal happen. You will also list your other nine goals (look back at yesterday's assignment), adding action steps/tasks to each. Below you will see a sample of my *Top Ten Goals List* from when I was getting my coaching business up and running. I have begun with my Key Goal and have then added my other goals as well as my action steps/tasks for each goal.

My Top Ten Goals & Tasks

1. KEY GOAL: Career: By next May (12 months), I will have established my coaching business by having at least 10 personal coaching sessions per week, one group session per week, and at least one business coaching contract each month that will together net at least $5,000 a month in finances. I will achieve this goal through the following tasks:

- Organizing office space.
- Ordering business cards.
- Establishing networking connections.
- Joining professional associations.
- Developing website.
- Developing blog.
- Signing up for coaching magazines.
- Reading books on coaching.
- Studying how to start and market my own business (articles, videos, courses).
- Marketing my coaching services.
- Developing a catchy Elevator Speech to tell others what I do.
- Attending at least one professional coaching conference a year to expand my coaching knowledge and contacts.

2. Self-Development: I will read 24 self-development books every 12 months by:
- Reading two books per month by committing to read 30 minutes a day.

3. Health: I will lose 10 pounds of fat and gain five pounds of muscle by September (4 months) by:
- Drinking a minimum of 10 glasses of water a day with a goal of one gallon, using a gallon jug to keep track of my daily drinking.
- Eating a "clean diet" (no sugar, flour, sodas) 98% of the time (one cheat meal per week).
- Exercising five days a week for 30 minutes.
- Improving posture by engaging muscles for better posture, strength and weight loss.

4. Significant Other: I will promote a better relationship with my husband over the next three months by:
- Giving him at least one compliment a day or thanking him for something he has recently done.
- Encouraging him by my choosing to be positive and to not react negatively or criticize.
- Booking us a date night at least once a month.

5. Family: Starting this week, I will establish a family night on Friday nights to promote family unity by:
- Going out to somewhere fun as a family or
- Having a family movie or game night at home.

6. Community: I will become more involved in my community by:
- Volunteering one to two hours a week at my children's school starting this new school year.
- Inviting families over for dinner to our house once or twice a month starting next month.

7. Self-Development: I will improve my photography skills by:
- Learning Photoshop through free YouTube videos over the next two months.
- Taking an advanced photography class.
- Offering to take free pictures for friends.
- Joining photography challenge groups.
- Reading photography blogs 2 to 3x week for 20 minutes.
- Creating a website to display my work.

8. Spiritual: I will develop a closer relationship with God by:
- Reading a daily devotional as soon as I wake up in the morning for five minutes.

9. Recreation: I will create three mini-vacations each year to promote family unity by:
- Researching, establishing specific dates (winter break, spring break, summer break), budgeting and making reservations at least two months in advance of specified dates.

10. Environment: I will de-clutter my home and attic by August by:
- Every day, my children and I will clean-up the house (and put away all "clutter piles") for ten minutes before bedtime.
- Every Friday afternoon, I will sort and organize boxes in the basement and attic for 30 minutes.

Assignment:

When you clearly define your actions toward your goals, your brain will begin to accept these goals and will then ALLOW you to move toward them. Without a crystal clear plan of action, the mind is confused and unfocused. Setting realistic goals brings clarity and focus as well as helps your brain to be less anxious, more solution focused and to produce feelings of happiness! Just imagine yourself becoming happily focused and productive toward what you really want in life!

> *"Goals in writing are dreams with deadlines."*
>
> *~Brian Tracey*

Therefore, remove ALL EXCUSES, and write your goals and plans of action on the next page (or in a journal/notebook) to begin to create the life you desire. You are the BOSS of your life. Your fortune lies in your daily routine of activities. The highly successful set big goals and then design **realistic** ways to achieve these goals within specific time frames. These successful individuals don't just live their lives by "chance," but instead plan their days hour by hour. They know exactly what needs to be accomplished each day in order to attain their desired results. Goals *with* action steps (tasks) are foundational to success. (The following exercise is also available to print at www.trainyourbrainworkbook.com.)

My Top Ten Goals & Tasks:

1. **Key Goal (written as a SMART goal):**

Tasks:

1.

2.

3.

4.

5.

6.

7.

8.

9.

10.

2. Goal:
Tasks:

3. Goal:
Tasks:

4. Goal:
Tasks:

5. Goal:
Tasks:

6. Goal:
Tasks:

7. Goal:
Tasks:

8. Goal:
Tasks:

9. Goal:
Tasks:

10: Goal
Tasks:

Writing these dreams and goals on paper is essential. Remember, the highly successful always put their dreams and goals on paper, thus taking them out of the world of ideas and bringing them into the now of reality. Please write your Top Ten Goals & Tasks, and hang them on your wall or in a place you will see them every day to remind you of the life you desire. Now say these goals, look at them, and think about them DAILY. If you do not, you will quickly forget about them and will maintain a life of the status quo. Remember, these are not silly exercises, but the techniques of the HIGHLY successful.

Creating Daily Task Lists

It's now time to find a system to daily review your Top Ten Goals & Tasks so that you can create **short, DAILY task lists**. We will begin creating a daily task list next Monday. Today you are simply deciding on how you want to review your Top Ten Goals and daily task lists.

For example, you may want to print out your Top Ten Goals & Tasks and tape them to your wall or desk (as suggested above) and then use my "Weekly Goal Setting Template" (at www.trainyourbrainworkbook.com or in your Toolbox at the end of the book) to write down the specific daily tasks you will complete each day. You may prefer to use a goals notebook, weekly planner, calendar, dry-erase/white board, chalk board, Google docs or to just write your specific daily tasks on a note pad or sticky (post-it) notes.

You may prefer to use a "Task" app on your mobile device (i.e. smart phone, tablet, etc.), so that you can list your goals and specific tasks and quickly review them when needed. Most mobile devices are already programmed with a "Reminders" or "Task" app. There are also many great (and free) task apps such as Any.do, gTasks, Cozi Family Organizer, Alarmed and so on. For example, in the Any.do app, you can easily create categories such as top ten goals, personal tasks, work tasks, school tasks and grocery list. This app allows you to print, export and sync your lists and can also remind you of your tasks as you can set alerts to go off at specific times. I will say that by keeping your goals and tasks in your mobile device, you will be able to view them on the run and quickly cross off, add to or adjust at any time. Again, most mobile device app programs will allow you to set off reminders at specific times to keep you on track. For example, every morning when you wake up, you could have an alert with your KEY Goal show up on your mobile device. <u>Do what works for **YOU**</u>. You are the boss of your life.

IMPORTANT!

If you do not create a system for reviewing your goals and tasks,
you will forget them in no time. Today find a system that works for YOU.

This is what I suggest to my Life Coaching clients:

In the mobile device app of your choice (or in a goals notebook, white board, chalk board, etc.), create four main sections: GOALS, GENERAL TASKS, SHOPPING and DAILY TASK LIST.

1. GOALS: Create a section that lists your Top Ten Goals & Tasks to refer to every day.

2. GENERAL TASKS: Create a section of weekly general tasks to refer to such as vacuuming, washing cars, repairs, taking trash out, de-cluttering, paying bills, doing laundry, dropping off dry-cleaning, etc. so you don't miss common things that need to be done each week.

3. SHOPPING: Create a section for keeping a shopping/grocery list so you don't end up at the store 15 times a week. Every time you walk into a store, your risk overspending. I highly recommend grocery shopping only once or twice a week and sticking to a budgeted list.

4. DAILY TASK LIST: Daily, refer to the three above mentioned sections (Goals, General Tasks, Shopping) and create a short list with your specific tasks that must be completed THAT DAY ONLY. Every day this section will change. Keep this daily task list to no more than **five or six** tasks altogether. Put these daily tasks on your Weekly Goal Setting Template (found at www.trainyourbrainworkbook.com), your calendar, daily planner, dry-erase board, a sticky note or whatever works best for you. Do what works for YOU! You are the BOSS OF YOUR LIFE!

What a tough week, but you are making major headway!
You are creating the path to make your dreams come true!
Now just keep going!

Day 5: Fearless Friday

Today you are facing your fears and obstacles. What FEARS and OBSTACLES are hindering you from achieving your goals?

It is said that your subconscious mind is over 30,000 times more powerful than your conscious mind as it controls 95% to 99% of your life. Your subconscious mind is your "primitive" and "emotional" brain. Studies[vii] show that your subconscious mind is an extremely powerful force with a primary role to protect—at all costs—your survival. This is great if you are being chased by a lion or bear but not if you are trying to create positive change in your life. As a result, if you are alive and breathing, the subconscious mind "thinks" it has done its job and works hard to keep you in exactly this same state.

Your subconscious mind dislikes change so much that when it perceives something as "threatening" to its current state, it will even try to dismiss it from your conscious thoughts so that change is not created.[viii] This is why you can set out to accomplish an amazing new goal but continually forget about it—the subconscious mind is resisting change in every way possible. Consciously you desire to move your life forward; however, the response of the subconscious mind is fear which causes these new and "threatening" thoughts to be blocked or dismissed. This results in you being unhappy with your current situation, yet too subconsciously fearful to change.

Further, research[ix] reveals that there are two main kinds of fear that hinder you from change: fear of past failures and fear of the unknown. Fear from the past keeps the subconscious mind from "growing up," thus holding you immobile as it has not forgotten the trauma of past failures, disappointments and emotional wounds. For example, if you were deeply hurt in a romantic relationship, the subconscious mind may try to sabotage future relationships in order to "protect" you. Consciously you desire love, but subconsciously you fear pain and rejection.

However, the greatest fear of all is the fear of the unknown. While fear (generated by the subconscious mind) is meant to protect you from real, life-threatening dangers, it can cause big blocks in your life when you try to step forward into unchartered territory. This new unknown risk seems too high to the subconscious mind, and therefore, it will fight hard to keep you stuck right where you are. This primitive, protective brain sees risk and says, "*Don't do it! Stay in your comfort zone! You're safe here.*" Further, your primitive brain "protects" you by *assessing* the situation and showing you everything that could possibly go wrong if you stepped out into something new. AND the longer you wait to step out, the more time your mind has to convince you to not take action!

Research[x] also shows that a fear response causes you to respond in predictable patterns such as to run for the hills or fight back (the fight-or-flight response), or to stand still as if completely paralyzed. How many times have you wanted to take a step forward into something new and have either run from it, fought or resisted it, or allowed it to completely paralyze you? In the end, fear keeps you unhappy, complaining and disappointed by your current situation instead of being able to take action to create the life you desire.

However, if fear is not protecting you from a true danger, then it is really just an illusion of the mind or **FALSE EVIDENCE APPEARING REAL**. This is fantastic news as it means that you can train your mind to overcome it!

To overcome FEAR, studies[xi] show you must:

1. Identify your fears and obstacles and determine simple ways to overcome them.

2. Create very clear, specific and realistic action plans to achieve your goals and dreams; thus, eliminating the brain's fear of change.

3. Identify resources and support needed so that you feel safe, supported, grounded and ready to meet any challenge.

By identifying and taking clear, concise, small and consistent steps forward, the subconscious mind will see that the "risk" is not too great or threatening. The subconscious mind will then come into agreement with the conscious mind and will accept significant change because **the change will happen slowly, step by step, instead of in an overwhelming, life-changing moment.** Slow and steady wins the race and is why yesterday's Top 10 Goals with <u>specific, small tasks</u> is so important.

Next, you must begin to specifically identify your fears and obstacles so that you can learn to overcome them and start to move your life forward. Therefore, take a minute to circle (or write-down in your journal/notebook) the following that apply to you.

What are my Fears?
- **Fear of Rejection**   (No one will like me, or what I'm trying to do or become…)
- **Fear of Failure**   (If I try, I will fail. I can't fail again. I can't face the embarrassment.)
- **Fear of Criticism**   (I always do it wrong. What I do will not be good enough.)
- **Fear of the Unknown**   (Change scares me…)
- **Fear of Abandonment**   (I'm scared to be alone. I'm scared others will leave me.)
- **Fear of Intimacy**   (I'm afraid to expose my true self. I'm afraid to be hurt/disappointed.)
- **Fear of Betrayal**   (I'm afraid to trust others.)
- **Fear of Poverty and Lack**   (I always worry about not having enough.)
- **Fear of Aging, Sickness and Death**   (I always worry about getting old, sick or dying.)
- **Fear of Loss**   (I worry about losing what I have, my reputation, or people in my life.)
- **Fear of Success**   (I'm afraid that I can't handle success. Success could ruin me.)

Internal Obstacles?
- **Feeling Unworthy**   (I am not good enough. I don't deserve good things.)
- **Procrastination**   (I can do it later, tomorrow, next week, next time, next year…)
- **Excuses**   (It's always someone else's fault. There is always a reason why I can't.)
- **Negativity**   (Constant negative view of myself, my life, my job, my spouse, my family…)
- **Grieving the Past**   (Dwelling on my past mistakes, failures, disappointments…)
- **Worry**   (Always seeing things not working out well for me or others.)

- **Self-Criticism**   (Always looking at my faults instead of my strengths.)
- **Lack of Confidence**   (I can't. I'm not smart enough, pretty enough, good enough…)
- **Lack of Time**   (Trying to do too much in a limited amount of time.)
- **Lack of Focus**   (Not creating clear focus for what I need and want to achieve.)
- **Lack of Specific Needed Skills**   (I don't have the skills to do what I want to do.)
- **Indecisive**   (It's hard for me to make decisions.)
- **Unorganized**   (I can't ever seem to find things or get things done. My life is a mess!)
- **Unmotivated**   (I don't really care. Nothing seems to get me excited.)
- **Undisciplined**   (I have little control over my life.)
- **Impatient**   (I get annoyed waiting, jump into things too soon, interrupt others speaking.)
- **Bad Habits and/or Addictions**   (Smoking, alcohol abuse, gambling…)
- **Poor Health**   (My health is hindering me from doing the things I want to do.)
- **Gluttony**   (Lack of control in food intake. Food controls me instead of me controlling it.)
- **General Poor Diet, Lack of Exercise and Water Intake**
- **Obsessive Behaviors**   (i.e. exercising 3 hours a day; incessant phone texting or social media use; obsessive spending, frugality or hoarding; obsessive cleaning…)
- **Consistent Poor Use of Time or Avoidance of Productivity**   (i.e. watching too much television, playing too many video games, wasting too much time on social media, laying around doing "nothing," shopping instead of completing important tasks or facing reality.)
- **Poor Boundaries in Work, Life, Relationships**   (Unable to say "*No*" and, therefore, consistently overcommitting to things that bring imbalance and distraction to my life.)
- **Always Blaming Others**   (Habitually blaming others for the outcomes of my life instead of taking personal responsibility.)
- **Always Needing to "Rescue" Others**   (Feeling others cannot help themselves.)
- **Always Needing to be "Needed"**   (I must always prove my worth.)
- **Always Needing to be in Control or Control Others**   (I must be "above" others.)

Highly Destructive Internal Obstacles?
- **Unforgiveness** (I can't forgive them/myself.)
- **Bitterness**
- **Resentment**
- **Anger**
- **Jealousy/Envy**
- **Victim Mentality** (It is never my fault, someone/thing else is always to blame.)
- **Guilt**
- **Shame**
- **Negative Coping Strategies** (Complaining, whining, criticizing, gossiping, backbiting, "the silent treatment," manipulation, temper-tantrums and so on.)

External Obstacles?
(Hindrances in my environment and through others).
- **Lack of Finances**
- **Lack of Resources**
- **Lack of Social support**
- **Negative or Criticizing Friends, Family, Neighbors, Co-workers, Employers…**

Other?
(For example: On-going negative thoughts/beliefs against myself, situation or my future.)

Great job! That was a tough exercise! Now let's take a minute and discuss how your current life is a reflection of all your life experiences. The fears and obstacles you face today are a culmination of your past experiences' imprint on your conscious and subconscious mind. Your mind is held captive by the negatives of the past and which subconsciously can affect *every area of your life*. Dwelling on these negative memories and feelings creates a wall around you, similar to a self-created cage or prison. No matter how hard you try, the wall won't seem to come down. Further, your brain is unable to distinguish between what is real and what is imagined and will literally "relive" these negative memories over and over every time you dwell on them—which only further reinforces their strong neural connections in your brain.

However, once you change your negative views of the past to positives, you can undo these deeply rooted "fear from the past" neural pathways.

Isn't it time to let go of your past hindrances? Isn't it time to be set free from your past and to begin to move your life forward? Either you can keep looking backward, or you can choose to keep your eyes on your bright and wonderful future. Plus, when you change your focus toward a desired result, the past will become trivial in comparison.

My husband and I have a wonderful friend and millionaire-mentor, Darin Kidd (a protégé of the late and great Paul J. Meyer). I've heard Darin say a millions times, *"Don't look back unless you want to go back!"* And neuroscience is proving him RIGHT! You will move in the direction of your focus. Reliving your past failures is not helping you to create the future you desire. And I have news for you: no one is perfect. If you didn't achieve your goal(s) the first, second or hundredth time around, it's okay! Mistakes, failures and missing the mark are part of life for EVERYONE. However, if you only dwell on your mistakes, you will go nowhere fast!

Today begin to see your past mistakes, hurts, disappointments and failures as building blocks instead of stumbling stones. Begin to turn these past negatives into wisdom to build your bright future. As your past is transformed into a resourceful wealth of wisdom and experience, your brain will disconnect the old negative associations with these memories. As you become grateful for these difficult times that made you stronger and wiser, your brain will then be able to use these memories to help build your new and amazing future!

By the way! Did you know that some of the greatest inventions and cures of the modern world were from "mistakes"? Did you know that Thomas Edison said he failed 10,000 times before he perfected the light bulb? Mistakes and failures are OKAY! They are part of life. However, you must choose whether your mistakes and failures will make you or break you. What if Thomas Edison had given up at failure #9,999? Failure was simply steps in the ladder to Edison's success. Therefore, you must choose to stop beating yourself up, and start turning your lemons into lemonade. The future belongs to you. You are the author of your destiny. So, let's begin TODAY rewriting the old chapters of your life so that you can create the beautiful and amazing future you deserve!

> *"Yesterday is gone. Tomorrow has not yet come. We have only today. Let us begin."*
>
> ~Mother Teresa

Assignment:

Take a moment to reflect and answer the following. (Please write below or in your journal.):

The greatest fear that has hindered my life is:

The greatest obstacle that has hindered my life is:

My three greatest successes/accomplishments are:

1.

2.

3.

What I learned from these successes/accomplishments:

1.

2.

3.

My greatest failure/disappointment is:

What I learned from this disappointment/failure:

Is this past failure/disappointment holding me back? Why? How?

I will use my past disappointments and failures as building blocks to create the future I desire by:

I am <u>thankful</u> for the wisdom and experience gained from these past good and bad experiences. This wisdom will help me to:

Now it's time to write your statements of action for overcoming your greatest fear and obstacle. Be as specific as possible.

Examples:

Fear of Rejection: I overcome my fear of rejection by acknowledging that others' opinions do not define me. I define what I want in life and choose to daily take small steps toward my dreams and goals.

Obstacle of Bitterness: I overcome my obstacle of bitterness by choosing to forgive that person and to release that bad memory. My future is worth letting go of my past.

My Statements of Action:

I overcome my fear of _____ by _____

_____.

I overcome my obstacle of _____ by _____

_____.

Please read your Statements of Action out loud. (You may want to add these action statements to your goals list. These statements are also in the Declaration Cut-Out section in the Toolbox.)

Now REPEAT OUT LOUD:

"I love myself deeply and completely. I acknowledge that I have allowed my fears and obstacles to hinder me, but I now choose to let go of the fear of _____ and the obstacle of _____. I release them from my life right now. (Breathe out a deep breath and see the fear/obstacle leaving you). I choose to forgive myself, to forgive others and to let go. (Breathe out another deep breath). I now invite joy, love, peace, faith, hope, happiness, confidence and success to fill this place in my mind, body, spirit and life. (Breathe in a deep breath as you receive these wonderful gifts). I allow abundance and freedom to flow through me. I now welcome new creative ideas for achieving my goals and overcoming my every fear and obstacle. I choose to live my mission, my purpose. I am powerful. I am worthy. I am lovable. I am capable. I am full of incredible potential. I am free to be who I was created to be. I welcome good things into my life from this day forward."

Today is a day of new beginnings!
It's time to bury those fears and failures six feet under. It's time to say goodbye to the limits of the past, and say hello to believing and achieving your desired future. You can, and you will! I believe in you! Now go do it!

Day 6: Celebrate Saturday

Congratulations to a week well done! The demands of this week were high as you have accomplished more in better understanding yourself than most people accomplish in YEARS! Did you feel the pull of your subconscious mind to quit? Was this week hard to push through? Did you want to give up?

Well, you are still here! You fought the urge to quit, so job well done!

This week you have learned what psychologists[xii] call pathways thinking. Pathways thinking is when you take goals and break them down into smaller "chunks" (or tasks) allowing the subconscious mind to see the goals as reasonable and realistic versus overwhelming and threatening. Pathways thinking also involves creating multiple pathways to achieving a goal. When goals are broken down into smaller and more realistic steps (chunks), it is easier for the mind to create multiple pathways to completing each step. This is also seen when you face a fear or obstacle, and you create a new way to overcome or get around this fear or obstacle, as you did yesterday.

Every day, you are moving closer to your dreams and goals. So give yourself a good pat on the back. Now look over all you accomplished this week and do something FUN to celebrate! You deserve it!

Suggestions:

- Go out with friends and do a toast to your accomplishments.
- Go to a movie/play/concert or have a quiet movie night at home.
- Go out to dinner or fix your favorite meal at home.
- Go to a ballgame or play a round of golf or tennis or your favorite sport.
- Sleep in or take a long deserved nap.
- Take a hike through your favorite trails or go for a bike ride.
- Take a relaxing bubble bath, get a massage or a manicure.
- Take a day-trip to a fun place you've been wanting to go.
- Go out for ice cream or make an ice cream sundae at home.
- Snuggle up with your favorite new book.
- Go for a walk in the park or by the ocean.
- Buy yourself/pick some pretty flowers.
- Buy an inexpensive keychain, bracelet or necklace to remind you of your accomplishments.
- Sign up for that new class you've been wanting to take.
- Go to the mall and find those new running shoes you need.
- Work on that fun project you've been so excited to start.
- Lay in your hammock or sun chair and drink a cocktail.

**This is not a suggestion but a REQUIREMENT!
Rewards are CRUCIAL to goal achievement!**

Rewards help establish new neural connections in the brain which create new behavior patterns and eventually new habits. Remember Pavlov and the dog that salivated when it simply heard the bell ring?

You see, studies[xiii] show that habits are not just frequent actions but ones done automatically through the subconscious mind. Therefore, you must begin to recognize your current habits and also initiate effort to create new positive behavior until the new behavior becomes a new automatic habit.

> **IMPORTANT:**
>
> Be sure to recognize WHY you are rewarding yourself so your brain makes the connection between the new behavior and the reward.

Rewards have a powerful influence on your brain in creating new habits...whether these habits are positive or negative. For example, when you are rewarded for certain kinds of behaviors, you will keep repeating these behaviors—*even when the reward is coming from an undesired place.* At this point, the conscious and subconscious mind are in conflict, and the subconscious mind wins as it is easier to maintain habits than risk change. However, if you can reward the behavior you *desire*, your subconscious mind will begin to accept this new behavior and with time will allow it to become a new habit.

> *Your habits directly shape your future because your daily activities determine the direction of your life.*

So, even if you didn't finish all the assignments for this week, reward yourself for what you did accomplish. Every little step you take is bringing you closer to your desired life. (Even setbacks and "failures" are steps forward as they teach and strengthen you.) Don't wait until you've reached your ultimate goal to reward yourself. Be proud of *every* step you take on your journey toward goal achievement. Celebrate your small successes, and watch how your life transforms!

Now go reward yourself by doing something that is fun to YOU! (Just be sure to stay within your budget.) Plus, adding FUN into your life is foundational to creating both happiness and success. You've accomplished a lot this week, and you *deserve* this!

I will reward myself by:

What a great week! CHEERS TO YOU!

Day 7: See It Sunday

Today is "See It Sunday," and the exercise you will do today is one of the most important tasks you will complete in this program as it will reprogram your subconscious beliefs. Today is "SEE IT" Sunday because you must "see" it to "believe" it.

According to neuroscience, if you only set your goal at the conscious level, you may be limiting yourself to only 1-5% of your potential. Your subconscious mind is estimated to control 95-99% of your life as it is constantly in motion behind the scenes in every moment and aspect of your life. The subconscious affects not only your thoughts and actions, but also your deeply rooted beliefs about yourself and your potential.

You see, your subconscious mind stores your experiences in memory form and from these memories creates your perspective (worldview), your belief system, and ultimately your "reality." If new information comes in that is not congruent with your current perspective and belief system, the subconscious mind will typically just reject it. Therefore, if you have subconscious beliefs that you will never be wealthy, attractive or loved, your subconscious mind will reject new outside information that says otherwise while continuing to uphold your current beliefs. Your life is, therefore, a reflection of your current subconscious beliefs.

Because the subconscious mind's goal is to protect your survival by promoting homeostasis (balance), this "primitive" brain likes for everything to stay the same versus creating change. As a result, the biggest problem you face today is overcoming your limiting subconscious beliefs which try to confine you in an invisible cage. Again, these subconscious beliefs define *everything* about your life, including what you can and cannot achieve. These beliefs set limits to your success, your relationships, your happiness and even your health!

However, there is a way to trick your mind into believing a new reality (and thus creating new perspectives and beliefs). It's called visualization. Studies[xiv] show that visualization exercises have been found to create an internal, real-life, perceptual experience affecting the mind, emotions and motor representations. In other words, the brain (especially the subconscious mind) does not know what is real from what is imagined.

Think for a second about biting into a lemon; can you feel the saliva excrete in your mouth as you "taste" the sourness? Neuroimaging studies[xv] show that **imagined** physical action uses areas of the brain relating to those involved in the actual physical motion. Further, this imagined physical action increases specific performance skills, persistence and confidence.

Listen to this! In the 1980 Olympics, an experiment was conducted where athletes were divided into groups. Which group do you think performed better?

A. The group that had 100% physical training.
B. The group that had 25% physical training and 75% visual training.

Yep! The group with only 25% physical training and 75% visual training outperformed because visualization is powerful and effective. During visualization, the muscles of these athletes fired as if they were physically practicing!

This is the POWER of MIND OVER MATTER!

We've all heard incredible stories about professional athletes who were injured and told they would never walk or compete again. Did they lie down and die? No! They SAW in their minds themselves walking again. They SAW themselves competing again. They SAW it, they BELIEVED it, and no one could tell them otherwise. Did they ever have bad days and get discouraged? You better believe they did! Did they give up? NO WAY! Why? Because they were determined that their vision would come to pass because the vision was REAL to them!

Visualization exercises show the subconscious mind a new reality that will begin to create a new internal belief system. Visualization reshapes the brain as it stimulates the creation of new neural pathways to help make your dreams a reality. In fact, visualization is even said to have a positive effect on reprogramming your genes, but that's for another discussion!

Visualize to make your dreams a reality!

Specifically, visualization exercises encourage daily goal setting, the positive mindset to expect the goal to happen, as well as the ability to cope and regroup when obstacles and setbacks present themselves.[xvi] By training your subconscious mind to accept your desired future, you will begin to achieve your desired life almost "effortlessly." Why? Because your subconscious mind will begin to be reprogrammed for success and will then come in *agreement* with your conscious mind's choice to move forward toward this new life.

What are visualization exercises? These are exercises that simply involve vividly imagining your desired future and then soaking in the deep positive emotions (happiness and gratitude) that they bring. Connecting the image with the emotion is *essential* for tapping into the subconscious mind (as it is also the "emotional" brain).

Further, utilizing relaxation techniques while visualizing activates alpha and theta waves in your brain, making your subconscious mind the most open and receptive to new ideas and information.

So, all you have to do is **relax and happily imagine** your perfect life!

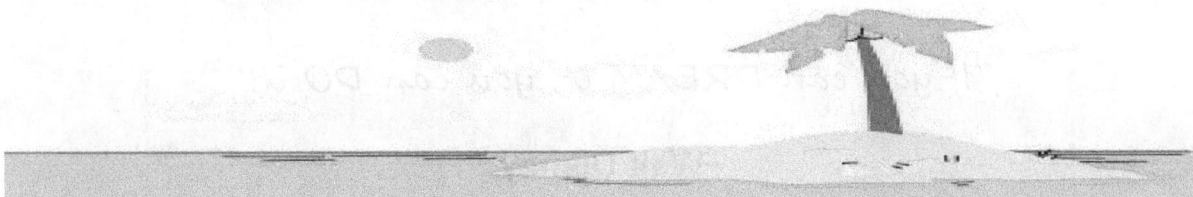

Insight

What is Your Vision for a Better Tomorrow?

Maybe you've heard the phrase, *"Where there is no vision, the people perish"* (Proverbs 29:18).

Why is this? Without vision, we have no clear and defined place to go because we have not given the mind anything specific to focus on or to inspire us. We have nothing more to do other than that which we are already doing. This is why Helen Keller once said, *"The only thing worse than being blind is having sight but no vision."*

Vision is a HOPE for something new—a better tomorrow. Vision breathes life and energy into our souls because vision creates that spark of hope that something better is possible. Hope then gives us FAITH and PASSION to pursue despite obstacles and setbacks.

Why? Because vision ultimately gives us purpose. It is in purpose that we persist until we have that which we envision.

Vision breeds hope. Hope breeds faith. Faith breeds action. Action breeds achievement.

Everything that has ever been created has come from a vision in the mind. Our thoughts operate at a spiritual level as they have the ability to create. Thoughts are not only creative, they know no limits. Thoughts are one of the most powerful forces in the universe.

What is in the imagination of your mind?

If you removed the limits of your current thinking and opened your mind to limitless potential, what would you see for yourself and your future? What is your vision for your better tomorrow? Not just a little better, but incredibly, even outrageously better. What are your great dreams and ambitions? What is your purpose? How will YOU make this world a better place? How will you live the EXTRAORDINARY life you are capable of?

There is only one YOU, and only YOU can do what you were put on this earth to do!

Are you ready to lose your small thinking?
Are you ready to use your imagination to start **DREAMING BIG**!?

"If you can DREAM it, you can DO it!"

~Walt Disney

THE MIRACLE QUESTION:

What would your life look like if you woke up in the morning and everything was *PERFECT*?

Now take a minute and describe this PERFECT life (think about your home, relationships, career, finances, health, spirituality, recreation, travel, etc.). Describe it in as much detail as possible. Give your brain something to RUN with! This will give you a head start before we begin the visualization exercise.

My Perfect Life Looks Like...

_____

_____

_____

_____

_____

_____

_____

_____

_____

_____

_____

_____

Also, **don't worry about the "hows"** of getting to your perfect future—just begin to "see" this future, and your mind will find ways to make your dreams a reality!

Are you ready to reprogram your subconscious mind for success?
Please listen to the "Day 7" visualization exercise at www.trainyourbrainworkbook.com.

(P.S. Don't be like I was when I first learned about this visualization exercise and passed it off as "silly." After I used it on my very first practice client, I was *shocked* by her amazing response. I then realized how powerful this exercise really is! Stop making *excuses*, and start *creating* the future you desire and deserve! Go to "Day 7" at www.trainyourbrainworkbook.com now!)

SEE IT! BELIEVE IT! ACHIEVE IT! You can do it!

Week 2: Getting Focused

This week you will create laser focus to move your life toward your dreams and goals. Plan to put several hours a week of effort into this program. Creating the change you desire takes time and effort as you must develop the thinking patterns, mindsets, attitudes, belief systems and habits of success. Through this program, you are literally rewiring and resculpting your brain for success—which is not something that happens magically overnight.

And remember, your subconscious mind is said to be over 30,000 times more powerful than the conscious mind, and it wants you to quit because it does not like change. Therefore, you must choose to press on if you want to bring the change you desire in your life. I cannot force you to start your race to victory, nor can I drag you over the finish line. This is your race, and you alone choose your results.

Today decide if you will live your dreams and goals or just maintain the status quo. Will you be like the highly successful or just settle for mediocrity? The future is yours—what will you do with it? Let's teach that subconscious mind to accept your dreams and goals!

Week Overview:

Day 8: Motivated Monday: Determining Action for the Week, Chunking

Day 9: Thoughtful Tuesday: Thinking About Your Thinking

Day 10: What and Why Wednesday: Establishing Your Values

Day 11: Thankful Thursday: Gratitude, Lack versus Abundance

Day 12: Fearless Friday: Overcoming Fears and Obstacles

Day 13: Celebrate Saturday: Celebrating Your Achievements, Agency Thinking

Day 14: See It Sunday: Visualization and the Subconscious Mind

> *"You are never too old to set another goal or to dream a new dream."*
>
> ~C. S. Lewis

Now is the time to create the future you desire!
Get your laser focus goggles on!
You can do it!

Day 8: Motivated Monday

Let's get motivated on Monday! It's time to start making your dreams a reality. Today you will determine your focus for the week (based on your Key Goal) and the specific <u>daily</u> tasks you will complete to bring your dreams into reality. You will begin by looking back at your Key Goal and action steps/tasks that you created last Thursday. Next, you will decide on five specific tasks to be completed this week, Monday through Friday, which will support your Key Goal. (I have included an example at the end of this lesson for you to refer to as well as a template to follow.)

NOTE: This is only <u>ONE TASK per WEEKDAY,</u> which equals FIVE TASKS per WEEK .

Now I am not asking for hours spent on each task; even giving ten minutes of focused time will keep you moving forward. Also, I recommend choosing a main focus for the week because many tasks are too broad (such as organizing your office, creating a website, or anything that would take multiple days). You will need to break this broader task down into smaller, more "doable" daily tasks. This broad task is now your focus for the week. However, some weeks you may not have a main focus as you work on simple, non-related tasks. Personally, I find having an overall focus each week keeps me more motivated and on track, but do what works for YOU.

You will then put these five daily tasks in your calendar, daily planner, white board, note pad, mobile device or wherever works best for you. Again, there are many great task apps available for mobile devices. You can also set alerts to go off on your mobile device at certain times to remind you to complete your tasks. So, no excuses. Find a way that works for YOU.

For some of you, focusing on just one task a day may be hard as you are accustomed to doing 100 things at once. However, the brain can only focus on **ONE** thing at a time. In fact, when you are driving and talking on your cell phone, your reaction time is that of a driver with a blood alcohol level of 0.08%! When your focus is stretched, you will not accomplish anything well and will often not complete your mission. However, by focusing 100% on one task, you will complete it well (and make daily advances) versus completing several tasks at 25%. The highly successful of the world have laser focus; they know their key goal and run after it with unwavering passion, faith,

---

Insight

If you want to become a forgetful person then multitask, don't get enough sleep, and keep up your high-stress lifestyle. When you are so overly busy, you stop learning and, therefore, stop remembering.

According to Dr. Rudolph Tanzi, Professor and Chair of Neurology at Harvard, often when we forget where we left something—such as our car keys—it is not that we have truly forgotten. It is that we were not "aware" or "focused" enough to "learn" where we placed the keys.

Is your life so busy doing so many things at once that you can't remember well? Becoming more self-aware and focused by slowing down, delegating, and/or eliminating non-essential activities will do wonders for your memory, your health and your life!

(Learn more through Dr. Tanzi and Dr. Chopra's excellent book, *Super Brain*.)

determination and persistence. The other 99% never devise a key goal, never create laser focus and give up when faced with fears or obstacles. Decide today whether you will be the mediocre 99% or the highly successful 1%. The choice is yours.

Chunking

I think it's fair to say that most people are the most productive when they are a little busier. Physics tells us that an object in motion will stay in motion, while an object not in motion takes a good push to get it moving (or maybe a swift kick in the pants!). However, this is not about being aimlessly busy. It's in being organized and productive toward your PRIORITIES (such as your Key Goal). When you have the hours of your day planned according to what you want to accomplish, you will find that you will accomplish so much more and so much faster because you will begin to build momentum. Momentum will keep you moving at a steady pace.

"Chunking" is a highly effective way to accomplish more and to do it faster. Chunking simply involves setting designated "chunks" of time where you are only allowed to work on a specific task. This chunk of designated time is now a **no multitasking zone**! The goal of chunking is to accomplish a specific amount of work, maintaining clear focus, within a specific time frame. When you give yourself focused time, you will begin to enter what is called the "flow state;" this is where you are totally engaged in what you are doing and will get much accomplished because you are "flowing" (or "on a roll") as you stay focused without interruptions. Chunking can be hours to even just five or ten minutes.

Listen to this! It is said that most people could accomplish all that they need to do in a typical 40 hour work week in only 20 hours. Why? Because most people waste a good portion of their day multi-tasking, getting side tracked and losing focus! Therefore, since I have been a habitual multitasker (and mind wanderer!), I now live by chunking. For example, I set aside two to four hour chunks of time throughout the week to work on this book. This is my uninterrupted time to push through and get as much accomplished as possible. If I become distracted, I pull back in my focus and push myself to complete the goal for that chunk of time. Therefore, I accomplish more because I know this is the time frame I *must* focus on this task and complete it.

Chunking is great for office work, such as establishing 15 minutes for reviewing emails, 15 minutes to reply, 15 minutes to return phone calls, one hour for presentation prep, two hours for big project work, etc.. BUT you must **stick to your time allotments**...no two hours milling through emails. Email and online social networks are major time suckers! (Also, with longer chunking time periods, take brief breaks every half hour or so.)

It is also helpful to plan your chunking according to your peak and non-peak times. For example, if you are most alert from 9 am to 11 am while from 1 pm to 3 pm you tend to get tired, schedule to work on your most demanding tasks during that 9 to 11 am time frame. Interestingly, research shows that during your peak or "most alert" times, it is preferable to work on your most attention-demanding tasks that involve logical, technical, detailed, planning or critical-thinking skills while reserving your creative, intuitive, brainstorming and unique problem-solving type projects for your sleepier times to better tap into the power of your creative and intuitive subconscious mind.

Chunking is also very useful at home. For house cleaning—set a timer, work quickly, and then stop when the timer rings. After school, I set aside one hour to totally focus on helping my kids with homework. They know they have my undivided attention during this time. At bedtime, I allow 30 minutes to help my kids clean up, get ready for bed, and do our nighttime family devotions (without focus this can easily take HOURS!). Then when I put the kids to bed, I know I have one hour to relax and unwind, take a bath, or read/listen to self-development materials (this is a no-work allowed time).

While I do not like to live by strict schedules (as they can make me feel "trapped"), I do find chunking to be a great way to think through my week and block off chunks of time to get specific tasks done. Now I don't always follow my time frames to a tee, but having some general "guidelines" gives my mind a "plan" to follow to keep me accountable. I prefer to plan out my whole week by chucks, but at the very least, I encourage you to plan out your next day. Always know your plan for the next day.

Either <u>YOU</u> will plan your day, or your <u>DAY</u> will plan you!

And listen, some days chunking will go fabulously well and other days, unexpected events may happen. You may even get knocked down for a period of time. However, even in setbacks, decide to get back up and keep moving (even if it's at a snail's pace) by setting aside small chunks of time to accomplish small tasks to keep you moving forward. For example, during the summer months when I have four kids at home, I purposely slow down my work schedule. However, even though my chunks of work time are more limited, I am still slowly moving forward. Then when summer ends, and the kids return to school, I get back into the full swing of things as chunking helps me to pick up good speed again.

It is also remembering that when setbacks come, pick yourself up and keep going. In getting back up, you may also need to start out slower and build up your momentum again versus trying to jump right back in at the speed you had built up to. There are seasons in our lives, and we have to learn to run when we can run and walk when we need to walk. Success is not an easy journey. But understand that if you want to accomplish great and amazing goals, it will take diligent focus and persistent effort, and chunking is a great way to help you do this.

> "If you can't fly then run, if you can't run then walk, if you can't walk then crawl, but whatever you do, you have to keep moving forward."
>
> ~Martin Luther King, Jr.

The goal of this program is to get you focused so you can begin moving in the right direction—whether that is creating movement because you have been totally STUCK, or whether it is in slowing down and refocusing because you have been moving so fast and out of control that you're burning out. Either way, focusing on your priority (KEY GOAL) is going to get you moving forward in the right direction. Start slowly, and build momentum with time.

Remember, your success lies in your daily activities.

It is those small, consistent daily tasks that will put you way ahead in life and will make your goals and dreams a reality. A steady pace wins the race. Be focused, determined and keep plugging away day by day. See your dream as a mountain that you must climb. With every little task you complete, you are taking another step up that mountain. If you keep a steady pace, you will get there in good time. There may be times when you can run, and there may be times when you can only crawl. However, no matter what, just keep going!

What will you do this week to move your life forward?

Take ten minutes at breakfast to decide on this week's schedule for completing your daily goal tasks. Again, you will have **one** KEY GOAL task **per day** Monday through Friday. Then you are also to add any other normal/general tasks that MUST be completed that day **only** (preparing for a work meeting, paying bills, appointments, shopping, cleaning, laundry, repairs, meal planning, picking up kids and so on).

Here's a sample weekly task list:

KEY GOAL: Career
This Week's Focus: Getting my office organized to advance my career   (This is a broad task so I have broken it down into five smaller tasks.)
Monday: Key Goal: Career: Organize work desk   General Tasks: Pick up office supplies, Call insurance
Tuesday: Key Goal: Career: Organize paper files   General Tasks: Grocery store, Drop off dry-cleaning
Wednesday: Key Goal: Career: Organize computer files   General Tasks: Laundry, Clean bathrooms, Pay bills
Thursday: Key Goal: Career: Organize and expand contact list   General Tasks: Take 20 minutes to dust and declutter house, Vacuum
Friday: Key Goal: Finalize organization of office, contacts, and determine anything missing   General Tasks: Sweep, Mop, Laundry
Saturday: Make-up day for any goal tasks not completed   General Tasks: Wash car, Go to son's ball game, Make dinner-date reservation

For highest productivity, research shows that you should keep your **total DAILY** task list (key goal task <u>and</u> general tasks) to no more than FIVE or SIX tasks altogether. A list of a dozen tasks per day will only overwhelm, confuse and distract you from accomplishing your **priorities**. Right now, decide on your key goal tasks for the week. If you prefer, you may add your general tasks the morning of each day. Do what works for you. (There is a printable **Weekly Goal Setting Template** at www.trainyourbrainworkbook.com as well as a copy in your **Toolbox** at the end of the book).

My KEY GOAL:

This Week's Focus:

_____

Monday:
Key Goal Task:
General Tasks:

Tuesday:
Key Goal Task:
General Tasks:

Wednesday:
Key Goal Task:
General Tasks:

Thursday:
Key Goal Task:
General Tasks:

Friday:
Key Goal Task:
General Tasks:

Saturday:
Key Goal Tasks: Make-up day for any goal tasks not completed
General Tasks:

Next, take 60 seconds and see yourself completing your tasks *with total EASE* (thus further removing the fear response). Also, put this week's key goal tasks (and general tasks) in your mobile device, daily planner, notebook, white board, Weekly Goal Setting Template (found at www.trainyourbrainworkbook.com) or *whatever system works best for YOU*. It is also important to remember that once you have completed one of your Top Ten Goals for the year, or it has become a very well established habit, cross it off, and replace it with a new goal. You should be continually accomplishing and creating new goals. This will keep you moving forward.

Great job! Now you know your plans for this week! Add them to your calendar, and block off the "chunk" of time you will accomplish them!

You are capable! You are powerful! You are AMAZING!
You can do anything you set your mind to do!
Now go do your tasks for today!

Day 9: Thoughtful Tuesday

Today is the day to think about your thinking. Did you know that your thoughts are powerful in determining the course of your life?

According to Napoleon Hill, in his world-renowned book, *Think and Grow Rich*, *"Your thoughts determine your behavior, your behavior determines your habits, and your habits determine your destiny."*[xvii] Napoleon Hill wrote this statement after twenty years of interviewing 500 of the wealthiest and most successful people of his day. While this statement was written almost 80 years ago, it has been proven true many times over through modern day research.

> "Your thoughts determine your behavior.
>
> Your behavior determines your habits.
>
> Your habits determine your destiny."
>
> ~Napoleon Hill

Neurobiologists have found that **your brain actually wires the way that you think.**

Whenever you have a thought, a brain cell called a neuron "fires" or sends a chemical message to the next neuron (through synaptic transmission), thus creating a connection or a pathway linking the two neurons together. The more the thought is repeated, the stronger the connection grows between neurons because **neurons that fire together wire together**. Also, the more the pathway is used, the faster, stronger and more efficient the transmission becomes. Eventually, the thought becomes an automatic response or habitual thinking pattern. This is what happens when we learn to play an instrument, play a sport or learn a new language. With enough practice, the response becomes automatic.

Think back to when you first learned to drive a car. You had to think about every single thing you did. However, with repetition, your brain eventually went on autopilot, and your mind was then free to daydream or carry on a conversation. Autopilot is how your brain conserves energy and becomes efficient. If we didn't have autopilot, we would be overwhelmed trying to relearn how to walk, talk, get dressed and brush our teeth every single day! Therefore, it makes sense that our brain always prefers to refer back to strong and established neural pathways.

We also go on autopilot for most of our conversations. The average person's conversational vocabulary is very limited because the brain's means of being efficient is to refer first to those words or phrases with the strongest neural connections (those words that we use most frequently). We, therefore, rely primarily on the same vocabulary for most conversations and thus form patterns of how we respond. Think for a moment. What do you automatically say when you see a friend? *"Hi. How are you?"* or *"Hey, how's it going?"* Or when you stub your toe, do you automatically say *"Ouch!"*? Yes! Because you have reinforced these responses, and they are now a part of your automatic programming.

However, since your thoughts become your responses (words and actions), you create perpetuating cycles. For example, when you repeatedly say *"I can't,"* you are wiring your neural connections to reinforce this thought which eventually becomes a habitual thinking pattern as it goes on autopilot through the subconscious mind. Once on autopilot, it is now a well-established belief. This belief then begins to affect your responses and thus runs your life! Can you now see how if your autopilot programming is to view everything in a negative, limited or self-defeating way, you will get STUCK in this negative cycle…and you won't even consciously know why!?

However, there is good news! Your brain is never hardwired or set in stone. It can ALWAYS be rewired. It's called neuroplasticity, and it's the brain's ability to reorganize itself by forming new neural connections. You can always create and reinforce (with repetition) new positive connections while weakening and deactivating old, negative ones with nonuse.

> *YOUR DAILY THOUGHTS BECOME A CYCLE OF THINKING PATTERNS THAT EITHER LOCK YOU INTO A STAGNANT STATE OR UNLOCK YOU INTO THE FUTURE YOU DESIRE.*

This is our GOAL!

BUT you must choose to get out of autopilot (become aware of your thoughts), and then choose to stop the negative thoughts and create new positive ones. With time, you will develop a new autopilot program that will allow you to continually see things in a positive light, create positive results and sustain new positive cycles. You will program both your conscious and subconscious mind for success! How exciting!

Simply stated, you are continually wiring your brain according to your current thinking patterns. This cycle of either positive or negative "thought reinforcement" then affects the direction of your life! Remember Napoleon Hill? Isn't this what he said almost 80 years ago? **Your daily thoughts** (reinforced and perpetuated by the brain) determine your **behavior** (how you see and respond to life) which become your **habits** (patterns and autopilot programming) that create your **destiny** (run your life and dictate your future).

Since thinking is where the direction of your life begins, you must start to recognize your thoughts in your daily life. As of now, you truly do not know what you are thinking. I know this sounds crazy, but it's true! Currently, you only consciously think about 1-5% of the time. The other 95-99% of your day, you simply "react" based on your subconscious programming. Again, your autopilot settings are there so that you don't have to relearn things over and over (such as walking, getting dressed, etc.) which then frees the conscious mind to learn and grow. However, most people allow the subconscious mind—which is typically programmed to see the negative in every situation—to completely run their lives. They, therefore, become *reactive* in life, instead of *proactive*. They simply respond (react) based on their negative subconscious programming.

Reflect for a moment. What do you say to yourself under your breath? This is your subconscious mind talking as it is simply reinforcing your current "thought habits." Do you say things such as *"I love my life,"* or *"My life stinks"*? Do you say, *"I'm so blessed,"* or *"Bad things always happen to me"*? Do you tell yourself, *"I'm a beautiful human being,"* or *"I'm fat, ugly and stupid*"? Are your thoughts mainly positive or negative? Do you think more on the problem or on finding the solution? If something goes wrong, do you keep a positive attitude, or do you immediately see yourself as having a "bad day" or see your situation as "hopeless"? Also, how often do you encourage yourself? Do you ever say, *"I can do this!"* or *"Good job me!"* or *"Way to go me!"* or *"I'm so awesome!"* This positive self-talk is extremely important!

**Positive self-talk is called agency thinking,
and studies[xviii] show it is <u>crucial</u> for goal achievement.**

This positive self-talk (agency thinking) is the kind of thinking we want to move toward over the next few weeks. Today begin to monitor your thoughts/self-talk. More than likely, you are very unaware of what you say to yourself because you have been running on autopilot. Begin to recognize common phrases that go through your mind on a daily basis. Begin to stop negative thoughts and replace them with positive and optimistic thoughts. Begin to use positive self-talk such as *"I can do this!"* to improve motivation and resilience (the ability to pick yourself back up after a setback).

Zig Ziglar is known around the world for his famous words:

**"*It is your attitude [thoughts and feelings],
not your aptitude [intelligence],
that will determine your altitude [level of success].*"[xix]**

Your attitude is everything. Guess who determines your attitude? You and ONLY YOU! Your attitude is directly controlled by your own thoughts and feelings. No one can make you feel bad unless you ALLOW yourself to feel bad. No situation or problem can make you quit; only you can CHOOSE to quit. Nothing can stop you from succeeding; ONLY YOU can stop your success. Today choose to become proactive instead of just reactive. Choose to live your life by design instead of allowing your old thinking patterns to dictate your life and future. Taking control of your life begins with taking control of your own thoughts. If you don't like your life or your thinking, change them.

It's simple. Negative thoughts will not produce a positive life!

Choose to rewire your brain to be positive and optimistic; to see opportunities for growth in challenges and set-backs; and to be kind, loving and forgiving. Remember, a little negativity (complaining, worry, bitterness, envy, etc.) spreads. A bad thinking pattern may start small but can eventually rewire your brain to see your entire life through the eyes of pessimism. Choose today to root out the negative that is keeping your life stagnant. Choose to believe in yourself. Choose to believe that you are capable—you are created with infinite potential. Choose to believe that success belongs to you. Choose to believe that you are AMAZING!

Now talk TO yourself. Say out loud:

*"You can do it (your name)!
You are powerful! You are capable! You are AMAZING! I believe in YOU!"*

Assignment:

At bedtime, in the box below or in your journal/notebook, write your main thoughts, feelings and overall attitude for today—both the positive and the negative. This exercise is simply about becoming AWARE of your current thinking patterns and attitudes. You cannot change something unless you are aware of it.

My thoughts for the day: (When you look in the mirror, what do you say to yourself? How do you talk to yourself throughout the day? What do you murmur under your breath? What do you tell yourself about your current situation/your life? What do you say sarcastically or "jokingly" about yourself or life? Do you complain, or are you thankful? Do you focus on the problem or the solution, the good or the bad? Do you focus on the best or worst in others? Do you think more about the past, present or future? How do you react in conversations: are you critical and judgmental or open, inquisitive and empathetic? What do you tell yourself about money and your current financial situation? What do you tell yourself about your future? <u>Be honest with yourself. You are uncovering your deep inner beliefs that are running your life</u>.)

My most repeated thought about myself or situation:

My feelings for the day: (What were your feelings for the day? Were they of happiness, joy, peace, excitement, sadness, fear, anger, frustration, stress, worry, doubt, anxiety or maybe all of the above? <u>Your emotions are simply a reflection of your thoughts. Positive thoughts create positive emotions while negative thoughts create negative emotions</u>.)

My overall attitude for the day: (How did you handle the events of the day? If one thing went wrong, did it ruin your whole day? Does everything have to work out perfectly in order for you to feel happy?)

My thoughts and reactions over the last week: (Do you see a pattern? Do you like what you see? Are there thoughts, words and attitudes that may have created your current situation?)

Warning: Reprogramming your thinking will not happen overnight.

Again, most people have no idea what they are thinking as they are running their lives on autopilot. I thought I was a pretty positive person until I began to apply this thought awareness exercise in my life. I was shocked by all the murmuring and complaining I was doing under my breath. I didn't even realize I was saying such awful things about myself and my situation. I was absolutely appalled at all the negativity and self-limiting thoughts I had been perpetuating. My bad "thought habits" were ruining my life! I had been STUCK in negative cycles but could never understand why. However, *now* I could see why. Once I became *aware* of my autopilot programming, I began to identify and uproot my ongoing negative thought habits. Then everything began to change for the better!

Therefore, every Tuesday we will revisit this topic. It takes time to become aware of your thinking patterns and begin to *consciously* change them. Remember, you are creating new neural connections and deactivating old ones. This is serious stuff!

However, it all begins with AWARENESS. Begin to pay attention to your thought life because it controls your emotions, your attitude and ultimately your success. A helpful tip is to record some of your conversations on a recording device. (For example, one day, my little girls were making a video and when they played it back, I could hear my voice in the background and was very surprised by some of the things I had said. I had been talking on autopilot! However, with awareness, I could then change what I didn't like.)

Don't forget! Take two minutes at breakfast to look at your key goal task today. Add any other tasks that MUST be completed today (preparing for a work meeting, meal planning, shopping, repairs, cleaning, picking up kids, phone calls, sending out invitations, running errands, etc.). Then visualize yourself completing these tasks *with total EASE*.

> "Whether you think you can,
> or you think you can't
> —you're right."
>
> **~Henry Ford**

Choose to take control of your thoughts, feelings and attitudes.
They belong to YOU! And remember, you have unlimited potential.
You CAN achieve anything you set your mind and heart to do.
Choose today to THINK IT, FEEL IT and BELIEVE IT!

Day 10: What and Why Wednesday

Today is about choosing to live by your values—the "WHATs" and "WHYs" in your life. Your values are those things that are the absolute most important in the world to YOU. Maybe family, career, being creative or a high achiever is of great significance to you. Maybe helping others, becoming a skilled athlete or building a business empire is what you hold most dear. Our core values stem from deep within us. They are based out of our personality type, our upbringing, our ethics, our beliefs and our vision for our lives. Our values are what drive us to be more and do more. Ultimately, we alone determine what values we want to uphold in our lives. Our values then become a reflection of who we are and what we want to become.

Therefore, become successful in those things that are of significance to YOU—instead of those things that don't really matter. When you build your life around your core values, you feel happiness, peace and fulfillment. For example, if someone holds the value of integrity as a core value, he or she will naturally demonstrate integrity in all that he/she does, and others will recognize it. Some individuals may have the core value of helping others as they work in a helping field or are always the ones to volunteer, donate, assist and support when needed.

Further, identifying your core values reveals what is most important in your life so that you can build all areas of your life around these important matters. Your core values are in essence part of your "calling" here on this earth and give you a sense of your personal purpose. Neglecting your core values will never bring you the true and fulfilling success you desire. When you do not live by your core values, you feel disappointed, conflicted and unfulfilled inside. You will sense that something is missing from your life or that your life is imbalanced in some way.

For instance, if your core value is family, and yet you are always working late and never making time for family, then you will feel internal struggle, imbalance and frustration. You may not be able to control your work hours, but there may be other ways to help the situation (such as choosing to turn off your laptop and work cell phone after 6 pm, going into the office a little earlier so that you can be home earlier some evenings, or even talking to your boss about possible solutions so that you can honor both your work and your primary value of family).

Choose today to live by your core values.

Sometimes your core values will conflict with each other which is often the case with career and family. However, if each core value (career and family) has their designated times and set boundaries, the two values can both flourish instead of competing with each other. It takes effort to design a plan that will properly honor your values, but it will be well worth the time and energy. When you recognize what is truly important to you, you will also begin to see unnecessary time and energy drainers that you can then remove from your life. Today choose to no longer dilute your focus on what doesn't really matter. Instead, put your time and energy into those things that are of significance to you.

Assignment:

The following is a list of "DOING" and "BEING" values. Read through the list carefully and circle (or write down in your journal/notebook) the ones that apply to you.

DOING VALUES

Serving, Helping, Giving, Teaching, Training, Equipping, Protecting, Empowering, Advising, Assisting, Solving, Pursuing, Entertaining, Performing, Ministering, Communicating, Mentoring, Inspiring, Influencing, Leading, Directing, Impacting, Excelling, Advancing, Promoting, Creating, Planning, Designing, Building, Beautifying, Collaborating, Organizing, Participating, Discovering, Exploring, Guiding, Nurturing, Growing, Connecting with Others, Honoring Family, Supporting Community, Improving Marriage, Developing Career, Making Money, Spiritual Growth, Love of Learning, Being a Role Model, Working Hard, Excellence in Service, Self-Development, Self-Discipline, Mastery, Expertise, Relaxation, Having Fun, Being in Nature, Playing Sports, Dancing, Developing Musical Skills, Competing, Winning, Being Successful, Being Challenged, Acting with Speed and Precision, Experiencing Pleasure, Intimacy, Upholding Spiritual Principles, Worshipping, Physically Disciplined, Obedience, Performance, Personal Power, Physical Vitality, Being Healthy, Productivity, Quality, Recognition, Respect for Life, Respect for People, Respect for the Environment, Risk Taking, Excitement, Tongue Control, Generating New Ideas, Playing, Good Decision Making, Good Listener, Ensuring Security, Becoming Famous, Being Goal Oriented

BEING VALUES

Integrity, Joy, Happiness, Love, Peace, Abundance, Balance, Truth, Uniqueness, Purity, Harmony, Loyalty, Empathy, Achievement, Spirituality, Authenticity, Godliness, Beauty, Flow, Energy, Transcendence, Unity, Accomplishment, Affirmation, Ambition, Attractiveness, Healthy, Caution, Compassion, Competence, Clarity, Creativity, Freedom, Organized, Orderly, Spontaneous, Determination, Diligence, Dependability, Devoutness, Discipline, Success, Efficiency, Elegance, Encouragement, Excellence, Enlightenment, Awareness, Excitement, Faithfulness, Forgiveness, Future Oriented, Freedom, Frugality, Fulfillment, Generosity, Gratitude, Grace, Gentleness, Genuineness, Good Taste, Honesty, Humility, Humor, Knowledgeable, Independence, Influence, Inspiration, Intelligence, Nurturing, Lack of Pretense, Patience, Perfection, Respectful, Reliable, Self-esteem, Originality, Intuition, Self-Expression, Sensitivity, Servanthood, Sincerity, Skilled, Detail-Oriented, Solitude, Stability, Temperance, Tolerance, Tranquility, Trust, Wisdom

---

Now choose (or create) your Top 5 Doing Values and Top 5 Being Values.

Here are my Top 5 Doing Values:

1. My top value is **spiritual growth**—honoring/ministering to God.
2. My next value is **honoring family**—honoring/ministering to my family.
3. My third value is **self-development**—honoring/ministering to myself which includes investing in and developing my skills and knowledge, taking care of my health, and allowing myself proper rest, relaxation and fun. (I combined some values here!)
4. My fourth value is **teaching and ministering to others**. (I must remember that if my first three values are not being upheld, then I am no good to anyone else.)
5. My fifth value is **creating** because if I cannot express myself creatively (through music, photography, writing, designing, etc.), I feel dead inside.

Here are my Top 5 Being Values:

Integrity, Love, Abundance, Achievement, Harmony

I know it's really hard to narrow these values down, but I want you to begin to decide what is truly important to you. You can add more values later, but let's start with these ten to give your mind something to focus on. Once you have determined your top values, write them below (or in your journal/notebook). Then think about whether or not your actions and decisions this week honored and supported these values.

My "DOING" Core Values   **Did I honor them?**

1.   Yes   No

2.   Yes   No

3.   Yes   No

4.   Yes   No

5.   Yes   No

My "BEING" Core Values   **Did I honor them?**

1.   Yes   No
2.   Yes   No
3.   Yes   No
4.   Yes   No
5.   Yes   No

How can I better honor my values this coming week?

1.

2.

3.

4.

5.

Insight

Living by our values is a choice we must make daily. Recently, I was approached by an amazing career transition and outplacement company that wanted to outsource work to me for a skill set I used years ago. I was so impressed talking with the world-renowned owner that I eagerly said *"YES!"* However, as I was set up in the company's system and received my first assignment, reality hit me like a ton of bricks. This high-demand position would require me to trade away time from my children on evenings and weekends as well as time to invest in my new businesses (and this book) that I am so passionate about...all for money and for a skill set that I'm not passionate about anymore. That night I struggled with my decision but woke up the next morning knowing that I had to honor my values—what is truly important to me, which is my family and creating a life I LOVE. I, therefore, turned down the job. This situation only served to make me more thankful for what I currently have and to help me realize that I wouldn't trade it for anything the world has to offer. Life is too short. Create a life you LOVE by living according to those things that are of significance to you—your values.

Never forget, your life has purpose, meaning and value. Living by your values brings happiness and fulfillment and enables you to truly be YOU. Don't live by someone else's standards. Be YOU! The world needs you to be YOU!

Now say out loud:

"I CAN DO IT! I choose to live by my values! I choose to be ME!"

Remember, agency thinking (positive self-talk) is crucial for goal achievement. I highly encourage you to print out your values, and put them in a place you daily see as it is easy to get caught up in life and forget about what is truly important.

Don't forget! Take two minutes at breakfast to look at your key goal task today. Add any other tasks that MUST be completed today (planning meals, repairs, kissing your spouse, shopping, de-cluttering, picking up the kids, going to gym, getting your hair cut).

> "The hardest battle you are ever going to have to fight
> is the battle to be just you."
>
> **~Leo Buscaglia**

Now go be YOU!

Day 11: Thankful Thursday

Did you know that being grateful is foundational to being happy? If you are always thinking about what you don't have, you are living out of a mindset of lack. A lack mindset keeps you stuck and unhappy. Think for a moment. Do you become easily dissatisfied with what you have when something "new" comes along as the new thing always seem better in comparison?

If you live a life of comparison, you will NEVER be happy or satisfied.

However, when you begin to see the daily things that you can be grateful for, you start to live out of an attitude of abundance. Living out of abundance allows you to feel content and grounded, instead of constantly striving for the next best thing. Living out of abundance allows you to be happy where you are now, but also thankful for where you are going (toward your dreams and goals).

Sadly, if you are continually focusing negative energy on your current situation, you will not be able to see the resources and opportunities available ("the abundance") to create a better life. Instead, you will only see "the lack" and will remain stuck. Due to the brain's Reticular Activating System, the brain filters out about 95% of the stimuli around you so that you can focus on what you deem important and what supports your current subconscious beliefs. Therefore, a negative focus will literally cause the brain to filter out the positive as well as the amazing opportunities of the situation. But good news! Living out of a mindset of abundance allows new resources and opportunities to be easily drawn to you simply because you become more AWARE of them (as they are no longer filtered out). Abundance surrounds you, but you must learn to see it.

We all have many things to be thankful for but are often so busy focusing on the "lack" that we overlook and take these "little blessings" for granted. Even the poorest of poor in our country are much better off than the majority of the world. You have no idea how many people would love to have what you currently possess—your physical possessions, relationships, talents, skills, opportunities and so on. However, gratitude is not just about realizing what you have compared to those less fortunate than you; it is in truly having *appreciation for what you have now.*[xx]

Studies[xxi] have found that keeping a daily gratitude journal or even just having higher daily levels of gratitude are associated with:

- ✓ Increased optimism, positive emotions and connection with others.
- ✓ Increased determination, attention and achievement of goals.
- ✓ Increased feelings of joy, compassion, forgiveness and generosity.
- ✓ Increased enthusiasm, energy, alertness and metabolism.
- ✓ Improved mood by reducing the stress hormone cortisol.
- ✓ Increased positive behaviors (especially improvements in exercise patterns).
- ✓ Reduced physical ailments (such as daily aches, pains and headaches).
- ✓ Improved sleeping patterns and lowered anxiety and depression.
- ✓ Increased life satisfaction and overall happiness.

Also, neuroscience shows that you can only have either positive <u>or</u> negative thoughts at any given moment—not both. This is great news for those employing gratitude. Gratitude not only stimulates the left prefrontal cortex (the happy brain) but also *blocks* the negativity of the right brain lobe, thus causing you to be even HAPPIER!

In addition, gratitude is literally addictive. Gratitude not only helps to regulate stress but also stimulates the sensation of pleasure in the reward centers of your brain.[xxii] Your brain craves these good feelings and thus searches for ways to create more gratitude. Employing daily gratitude creates an ADDICTIVE habit that will not only increase your happiness but also positively transform your life!

Gratitude creates more gratitude and thus more happiness!
It's a wonderful cycle! Why don't you try it today!

Assignment:

What are ten things in your life that you are thankful for? Write them below (or in your notebook or journal).

I Am Thankful For:
1.
2.
3.
4.
5.
6.
7.
8.
9.
10.

I highly encourage you to think about something you are grateful for every night before you go to sleep to allow your subconscious mind to go to work. This action of gratitude will begin to reprogram your subconscious mind as it will begin to seek and find new solutions and opportunities to create more gratitude. As you sleep, you brain will work to bring your dreams and goals closer and closer! How exciting!

Now say out loud:

"I love my life. I am so blessed.
Good things come to me!"

I will tell you later how this little phrase changed my life. For now, write this phrase down (or create your own positive phrase of thanksgiving), and put it where you will see it DAILY. I highly encourage you to put this phrase in your mobile device as a reminder or alert to go off often throughout the day. See it, and say it at least once a day.

> *"Gratitude unlocks the fullness of life. It turns what we have into enough, and more. It turns denial into acceptance, chaos to order, confusion to clarity. It can turn a meal into a feast, a house into a home, a stranger into a friend. Gratitude makes sense of our past, brings peace for today, and creates a vision for tomorrow."*
>
> ~Melody Beattie

Now when life throws lemons at you, you can choose to look for the amazing opportunities of the situation. You can choose to be grateful knowing that this tough situation is making you learn and grow, teaching you to become better and stronger, and launching you into much greater things. You become thankful knowing that life is helping you to see from an abundance perspective so that new, amazing doors can open before you.

Don't forget! Complete today's key goal task and general tasks, and visualize yourself performing these tasks quickly and easily. Your life just keeps getting better with each new day!

> "We tend to forget that happiness doesn't come as a result of getting something we don't have, but rather of recognizing and appreciating what we do have."
>
> **~Frederick Keonig**

Every day you are becoming more grateful. You see the good even in bad situations. You are finding ways to be thankful in ALL things! You turn your lemons into lemonade and amaze those around you. You are developing a truly thankful heart that is attracting good things into your life. And most importantly, you are thankful to BE YOU!

Day 12: Fearless Friday

Last week we learned that to overcome fear, a person must identify their fears and obstacles and then create very clear and specific action plans for overcoming these fears and obstacles. By taking these clear and simple steps, the subconscious mind will see that the risk of change is not too great or threatening. The subconscious mind will then come into agreement with the conscious mind and will accept significant change, because the change will happen slowly, step by step, instead of in an overwhelming, life-changing moment.

Remember, slow and steady wins the race. Quick success, quick riches, and quick gratification are fleeting. We live in an instant society; this is the mindset of the 99% who live the status quo. They think, *"If I could just win the lottery or get my big break, then all my problems would go away."* However, in the quick and instant results, there is no time for new habits and mindsets to be established.

It is a fact that almost all mega-lottery winners end up broke and worse off within several years of winning. These "winners" have won quick riches, but they have not won the battle of the mind. These winners are still operating on old mindsets, fears, habits and behavior patterns. These winners also feel guilt, shame and unworthiness as they subconsciously believe that they do not deserve this money. Therefore, they subconsciously self-sabotage themselves because of their own internal and external fears and obstacles.

Instead, it is those things which are gained slowly and steadily with time that will last. Slow and steady allows the mind to process and internalize new positive mindsets and behaviors, thus allowing these behaviors and mindsets to become habits. These new positive habits are then what the brain uses to not only create but also *maintain* a new and positive future.

> **"Your thoughts determine your behavior.**
> **Your behavior determines your habits.**
> **Your habits determine your destiny."**
> **~Napoleon Hill**

To produce a successful life, you must develop the *daily habits of success*. If you look at the daily habits of the highly successful, what do they have in common? Simple activities such as getting up early, planning their day, taking quiet time to write down and visualize their goals, exercising, reading, and employing positive-self talk and gratitude. These daily habits may seem very simple; however, they produce much *over time*.

In creating new habits, it is wise to start slowly and consistently and then build momentum with time. Taking baby steps are crucial to creating and maintaining success. When you are starting on your journey to success, don't overwhelm yourself with ideas of accomplishing grand goals in ridiculously short time periods. You will only create fear and resistance (procrastination). Life is a marathon not a sprint. While yes, starting something new may require you to take a "leap of faith," jumping off a gigantic cliff is typically not in your best interest.

> *Starting slowly eliminates fears and excuses.*

Unfortunately, most people have an "all or nothing" mentality. They think, *"If I can't go all out, then I just won't do anything."* Or they say, *"When I have the time and money to go 100%, then I will start."* What is this? This is just another excuse. This is a "jumping off a cliff" mentality. This is just another way the subconscious mind sabotages people from moving their lives forward.

Even five, 10 or 15 minutes a day goes a long way. For example, how many times have you set out to read a great book only to read a chapter and never pick up the book again? Don't try to read a book in a day or even a week. Start by making your goal to read a book in a month. Read five to 10 pages a day or a couple chapters a week. Set your goal to start a new book the first of each month. A book a month equals 12 completed books a year versus several partially and inconsistently read books.

Baby steps (slow and steady) are your secret to success. You may even find yourself craving your baby steps as you will see how far they have brought you on your path (as they have now become a new habit or lifestyle). Sometimes just dedicating five minutes to a task is enough to get you on a roll, and you might get more accomplished than you expected! Plus, you will find that *with time it will become easier to DO MORE.* With time, you will gain good *momentum.*

Start slowly and gradually build <u>momentum</u>.

So, let's think back to the reading of a book again. Some of the wealthiest people in the world claim that they read a book a day. It is said that Warren Buffet reads at least five to six hours a day. Why? Because knowledge (with action) is extremely powerful. The highly successful are VORACIOUS READERS—this is a "success habit." But did they start off reading at this high level? Of course not! They built up to this amazing standard.

For you, is reading a book a day a scary thought? My guess is that you would answer a definite *"Yes!"* Would it make you feel stressed or overwhelmed? Quite possibly! However, is reading a few pages at bedtime scary? No, it is very DOABLE. Is playing an audio book for 10 minutes a day while you get ready in the morning, drive to work, exercise, wash dishes or before you go to sleep at night an overwhelming thought? Probably not.

Why?
Because the subconscious mind will allow change in small and realistic amounts.

> *Think about what you CAN DO, not about what you can't.*

Further, it is the small, daily "doable things" that will give you what Jeff Olson calls the "slight edge" in his book called *The Slight Edge*. With consistency over time, your small, daily actions will *compound* to produce big results. This "slight edge" can be applied to any area of your life—health, relationships, finances, career and so on. For example, by consistently giving small, daily amounts of time to self-development, you will accrue knowledge and skills way above your peers, thus giving you the "slight edge."

I can see this true in my own life. When I was a teenager, I began reading about health and nutrition and have continued over the years to read on this subject for a few minutes a few times a week. With time and consistency, I have amassed a wealth of knowledge to the point that many people ask if I am a natural health professional.

Another example is exercise. Many people think that they must make a huge commitment (hours in the gym every day) to get in shape and, therefore, procrastinate and end up doing nothing. However, instead, what if they committed to exercising only 10 minutes a day or maybe 20 minutes three times a week? Isn't that a more _doable_ place to start? Start where you can, but just start! Over time, small, underline consistent actions add up to big accomplishments. Plus, you can always build up to greater things along the way (as you gain _momentum_).

By the way, did you know there are millions of FREE exercise videos on YouTube that you can do in the comfort of your own home? AND did you know there are zillions of FREE audio books and tutorials on just about any subject imaginable on YouTube and the internet? At the click of your fingers, you have access to just about anything you might ever need to give you that "slight edge." We truly live in the greatest times ever in terms of easily available information.

Listen to this. When my oldest daughter was eleven years old, she started watching YouTube videos on making decorative cakes. By the time she was twelve, her cakes were so impressive that people began to pay her to make these specialty cakes. _If she can do it, what's your excuse?_

No more excuses. The resources you need are more available than you ever thought possible. You just have to take advantage of them. Start somewhere. Start slowly. You can build with time. You will gain momentum and speed as these new behaviors eventually become habits. Your new success habits will then almost "effortlessly" guide you to even greater success.

Just START! You can't finish if you don't start.

No matter how busy you are, you can always fit a couple of minutes into your schedule to work on something that will take you farther on your path to success. (If you can't fit a couple minutes into your day, then you need to sit down and _re-prioritize_ your life.) This little bit of action a day (or week) gets you—with time and consistency—way ahead in life.

Unfortunately, most people live in a continual state of focusing on what they cannot do and why they cannot do it. They have defeated themselves before they have even given themselves a chance! WHY? There are two main reasons this happens:

1. **They take on too much, too soon, get overwhelmed and quit.**
2. **Their continual negative focus on life's problems creates and breeds fears and obstacles that hold them immobilized (paralyzed) in their current state.**

So, what are you telling yourself? What does your self-talk sound like? Is it problem focused or solution focused? Choose to be solution focused, not problem focused. Choose to take baby steps, gaining momentum with time. Focus on what you CAN DO versus on what you "can't."

The highly successful have a solution-focused mindset that sees their desired future and goals and creates practical ways to achieve them…step by step and day by day. The solution-focused mind says, *"No matter what obstacles are thrown my way, I AM finding a way to overcome them. My dream, my will, my passion are bigger than any fear or obstacle that could ever get in my way. If one path doesn't work, I create a new path. I always find ways to achieve my goals. Step by step and day by day, I am winning my race in life."*

> Give no mental attention or recognition to defeat…not even 1% of a thought!

Here's another example. If a football player goes out onto the field seeing only defeat because of the giants he is facing (the problem), will he be motivated to win? Of course not! He lost the moment he walked onto the field. Why do you think pep talks and visualization exercises are so popular with sports teams? Because they work!

What coach would ever say, "*Sorry guys, those other players are giants, and they are going to crush you!*"? No! That coach would say, "*Those guys may be big, but you have more guts and talent than all of them put together. You know the plays. Now dig deep, go out, and give it your best. You can do this! I believe in you!*" The coach's goal is to root out any thoughts of defeat and to deeply instill beliefs of success. The coach would go over the plays to help the players visualize outcomes. And if he was a really good coach, he would have the players visualize and feel the emotions of winning the game. By the way, a lot of positive emotion is created through the team "chant" before the team walks on the field to play.

Thinking, speaking, visualizing, and seeing the solution (winning) allows the mind to create strategies to win. In setbacks, the brain reroutes and creates new strategies (this is called pathways thinking). When the football player has trained his mind to be solution focused, even if he does lose the game, he knows that he will try, try again until he does succeed. Over and over, he creates new pathways to better help him obtain his goal.

Remember! Fears and obstacles will ALWAYS come your way. You must choose whether these fears and obstacles will control you (problem focused) or whether you will control and conquer them (solution focused). Decide today to be a conqueror!

It's time to look at the giants in your life. Think about the fears and obstacles that hindered you this week in achieving your goals. We have layers of subconscious sabotage that we have created over the course of our lives that must be peeled away. Each week, as you complete this exercise, you will be shocked at the layers that will be revealed to you. Plus, you can develop new fears as new opportunities present themselves, making this a valuable on-going exercise.

Identifying your fears and obstacles is like peeling the layers of an onion.

For example, it was after several months of completing this weekly exercise that I identified one of the greatest obstacles hindering me from moving forward into one of my biggest dreams and goals. That particular week, an occurrence triggered a thought that had gone through my mind about a possible negative effect that could happen to my family if I obtained this great life goal.

While it was all theoretical, my subconscious mind saw this "negative consequence" as being a very REAL threat and, therefore, had been blocking me from moving forward. Over and over, I had taken a step forward, only to stop dead in my tracks. I would then make up an excuse to make myself feel better. Finally, I decided to tell that fear that it was time to die. I then visualized what I *wanted* to happen with my family upon achieving my great goal, instead of what I feared.

Now it's your turn. Circle (or write down) your greatest fears and obstacles for this past week.

What are my Fears?
- Fear of Rejection
- Fear of Failure
- Fear of Criticism
- Fear of the Unknown
- Fear of Abandonment
- Fear of Intimacy
- Fear of Betrayal
- Fear of Poverty and Lack
- Fear of Aging, Sickness and Death
- Fear of Loss
- Fear of Success

Internal Obstacles?
- Feeling Unworthy
- Procrastination
- Excuses
- Negativity
- Grieving the past
- Worry
- Self-Criticism
- Lack of Confidence
- Lack of Time
- Lack of Focus
- Lack of Specific Needed Skills
- Indecisive
- Unorganized
- Unmotivated
- Undisciplined
- Impatient
- Bad Habits and/or Addictions
- Poor Health
- Gluttony
- General Poor Diet, Lack of Exercise and Water Intake
- Obsessive Behaviors
- Consistent Poor Use of Time or Avoidance of Productivity
- Poor Boundaries in Work, Life, Relationships
- Always Blaming Others
- Always needing to "Rescue" Others or to be "Needed"
- Always needing to be in Control or Control Others

Highly Destructive Internal Obstacles?
- Unforgiveness
- Bitterness
- Resentment
- Anger
- Jealousy
- Victim Mentality
- Guilt
- Shame
- Negative Coping Strategies   (Complaining, whining, criticizing, gossiping, backbiting, "the silent treatment," manipulation, temper-tantrums and so on.)

External Obstacles?
(Hindrances in my environment and through others).
- Lack of Finances
- Lack of Resources
- Lack of Social support
- Negative or Criticizing Friends, Family, Neighbors, Co-workers, Employers

Other?
(For example: On-going negative thoughts/beliefs against myself, situation or my future.)

_____

The biggest fear and obstacle that I faced this week in achieving my goals:
Fear:
Obstacle:

Next, it's time to create a statement of action to overcome these fears and obstacles.

Examples:

Fear of Being Incompetent: I overcome my fear of being incompetent by studying those whom I want to be like, reading relevant and informative websites and books, and watching pertinent YouTube videos, thus growing my knowledge, expertise and confidence level.

Fear of Failure: I overcome my fear of failure by recognizing that failure is simply a stepping stone to success. I choose to daily complete one small task toward my dreams and goals and choose to pick myself up anytime I may fall down.

Fear of Rejection: I overcome my fear of rejection by choosing to love and accept myself knowing I am not perfect, but I am daily growing as a person. Daily, I look in the mirror and tell myself how amazing and capable I am!

Obstacle of Limited Finances: I overcome my obstacle of limited finances by finding free and inexpensive resources to get my business moving forward.

Obstacle of Lack of Skills: I overcome my lack of skills by learning what skills are needed for what I want to accomplish. I study from those who have these skills and read books/articles/blogs on how to develop these skills. I practice these skills in my daily/work life.

Obstacle of Complaining: I overcome my obstacle of complaining by choosing to focus on the positive and to be thankful for my life (my job, my spouse, my kids, my family, my health, my home). I choose to stop negative thoughts and words, replacing them with positive words and thoughts that will create the life I desire.

Obstacle of Critical People: I overcome my obstacle of critical people by limiting my time with these negative influences. I recognize that these people are dream killers because of their own past failures and negative subconscious beliefs. These critical people do not define me or control my destiny. I control my life and destiny.

Obstacle of Social Media: I overcome my addiction to social media that is taking important time away from my family and my work by limiting social media time to my lunch breaks and after my children go to bed.

My Statements of Action:

I overcome my fear of _____ by _____

_____

_____.

I overcome my obstacle of _____ by _____

_____

_____.

Please REPEAT OUT LOUD your new positive statements of action. Write them on a sticky note, and place them on your bathroom mirror. Repeat every time you brush your teeth.

Now also repeat out loud the following:

I let go of the fear of _____ and the obstacle of _____. I now release them completely from my life and allow love, joy, peace, abundance, success and freedom to flow through me. I choose to live my mission, my purpose. I am powerful. I am worthy. I am lovable. I am capable. I am free to be who I was created to be. I welcome good things to come into my life from this day forward. I am a winner! Today I am finding a way to make my dreams a reality!

(P.S. If you are having a hard time releasing the past, please use the visualization exercise *Day 28: Releasing and Embracing* at www.trainyourbrainworkbook.com.)

Insight

What if your fear is actually protecting you from a "REAL" danger?

Here's my little story. I decided at the ripe, young age of 39 to learn snowboarding with my kids. The first season I went out thinking I was going to easily conquer the mountain and instead it conquered me as I took some bad falls. As the next season approached, I practiced my balance using special equipment, visualized my turns and decided I would stay on the bunny hill until I gained my confidence. However, when the day came, I stood at the top of that bunny hill literally shaking with fear. At times, I would actually "freeze," paralyzed with a fear of falling and getting hurt again. I was, honestly, shocked that I was reacting in such a fear-based way.

While my subconscious mind was doing a great job of trying to protect me from getting physically hurt, it was also causing massive anxiety concerning learning this new sport. I watched as little children flew by me effortlessly; while there I was, a grown woman, having an emotional breakdown at the top of a bunny hill! It was ridiculous! I was allowing my fear to control me instead of me controlling my fear. At this point, everything in me wanted to quit. However, I had to make a choice of what I wanted to do. Did I want to quit, or did I want to press through and create a fun sport to participate with my kids? It was my choice and my choice alone. I finally decided to say *"enough"* to the fear and to take control of my emotions so I could continue to pursue my goal—I would conquer that big, bad bunny hill!

As a result, I began to research new studies[xliii] that show how anxiety, panic disorders and phobias stem out of the fight-or-flight response to momentarily "paralyze" us with fear, so we can "assess" the situation. This was exactly what was happening to me! I would sit at the top of the hill feeling paralyzed as my thoughts were going wild! Research also reveals that by simply taking a few deep breaths, I could help reset my parasympathetic nervous system to get out of this debilitating fear response. Therefore, the next time I got to the top of the bunny hill, I took a few deep breaths. Then I assessed the situation—I was not going to die on this little hill.

But WHAT IF I did fall? This was a very real possibility! Therefore, I took a few moments to <u>visualize</u> myself falling, not getting hurt and quickly getting up and continuing on. At this point, something switched in my brain as I now knew that I was going to be okay. Falling was OKAY! I might get some bruises, but I was not going to die! I, therefore, breathed out all fear and worry and breathed in victory as I then *visualized* what I needed to do and pictured everything going smoothly. Over and over, at the top of the hill, I would smile and say, *"I do can this! I got this! This is so EASY!"* At the bottom of the hill, I would say, *"Just do it one more time,"* and would end up going up many more times. Slowly but surely, I took it one slide down that bunny hill at a time. And you know what? I may have stayed on that bunny hill for a while (and my kids teased me about it), but I knew that slow and steady would get me on that big mountain. And it did!

Another important lesson I learned from snowboarding is that you will move toward whatever you are looking at. For example, if you are looking directly at the obstacle you want to miss, you will automatically move toward it. However, if you look in the direction you want to go, you will move in that direction instead. When our focus is on our obstacles, we will end up smacking right into them. **However, when our focus is on where we want to go, we will easily glide around any obstacles that come in our path.**

No fear or obstacle will stand in your way. You are a winner!
Remember...where there is a will, there is a way!

Day 13: Celebrate Saturday

CONGRATULATIONS on another amazing week! This week you created focus by deciding on your main objective for the week, learning the skill of chunking, creating agency thinking (positive self-talk) and defining your values. You have also begun to understand the importance of focusing on gratitude (versus lack), solutions (versus problems) and on how "slow and steady" creates momentum and great achievement over time. This new focus will allow you to easily begin moving toward happiness, abundance and success!

Now take a moment and reflect on your AWESOME accomplishments for the week. Did you feel the pull of your subconscious mind to quit? Was this week hard to push through? Did you want to give up? Well, you are still here! You fought the urge to quit, so job well done!

Next, I need you to say out loud, **"Good job (your name)! You did it! You are AMAZING! I am so proud of you! GOOO (your name)!**

This may sound silly...and I bet it made you smile....but again, this is agency thinking, and it is a powerful key to training your brain for achievement. You are reinforcing new behavior or habit formation while also creating new positive neural pathways in your brain.

> *Insight*
>
> Studies show that one of the top reasons for unhappiness in the workplace is lack of praise and recognition. If you want your employees to succeed, then encourage them. Give them honest (not artificial) praise for what they have done *well*. This goes for your kids, spouse, and loved ones too! Wire those around you to excel by recognizing and praising their good work and effort. Further, recognize the potential and purpose within them and remind them just how special they are. They NEED to hear this from you! Make a positive difference in the world today... starting with those around you!

Now it's time for **FUN**! Go do something special to celebrate and reward yourself!

No skipping this step! Your brain needs this positive reinforcement to begin to establish these new behaviors as habits. So go out with friends, go to a movie, go for a long walk, go to the ballgame, take a bubble bath, treat yourself to ice cream, go for a hike or bike ride, take a nap, get a massage or manicure...whatever is fun to YOU! And do it all while congratulating yourself!

I will reward myself by:

Remember to take two minutes at breakfast to look at your task list for today. This is also your day to catch up if you missed an assignment this week. Add any other tasks that MUST be completed today (shopping, repairs, cleaning, activities, etc.).

Cheers to a job well done! You are on your way to living your dreams!

Day 14: See It Sunday

Today we will "see" your future as it is "SEE IT SUNDAY." It is tempting to skip this step, but visualization is KEY to teaching your brain (primarily your subconscious mind which creates your belief systems) to accept the future you want as reality.

WHAT IS the Conscious and Subconscious Mind?

The brain is very complex. Therefore, I will attempt to explain, in as simplified and elementary form as possible, the three brain layers (reptilian, mammalian and neocortical) that make up what we call the conscious and subconscious mind.

The inner most layer of our brain is often referred to as the reptilian brain; it does not communicate logically but more instinctually and acts automatically as its focus is on keeping us alive by regulating our vital body systems. Next, the middle brain layer is known as the mammalian or "emotional" brain and communicates through intuitions and emotions as it reacts based on experiences and memories to…yes, protect us. These two interconnected brain layers are focused on survival (homeostasis) as they run our autonomic nervous system (ANS). Our ANS oversees our sympathetic nervous system (regulating our stress or "fight-or-flight" response) and our parasympathetic nervous system (regulating our "rest and digest" response). As a result, these self-focused, "reactive" brain layers can only focus on the "now," not the future, and desire immediate gratification (a survival response). Most importantly, these primitive brain layers contain the limbic system which is involved in motivation, emotion, learning and memory. These primitive brain layers are what we will refer to as the subconscious mind.

The outer brain is the neocortical brain, also referred to as the neocortex or grey matter. The neocortex is the "human," logical brain and comprises 85% of the brain's mass. The neocortex is responsible for such functions as conscious thought, language, long-range planning, big-picture thinking as well as voluntary muscle movements and is what we will refer to as the conscious mind. Further, the neocortex can be broken down into four lobes (frontal, parietal, temporal, occipital) as well as two hemispheres. The left hemisphere is more logical and rational, while the right hemisphere is creative, intuitive and emotional as it is connected to the primitive brain.

Ultimately, it takes the whole brain positively working together to create productive results—this is our goal. Now I must remind you that I am not a neurobiologist or neuroscientist. Considering the brain has around 86 billion neurons and several 100 TRILLION connections, my teaching you every detail, function and interrelation of the brain is out of my expertise. Instead, my job is to show you how the brain affects goal achievement, thought processing, motivation, habits, beliefs and happiness…the ingredients of success.

**I want to teach you how to
MAKE YOUR BRAIN WORK FOR YOU,
instead of you working for your brain.**

So, let's start by taking another look at the subconscious mind which never sleeps and never stops taking in information—it is a nonstop recording device. Scientists, physicists and neurophysiologists have estimated that your brain is inundated with around 200 to 400 billion bits of data every second. If your conscious mind had to constantly deal with this much data, you would be completely overwhelmed and would short-circuit!

As a result, the subconscious mind decides what data is relevant and stores information in memory form. It is from these stored memories and experiences that your belief system (based on your current perspective and "reality") are created and which influence every moment of your life. If new data comes in that is not congruent with your current belief system, the subconscious will typically just reject it. Therefore, if your subconscious mind has been programmed to believe that you will never be wealthy, attractive or loved, it will fight tirelessly to uphold this belief and will reject new outside information that says otherwise. Because this primitive brain's goal is to protect you by promoting homeostasis (balance), it likes for everything to stay the same versus creating change. This protective brain also prefers the familiar as the familiar is a "safe" option.

Further, this non-rational mind communicates to the logical conscious mind not in words but through emotions, "gut feelings," intuitions, automatic reflexes (increased heart rate, running from danger), images (daydreaming) and dreams. The subconscious is constantly at work behind the scenes determining the "best" response to any given situation and then communicating to the conscious mind what should be done next. Because this instinctive, primitive brain's primary goal is survival, it is always on guard to find and warn against a threat. Therefore, it is more negatively focused. Since change is seen as a "threat," the fear response is produced, and your automatic (instinctive) reaction is to run, fight back or become completely "paralyzed." This response is helpful when you are being chased by a lion or bear but not when you are trying to bring positive change to move your life in a new direction. Instead, your subconscious keeps you stuck where you are since you are currently "safe" and "surviving."

However, I have fantastic news! When you use visualization exercises, the brain is tricked into believing a new *reality*. Also, your brain will take in this new reality (into your memory database) according to the emotions you are having at that moment in time. This is why positive emotions (such as happiness and gratitude) with this new visualized life will show the subconscious mind that there is *nothing to fear*. <u>Once fear is removed, your subconscious mind will be like a sponge soaking up your amazing ideal life images</u>. Your subconscious will then begin to develop new beliefs about you and your life to support these images and positive emotions. AND it will do everything in its power to see that your new beliefs come true!

Does this make sense? Seeing your future *must* involve your emotions—your feelings—if your subconscious mind is to make the connection. When you close your eyes for the visualization exercise, not only see yourself in your dream future...in your dream home, car, business, ministry, body, vacations and relationships, but also FEEL what it is like to be in this perfect future. Imagine a future free of worry, full of peace and overflowing with joy and thanksgiving. Take in a deep breath, and soak in these powerful positive feelings. Let them become a part of who you are *now*. Continue to remember these great feelings as they will motivate you to move your life forward.

**In essence, you are "tricking" your mind to believe the future is "NOW,"
and telling it that this "now" is <u>SAFE</u>.**

With *repetition*, your mind *will* begin to accept this dream future as a true possibility (as the subconscious mind learns through repetition). You will, therefore, find yourself doing things to move yourself forward to obtain these goals and dreams. The mind-blocking obstacles will gradually be removed and be replaced with positive thinking, positive images and positive feelings that will motivate you to take steps toward these goals. You will feel your future being drawn toward you as you attract what you focus on. In essence, you are establishing a new belief system—an unshakable belief in your heart that says, *"The life I desire is MINE!"*

Feeling Worthy

Visualization also plays a critical role in creating within you the feeling of being worthy to have the future you desire. A big subconscious block for most people is in not feeling worthy or "good enough" and which is instilled in them from past negative experiences and relationships. These hurtful memories are very real to the subconscious mind. Therefore, the subconscious works in the background trying to "protect" you from new hurts and disappointments by *reminding* you of your past traumas, failures and disappointments. This all results in you feeling unworthy of creating new and better experiences and relationships and is how you become "stuck" in repeating life cycles.

This is why positive visualization is so powerful to the subconscious mind. The more vivid and real your visualization becomes, the more real it will seem to the subconscious mind. Then your mind will accept that you deserve this desired life (because it will think you already have it!). As you soak in the great emotions of the visualization, *tell* yourself that you are worthy to live your life purpose and have an abundant life. At first, the visualization will seem like a fantasy (as you will still feel unworthy), but with time, you will begin to feel worthy and will have an overwhelming desire to obtain this great future.

However, if time continues and you are still fighting feelings of unworthiness, take time to look deep inside yourself to see what is holding you back. You may need to forgive or apologize to someone. You may need to right a wrong. You may need to forgive the person who spoke terrible things about you or to you. You may need to forgive your parents for modeling and instilling in you a victim or poverty mentality. Begin to search deep within to reveal the "lies" that are telling you that you don't deserve a better life…a life of love, happiness and abundance. Maybe you need to forgive *yourself*!

Feeling worthy starts by LOVING YOURSELF.

Love yourself. No matter your age, gender, size, nationality, intelligence, social or financial status, choose to love yourself exactly as you are NOW. If you don't accept yourself as you are, you will hinder yourself from moving forward into what you want. If you need to lose 30 pounds but cannot accept and love yourself as you are now, then your subconscious mind, and thus your body, will think that it does not deserve to be thin and healthy.

Make a conscious decision to accept and love yourself exactly as you are NOW.

We love and accept our children for all their imperfections because we see the potential within them. You are perfectly imperfect, and that's a wonderful thing! Loving yourself is a choice and is foundational to creating the life you desire. When you love yourself, you will respect yourself. You will respect your body, your time, your abilities and your right to live a life of love, happiness and success…a life of abundance. Also, only when you love yourself can you truly love others.

You will only **ALLOW** love and abundance into your life to the degree that you love and accept yourself. If you do not love yourself, you will sabotage every relationship where someone loves you more than you love you. And you will not be able to accept or keep the wonderful blessings that await you. Not being good enough is a lie.

Admit it. You've been lying to yourself all these years.

Every day, look in the mirror, look yourself in the eye, and tell yourself, "*I love you, and I respect you.*" Daily, say to yourself that you are amazing, smart, capable, attractive, and you deserve to live an abundant life. You may feel resistance at first as you might not believe these statements. Don't fight with yourself. Instead, tell unworthiness, resistance, and negative beliefs to go from you, to leave you. Then say what you want to come into your life. For example, "*I let go of all feelings of unworthiness, and I welcome love and abundance into all areas of my life.*"

You DESERVE an ABUNDANT LIFE

You deserve not only a better life but also a chance to make this world a better place. No one on this planet is better than another. We are all precious, and we all deserve to live out our God-given purposes and potential. We owe it to ourselves, to others and to our Maker (Universe, Higher Power)! Remember, there is only one YOU, and only you can do what you were put on this earth to do! You are incredibly special and unique! Your potential is limitless!

Still not sure you deserve (are worthy of) *incredible abundance*?

You're not alone. Why does the highly successful 1% of the population own more wealth than the 99% combined? It's because the 99% subconsciously feel they don't deserve a life of abundance—they do not feel worthy of having "more." They have been programed this way from childhood and, therefore, go through life on autopilot with this belief system. They have been told that money doesn't grow on trees and that there is not enough to go around. They are programmed to believe that only certain people have what it takes to become financially well off. They are taught that wealth only comes as a result of grueling, hard work as a person must sacrifice everything and everyone to become wealthy. They associate wealth with becoming selfish, greedy and making money into a god. They are told that rich people are lying thieves and cheats. They watch television shows that portray the rich as wasteful, vain and eccentric.

Therefore, the 99% create subconscious excuses as to why they cannot live a financially abundant life.

Think about this: why are most spiritual people broke? It is because they have a subconscious view that money is evil and will ruin them. They internally think that if they have wealth, they will become selfish and greedy. They often think that it's wrong to desire money or to be wealthy. Or maybe they think a lowly and humble life is being submissive to God.

Let me ask you a question? How are you going to make a difference in this world if you are constantly broke, struggling, defeated and depressed? Think of all the starving children you could feed if you allowed abundance to flow to you. Because it's not really about YOU, it's about how you can give back and SERVE OTHERS. It's about your CONTRIBUTION to this world.

**Let me tell you what I consider to be selfish and greedy;
it's when you have a powerhouse of potential within you,
and you don't use it to make this world a better place.**

And, yes, abundance is more than just money—it applies to ALL areas of your life. However, if you can recognize that money is simply a *vehicle* for you to live out your greater purpose and to make a positive difference in this world, then your old "autopilot" view about money will finally change. You can have as much money as you *allow* into your life. Your current money situation is a reflection of your current autopilot view of money.

What is your *current* autopilot view about money?

_____I don't feel worthy or deserving of having "more."
_____I don't think it's possible for me to have more.
_____Money doesn't grow on trees.
_____There is not enough money to go around.
_____Only certain people have what it takes to become financially well off.
_____Wealth only comes as a result of grueling, hard work.
_____A person must sacrifice everything and everyone to become wealthy.
_____Wealthy people are selfish and greedy.
_____Wealthy people make money into a god.
_____The rich are lying thieves and cheats.
_____Rich people are wasteful, vain and eccentric.
_____Money is evil. Money is the root of all evil.
_____Money will ruin me. Money will make me become selfish and greedy.
_____I can't handle money. I don't trust myself with money.
_____I'm not smart enough to become wealthy.
_____Others will dislike me if I make too much money.
_____A lowly, poor and humble life is being submissive to God.

What did your parents always say or imply about money?: *"We don't have enough," "Being broke/struggling is the way it is," "Debt is normal," "Everyone lives paycheck to paycheck," "Money ruins lives," "You can't be happy and rich," "It's shallow to want money."*

My New Money Mindset
(Which statement most resonates with you?)

- ✓ I can have as much money as I want and allow into my life.
- ✓ I live in an abundant universe where there is no lack.
- ✓ I am a magnet for incredible things...including wealth!
- ✓ I walk in an attitude of gratitude and abundance.
- ✓ I am a lender and not a borrower. I am an amazing and generous GIVER!
- ✓ I ALWAYS have MORE than enough.
- ✓ I attract ALL that I need. All that I need comes quickly and easily to me.
- ✓ I attract abundance, exceeding abundance!
- ✓ I continually find and create new sources of revenue that easily flow to me.
- ✓ Money chases me. I attract money and build wealth easily.
- ✓ Money flows to me and through me easily and appropriately.
- ✓ I rule over money. I am a good steward of money. I take control and ownership of my finances.
- ✓ Money obeys me as it is my tool to create an extraordinary life and world around me.
- ✓ I have total peace and freedom in my financial life. I am financially FREE!
- ✓ Prayer: *Thank you God (Universe) that You are the source of all abundance and that through You, I always have more than enough. Thank you that You are blessing the works of my hands and daily guiding me into a life of abundance that I might be a BLESSING in this earth.*

Begin to change your perspective, and you will change your life.

The fun thing is that when you follow your dreams, the money will *follow* you...if you *allow* it! By opening yourself up to receive more, you will attract all that you need to make your dreams come true. So, are you now beginning to understand that you deserve abundance...in ALL areas of your life? The world is counting on you to be the best possible you, which starts by loving and believing in yourself! You must see yourself as worthy and deserving of these good things. *Allow* these good things to come to you by clearly visualizing them as yours NOW. Don't worry about the "HOWs," you will figure them out in time.

Stop Stressing and Learn to Relax

If you find yourself fretting about all the HOWs, then you're simply holding yourself back. Stress and worry wreak havoc on your nervous system (which includes your brain). By taking time to relax and be still, your subconscious mind will begin to find the answers and will speak to you through intuitions. A journal can be a great way to allow your subconscious mind—as well as your spirit and God (Universe, Higher Power)—to talk to you. I encourage you to complete your visualizations at night before bed, and then soak in the happy, positive and grateful emotions you create. All night, your subconscious mind will search for solutions, and you may just wake up with answers to your HOWs. The solutions are there, you just have to give them a chance to come forth. So choose to fully release yourself to the dreams in your heart. SEE these dreams as so real and crystal clear in your mind, and then just watch what happens!

So RELAX....
The answers will come. Just keep dreaming!

Insight

The Power of Visualization and Goal Setting

Visualization and goal setting have been very powerful in my own life. For example, after years of my husband and I talking about the kind of house we wanted to purchase, we finally began to act. We knew that we wanted a home with a lot of space and a large plot of land to provide plenty of room for our family of six and also to hold meetings and other functions that we desired. However, in our small town by the ocean, half a million dollars doesn't go far, and property taxes are sky high. Therefore, we had to make the choice to either keep making excuses and settling for less OR to step up to the plate and set a concrete goal of buying the house we wanted. (I will tell you more about our story of negative financial cycles later in this book). We decided to set the goal and to accomplish it in the next nine months.

We didn't know HOW we were going to do it, but we committed that we would find ways to make it happen. We looked at houses online during those months and went to open houses to tour homes we liked. We kept clear in the forefront of our minds what we wanted, and we were determined we would get it. We visualized ourselves living in these types of houses, hosting events and enjoying this kind of "lifestyle." With time and consistency, we began to feel "worthy" of living in the home we desired.

During this time, we also found ways to pay down our debt, save more money for the down payment and increase our credit score. We ended up paying off most of our debt including both of our vehicles. My husband qualified for many top bonuses, and my coaching business began to grow. In addition, I had taken some photography classes, and friends and acquaintances began to offer to pay me to take their family portraits.

It wasn't always easy, but we both DECIDED to keep our minds 100% positive toward finding and buying the house we needed and wanted. In the meantime, my husband's newly paid off car was totaled in a car accident, and we discovered we had an old debt reported against our credit. In the past, we would have been discouraged. But not this time! We agreed to stay positive (telling negativity to leave us), to take care of these matters and to KEEP GOING!

Again, we didn't know how it would happen, but as time went on, we found ways. Why? Because the VISION was REAL in our minds and hearts. We fully believed that we would receive our belief. We were DETERMINED to keep the mindset of abundance and quench out any thought of negativity against our plan (which takes serious effort!). We continually envisioned ourselves in our new home, happy and with all that we needed.

After months of searching, we found the home we wanted—a good investment with a great price and a big profit potential with a few upgrades. However, we then faced more obstacles in qualifying for this big of a home loan, as we were labeled "high risk" because of the nature of our commission-based businesses and our past financial ups and downs. After facing rejection, we picked up our pride off the ground, kept going and found a lender who helped us to get our finances and credit in order…and we ended up qualifying for even MORE than we needed!

Guess what? We bought the house we wanted within our EXACT timeline. However, it wasn't until we stopped making excuses; set a clear goal with a deadline; and followed through that our dream became a reality. We thought it, saw it, felt it and believed it!

SET a clear goal with a deadline, SEE it as real in your mind, and then GO fiercely after it!

Never forget!

Tell the lies to go! Tell unworthiness to go! Tell resistance to go! Tell stress and worry to go! Forgive yourself, forgive others, and let go. Then welcome love and abundance into all areas of your life. You deserve to live your dreams! You deserve to fulfill your potential! You deserve a good, happy, successful and ABUNDANT life! You deserve to make this world a better place! You deserve to be the AMAZING person you truly are and to live the AMAZING life you were created to have!

Are you ready to reprogram your conscious and subconscious mind for success?

Visualization is powerful. Please now listen to the Day 14: *A Day in Your Perfect Life* audio recording at www.trainyourbrainworkbook.com, and then write down the positive feelings you felt during the visualization exercise.

"Seeing" my future made me feel:

1.

2.

3.

4.

5.

> *"The best way to predict your future is to create it."*
>
> ~Abraham Lincoln

Feeling ambitious?

Begin to design your tasks list for the week— Monday through Friday. (Look at Monday's assignment). Some of you will find it easier to design your weekly schedule on Sunday rather than Monday morning. If not, just stick with Monday morning.

Another week well done! Keep up the good work! You should be incredibly proud of yourself!

THINK IT, SEE IT, FEEL IT, BELIEVE IT!

Week 3: Breaking Limiting Habits & Mindsets

This week is about breaking old, limiting habits and mindsets that have held you back. Are you ready to create the habits and thinking patterns of success? Creating the change you desire takes time and effort. Your life is like a garden—it will grow what you sow into it. If you don't like what you are growing, then begin to plant the seeds that will produce the kind of crop you desire. You must also uproot the weeds that are trying to kill your harvest. This week we will do some planting and some uprooting. Are you ready?

Decide today if you will live your dreams and goals or just maintain the status quo. The choice is yours. I cannot force you to start your race to victory, nor can I drag you over the finish line. This is your race, and you alone choose your results. Choose to be an overcomer in this life! You were created to be EXTRAORDINARY!

Week Overview:

Day 15: Motivated Monday: Determining Action for the Week, Eat Your Frog

Day 16: Thoughtful Tuesday: The Power of Your Thoughts and Words

Day 17: What and Why Wednesday: Evaluating Values, Boundaries, 80/20 Rule

Day 18: Thankful Thursday: Gratitude, Happiness and Success

Day 19: Fearless Friday: Facing Your Weaknesses, Creating Confidence

Day 20: Celebrate Saturday: Celebrating Your Achievements, Habit Formation

Day 21: See It Sunday: Dreaming Big, Vision Board

> *"What you get by achieving your goals is not as important as what you become by achieving your goals."*
>
> **~Zig Ziglar**

Now is the time to create the future you desire!
You can do it! You are extraordinarily AMAZING!

Day 15: Motivated Monday

Today is about getting motivated to make your dreams a reality!

First thing Monday morning (or Sunday evening), look at your Key Goal and the specific tasks listed under it. Decide on your focus for this week, and then choose five specific tasks that support this focus to be completed Monday through Friday. This is only **one task per weekday**. I am not asking for hours spent on each task, even giving ten minutes of focused time will keep you moving forward. Write down, put in your calendar and/or phone task app these five tasks/actions that support your goal. (If you feel ambitious, add another SMALL goal task from your secondary goals. However, I would rather you do one task well than add on too much too soon—only add another goal task when you feel ready.) Then take 60 seconds and visualize yourself completing each of these goal tasks *quickly and easily*. You can add your daily general tasks too or wait until the day of.

> *"Never give up on a dream just because of the time it will take to accomplish it. The time will pass anyway."*
>
> *~Earl Nightingale*

Example:

My Main Focus this Week: Career—Marketing my services

Monday:
Key Goal: Career—Research marketing techniques of those with similar services
Secondary Goal: Health—Drink 9 glasses of water
General Tasks: Go to bank, Take son to baseball practice

Tuesday:
Key Goal: Career—Create a strong "elevator pitch" to explain what I have to offer
Second Goal: Health—Drink 9 glasses of water
General Tasks: Pay bills, Grocery store, Mail Invitations

Wednesday:
Key Goal: Career—Create business cards through an inexpensive online site
Secondary Goal: Health—Drink 9 glasses of water
General Tasks: Laundry, Dust, Vacuum

Thursday:
Key Goal: Career—Finalize and order business cards
Secondary Goal: Health—Drink 9 glasses of water
General Tasks: Fold laundry, Mop

Friday:
Key Goal: Career—Research professional networking groups and choose one to attend
Secondary Goal: Health—Drink 9 glasses of water
General Tasks: Have oil changed in car, Pick up birthday present

Saturday:
Goals: Make-up day for any tasks not completed
General Tasks: Wash cars, Mow grass

My Main Focus This Week:

Monday:
Key Goal:
Secondary Goal:
General Tasks:

Tuesday:
Key Goal:
Secondary Goal:
General Tasks:

Wednesday:
Key Goal:
Secondary Goal:
General Tasks:

Thursday:
Key Goal:
Secondary Goal:
General Tasks:

Friday:
Key Goal:
Secondary Goal:
General Tasks:

Saturday:
Goals: Make-up day for any tasks not completed
General Tasks:

(Note: There is a printable Weekly Goal Setting Template at www.trainyourbrainworkbook.com as well as a copy in your Toolbox located at the end of the book. Also, whenever you complete one of your Top Ten Goals for the year, cross it off and replace it with a new goal. From time to time, you may need to determine a new Key Goal to focus on…this means you are moving forward!)

Next...Mark Twain has a great saying called *"Eat your frog."*

Am I asking you to go eat a frog or maybe some frog legs? Thankfully, no! Eating your frog means to do the task you like the least FIRST. Get this task over with before you even have time to procrastinate about it. Because guess what? If you wait until you *FEEL* like doing it, it will never happen. AND the longer you wait to do something, the more time your mind has to convince you to not take action. Procrastination is one of the biggest causes of failure.

What's the answer? Just do it! Take action before you have time to even think about it. The highly successful are not just planners but doers; they quickly make decisions and then immediately follow through. The unsuccessful take forever to make a decision and then change their mind a thousand times. Therefore, take on the habits of the highly successful, and just do it! Get out of bed before you have time to hit the snooze button; exercise before you have time to talk yourself out of it; pick up the phone and make that call before you have time to hesitate; create your plan of action for the day and start doing it before you have time to make a list of excuses as to why you can't do it. Don't wait. Just do it!

For me, my frog is exercising. It's not that I don't like to exercise; however, if I don't do it as soon as I get up, I will often put it off, get busy with other things, and in the end, it will not get done. Therefore, by doing it BEFORE I do ANYTHING else, I don't get distracted or procrastinate.

Insight

If you want to be unfocused and distracted (which can promote procrastination), have a lot of clutter around you as you work. Clutter distracts the brain. This is why you feel peaceful when the house/office/desk is clean and orderly, and why you feel chaos when clutter is piled up everywhere. Instead of waiting until the clutter is out-of-control, set aside five to 10 minutes a day for the next few days to get all the clutter out. Your brain will thank you, and I bet you will be more excited to get working too!

Maybe eating your frog means starting on a project before checking your email or social media. Maybe it's about working on self-development before turning on the television. Maybe it involves making phone calls, doing laundry or paying bills before you start doing anything else.

So, what's your frog? What task is the easiest for you to procrastinate on (at home, at work, etc.)? Maybe it's creating your task list! Choose your frog, and then go do it! However, if you still feel hesitant, visualize yourself completing this task with *total EASE*. We hesitate because of fear and dread. But *WHY* does something have to be hard or dreadful? It doesn't! Choose to see yourself accomplishing your tasks quickly and easily! And just think how GREAT you will feel when the task is completed! Now go EAT YOUR FROG!

Eating your frog is another great habit of the highly successful.
Procrastination is a sure sign of living the status quo.
Conquer this bad habit by eating your frog today!

Day 16: Thoughtful Tuesday

Today we are thinking about our thinking again. I am going to cover a lot of ground, so get your running shoes on! Did you know that your thoughts create your words and your emotions? Therefore, let's take a look at the powerful impact of your thoughts and words on your life.

Studies[xxiii] show that positive thoughts and words increase a person's capabilities by:
- Creating optimism about life which helps the person to not only commit to goals but also be more successful at achieving them.
- Promoting overall happiness, life satisfaction and improved self-concept.
- Stimulating the brain to think bigger, more creatively and productively as it becomes more mentally alert, able to make quicker and better decisions and to solve problems faster and easier.
- Helping the person to more quickly and easily cope and rebound from setbacks.
- Increasing positive feelings/emotions about one's self, others and life in general.
- Strengthening the cardiovascular and immune systems.
- Reducing stress, increasing energy levels and promoting healing and overall health, thereby assisting in slowing aging and increasing life span.

That's a few pretty good reasons to choose to employ positive thoughts and words!

HOWEVER, negative thoughts and words produce all the opposite effects such as lowered self-esteem/self-concept, limited creativity, increased stress, inability to cope, weaker immune system and reduced over-all energy and functioning. Negativity is *toxic* to our lives and bodies.

Life and death are in the power of YOUR tongue...literally. Your words reveal the thoughts of your heart. Out of the abundance of your heart, your mouth speaks. So, what are you speaking? Are you speaking positive words into your life—your daily situations? OR are you speaking death? When things start to go wrong, what comes out of your mouth? Are your words building a highway to your future or a ditch to get stuck in?

It is so easy to have a setback and begin to have a pity party for yourself as you begin to tell yourself everything that is wrong with your life. Did you realize that when you have a pity party, you are totally focused on yourself and your own needs? You are being completely selfish and self-absorbed! (OUCH!) When you find yourself slipping into a complaining, *"Poor me"* state, STOP yourself. Instead, begin to think about what you have to be thankful for—remember, there are many in far worse situations. Most of us in our worst day are far better off than the majority of the world. Instead of turning your thoughts inward, turn them outward.

Turn your thoughts toward how you can help others. Get your thoughts off of yourself! Shake yourself out of your pity party! Negative thoughts and words create negative emotions which are all negative energy. Negative energy turns inward and like a vacuum sucks the life out of you and those around you; you begin to feel tired, down and miserable.

In contrast, positive energy gives outward. It gives life to you and those around you. Positive energy energizes, excites and even stimulates your immune system.

Your thoughts, words and emotions are simply energy in motion, and you have control over them. When the negative thoughts and feelings like frustration, irritation, stress, envy, rejection, despair, anxiety, worry and the like come at you like a flood, STOP them! By entertaining these strong negative emotions, you are only allowing your brain to enter into the fight-or-flight response as your primitive/emotional brain (the limbic system) takes over, and your logical brain is completely overridden. This is why people make irrational decisions and say irrational things when they are either stressed, highly emotional or when a subconscious fear is triggered. Further, this "limbic storm" of irrational thoughts and emotions reinforces this negativity into the neural pathways of your brain. The sooner you choose to calm your emotional brain, the less neurons will be involved.

Therefore, when a limbic storm of negative thoughts, words or emotion hits you, choose to STOP, take a deep breath, and TELL those negative thoughts and emotions to LEAVE you (specifically naming/labeling each one). SEE them going out of you. They cannot stay unless you give them permission. Then invite and envision love, joy and peace being poured into you from above (from your Higher Power, the Universe) like a refreshing river. And **choose** to rest in peace fully believing that everything is going to work out (lean on your Higher Power).

So, even when life hits you with unfair circumstances, **choose** to walk in peace and joy. **Choose** to find something positive in the situation to help you learn and grow. **Choose** to find ways to be thankful despite the hard times. **Choose** to find solutions even in the midst of the mess. **Choose** to see yourself coming out of the situation as stronger and better and farther along on your path to success. **Choose** to tell yourself that you will overcome every hindrance and obstacle. You *can* do *anything* you set your mind to do.

What it boils down to is this: in every situation you must choose to either be a *victor* or a *victim*. A victor strives to overcome. A victor sees himself conquering the finish line. A victor stays positive even in the midst of difficult circumstances and keeps going. However, a victim defeats himself by his own actions and beliefs. Think about that for a minute. **A victim defeats himself**. No one can defeat you unless you allow them to.

Are you going to be a victim of your circumstances (of your past), or are you going to be a victor? Will you determine to overcome whatever comes your way, or will you continue to make excuses that it is out of your control? Life is not always easy. Life is not always fair, and everyone gets knocked down. However, the victor chooses to get up again, while the victim chooses to lie down for a pity party. Your life outcomes are your choice.

Don't say *"I can't or I'll try."*	Say *"I can!"*
Don't say, *"I can't do anything about this situation."*	Say, *"I shape my circumstances. I determine my future. I take control of my life! Good things are coming to me!"*

Therefore, today let's start replacing negative thoughts and words with positive thoughts and words. Let's turn your lemons into lemonade! To do this you must FIRST root out those ugly negative thoughts and words that limit you and hold you back; they limit your belief in yourself and thus limit your success. These negative beliefs lie deeply rooted in your subconscious mind. The only way to root out old negative belief systems is to create new positive belief systems. We do this through creating new thinking patterns. With *repeated* use of these new positive thinking patterns, new neural connections will be formed, while negative connections will be deactivated and rendered obsolete with nonuse. It's simple: *whatever you repeatedly tell yourself will become your beliefs.*

Take a moment and reflect on the ten most common negative thoughts/words you have about yourself and your life (health, work, relationships, money, success, self-concept, etc.). Think hard and be honest with yourself. This is a very personal exercise. You may feel uncomfortable as you are identifying your deeply rooted internal belief system and also facing your hidden fears and self-perceptions. I know this is difficult, but I know you can do it! The goal is to identify your negative thinking patterns/habits and to replace them with positives. (You will write your positive statements at the end of this lesson.) For example, replace the thought or comment of:

"I'm not good enough"	with	"I am good enough. I am capable. I am valuable. I am worthy. I am full of potential! I am AMAZING!"
"I'm so ugly"	with	"I am a beautiful human being. I am beautiful in mind, body and spirit. My beauty radiates from the inside out and blesses those around me."
"I'm so fat"	with	"I am attractive. I love my body. Every day, my body is changing for the better. Daily, I am leaner, healthier and stronger. I choose healthy foods and take care of my body. I am my perfect size."
"I'm unlovable" "No one likes me"	with	"I am lovable. I deserve to love and be loved. I give and receive love freely. Daily, love increases in my life. I love people, and people love me."
"I can't do this anymore" "Life is too hard" "Everything is against me" "My life is a wreck!"	with	"I love my life! I can do this! I choose to keep going and to press through. I am making the best of this situation. I see opportunity instead of obstacles. Everything is working out great for me.
"I'm such a failure" "I'll never succeed" "I'm stupid" "I can't do anything right" "No one believes in me"	with	"I am smart. I am capable, and I can do anything I set my mind to do. I choose to pick myself up and keep going despite any obstacle or setback. I am a victor! I attract everything I need to be a HUGE success. Watch out world, here I come!"
"I don't deserve good things" "I'm worthless" "I hate myself" "I'm not enough"	with	"I am worthy to have the life I desire. I am worthy to have wonderful relationships, health, wealth, happiness and abundance. I LOVE and respect myself. I love who I am and who I am becoming."
"I'm so broke" "I can never get ahead" "I have to kill myself to make a living" "Becoming wealthy is too hard" "Money will make be selfish and greedy"	with	"I have all the money I need. I allow money to come into my life. I am a magnet for money. I continually find new sources of revenue that flow easily to me. Money flows freely to me and through me so I can be a blessing to the world."

Notice how these new positive statements are all present tense, not something far off in the distant future that you can't quite grasp. They are **NOW**. The subconscious mind understands *now*, not the future.

The Subconscious Mind

It is said that if the brain were compared to a giant iceberg, the conscious mind would be the tip above the water, while the subconscious mind would be the giant mass submerged beneath the surface. Further, the subconscious mind does not "think," but rather stores information, emotions and experiences received and "reacts" accordingly. The subconscious mind could be compared to the hard drive of a computer as it stores and views information very LITERALLY.

Therefore, if you keep saying "*I am fat,*" the subconscious mind receives the information that you are fat and should remain fat. If you state you "*will*" lose weight (future tense), the subconscious mind may process this as you will lose weight in the future, not now (thus, possibly blocking you from currently losing weight). As a computer simply obeys (reacts) according to how it is programmed, so your subconscious mind obeys (reacts) according to its current programming. Your current life is a reflection of how you have programmed your MIND!

For example, if you have repeatedly told yourself that you can't lose weight, it's too hard for you to lose weight, or you have continually stated, "*I AM fat,*" your subconscious mind will simply uphold these beliefs. Even more, your subconscious will often work by creating internal excuses as to why you can't exercise or as to why you really *need* those unhealthy foods. Your mind can even manifest physical symptoms to hinder you from exercising as it controls your automatic bodily functions. This is why repeated, present tense statements are so important to the subconscious mind—statements such as "*I AM lean and healthy,*" or "*I AM creating a lean and healthy body,*" or "*Every day, I AM more fit and healthy,*" or "*I AM losing weight with total EASE!*"

Next, it is important to note that because the subconscious mind is so literal, it does not always register "not's" and "don'ts," but instead downloads key words and emotions. To illustrate, what if I said, "*Don't think about chocolate cake. Don't think about slicing through layers of creamy, decadent icing and light fluffy chocolate cake. Don't think about taking a delicious bite.*" I bet you thought of chocolate cake, right? I bet you could even taste it! Or what if I said, "*Absolutely do NOT think about a beautiful sunset full of vibrant pinks, oranges, purples and reds.*" Your mind can't help but think about what is being said and paints a picture of it in your mind's eye. This is how the mind works.

Therefore, if you repeatedly tell yourself, "*I will not smoke.*" Guess what? You are really just reminding your brain to smoke! Therefore, say what you want: "*I AM smoke FREE,*" or better yet, "*I AM making healthy choice,*" or "*I AM creating a healthy body and lungs*" or "*I desire only healthy habits,*" or simply say, "*I AM FREE!*" while happily and thankfully visualizing your smoke-free life. (You may also need to forgive yourself for this destructive habit, and forgive those who modeled it to you. Ask your Higher Power for help, assistance and forgiveness as well.)

When you are changing eating habits, instead of saying, *"I won't eat cookies"* (which reinforces the image of "cookies" in your brain and makes you want them all the more), say *"I choose healthy snacks and activities such as…,"* or *"I am creating a healthy, fit and strong body,"* or *"I respect my body and love feeding it with healthy foods."* If these statements seem too farfetched for you, then just begin to create "want" by stating, *"I want to be healthy,"* *"I want to eat healthy foods,"* *"I want to be lean and fit."* (Also, visualize and/or show yourself pictures of your ideal body/health. Walk with confidence feeling/imagining how good it FEELS to be fit and healthy.)

> "To get what you want, want what you get." Therefore, clearly tell and show your brain what you WANT.

Concerning money, instead of just focusing on debt by saying, *"I don't have debt,"* say *"I am debt free."* Or better yet, eliminate the word "debt" and focus on the "abundance" that you WANT. *"I am financially free,"* *"I continually attract abundance,"* *"I always have more than enough,"* *"Money flows easily to me,"* *"I am a wise steward of money,"* *"I am so incredibly blessed!"*

For relationships, instead of focusing on your unhappiness, focus on what you WANT. *"I have loving and thriving relationships,"* *"My relationships are in perfect balance,"* *"I attract amazing people and relationships into my life,"* *"I am so thankful for my spouse (family member, boss, co-worker, neighbor),"* *"Every day, my relationship is improving,"* *"I love being married,"* *"My marriage is full of love and joy,"* *"I am so happy. I love my life and my relationships/spouse/family!"*

Regarding your work, instead of focusing on how much you dislike your job, focus on what you WANT. *"I excel at my work,"* *"I love finding ways to use my talents and abilities,"* *"My boss is so pleased with my excellent work and attitude,"* *"My skills and abilities are daily increasing and opening new doors for me,"* *"I love my job!"*

Concerning your children, as an alternative to just telling a child NOT to do something, such as *"Don't hit"* (which puts the focus on "hitting"), also say what you WANT, such as *"Play nice"* or *"Be kind."* When my children start acting less than kind, loving and obedient, I often ask them, *"Are you being kind, or are you choosing to act selfishly?"* (Don't tell others that they ARE selfish. You don't want to program their minds to BE SELFISH. State that they are <u>choosing</u> to <u>act</u> selfishly.) I may also ask, *"What is the kind/best choice in this situation?"* Or *"Are you obeying, or are you <u>choosing</u> to disobey?"* Begin to wake up children's brains to think for themselves. Finally, end the conversation by *focusing* on making good choices (or even role playing) of being kind, playing nice, obeying, etc.…and of course, hug and love on them!

Insight

Children's minds are extremely impressionable, especially before the age of seven when their brains are often in a highly receptive theta wave (hypnotic-type) state. Therefore, don't repeatedly tell a child that he/she is a *"rude, disobedient kid who never listens,"* unless that's what you want him/her to be! Be aware that you are continually programming your children's thinking patterns, self-image and beliefs!

Many of your current beliefs are from your childhood. Think back to your early years and to your perceptions about yourself, love, money, health, success and so on. (Ask your brain and your Higher Power to reveal your hidden negative beliefs.)

Focus on what you WANT:

"Healthy Habits," "Financially Free," "Happiness," "Thriving Relationships," "Abundance," "Eat Healthy," "Love," "Good Choices," "Promotion," "Fit Body," "Kindness"

The highly successful focus on what they WANT, the unsuccessful focus on what they DON'T want. Your life will move toward what you focus on. A runner looks ahead to see where she is running. If she is always looking sideways, she will end up going sideways, tripping or falling flat on her face! A ball player focuses his attention to exactly where he wants to throw the ball. If he wants to throw the ball to the right but keeps telling himself "not" to throw the ball to the left, his brain will keep hearing "left." It will, therefore, be difficult for him to hit his target on the right.

Your focus determines the direction of your life. Can you now see why focusing on what you *want* and not on what you don't want is so CRUCIAL? Therefore, show your mind (especially your subconscious mind) what you *want* by creating a clear vision. *Focus* on those wonderful things you *want* in your life such as abundance, love, joy, peace, balance, favor, health, wisdom, intelligence, promotion, success, confidence, creativity, wonderful relationships, prosperity, greater spirituality, thankfulness, positive energy and so on.

Finally, another step in conquering the subconscious mind is to choose to accept and love yourself as you are NOW (faults included) and to find peace with your current situation. If you do not, then you are only fighting your current state which only brings more fear and resistance to change. When you fight something, there is strong thought and emotion which further seals it into your subconscious mind (the "emotional" brain). Statements such as *"I hate my life...my body...my job...my marriage...my bad habits...being broke...being single...being unhappy"* create strong negative emotion.

Instead, you want to seal into your mind those good things that you DO want. This is why the *"I AM"* statements are so powerful. *"I AM happy, healthy, wealthy and wise!" "I AM becoming the best possible me!" "I AM creating the amazing life I desire!" "I AM so thankful for my life!"* These statements begin to reprogram your current belief system to accept yourself for what you are now *and* for what you want to become. These statements help you see yourself as worthy of the life you desire.

> **"What you resist not only persists, but will grow in size."**
>
> **~Carl Jung**

With *consistent* repetition, your subconscious mind will finally "get the message" and understand what you truly WANT. When this happens, you will feel a sort of "internal shift" as you easily begin to move toward what you WANT. For example, you will notice that you will no longer even desire unhealthy foods and will find yourself doing things to work toward your health goals because you will WANT to be healthy MORE THAN you want those bad choices. Those bad choices will no longer be "worth it" as you have created a *greater desire* to be healthy. However, don't be discouraged if "the shift" doesn't happen in a day or even a few weeks...just be persistent! When the belief comes, it will happen! Simply resisting will not accomplish anything. You must create enough desire within you (by clearly showing your subconscious mind what you truly WANT) so you can begin to easily move toward your dreams and goals.

Are you ready to rewrite your life to be *AMAZING?!*

Assignment:

Today you will determine the ten most common negative thoughts/words you have about yourself and your life and then rewrite them as new positive statements in the box below. In doing this, you will be deciding what you WANT in your life so that you can begin to move toward these wonderful and positive things. If you have religious beliefs, I encourage you to rewrite your negative statements using your spiritual texts. (This exercise is also in printable format at www.trainyourbrainworkbook.com.)

My Ten New Positive Statements about Myself/Situation:

1.

2.

3.

4.

5.

6.

7.

8.

9.

10.

Great job! You are weeding out those old, ugly self-sabotaging thoughts!

Now go stand in front of a mirror, look yourself in the eye, and repeat these new statements out loud. Most importantly, see yourself in *full possession* of them *now*. Since repetition is key to reprogramming both the conscious and subconscious mind, I HIGHLY encourage you to review your positive statements DAILY, and put them in a place you will frequently see (bathroom mirror, refrigerator, night stand, door, etc.). In addition, when you say your new statements, SMILE and FEEL the good emotions associated with these positive words.

> **Remember,
> agency thinking
> (positive self-talk)
> is CRUCIAL
> for goal
> achievement.**

Here's a helpful tip. To assist the brain in its natural tendency to create habitual patterns, add your positive statements to specific actions that are already habits (and **SMILE** while you say them).

For example, when you brush your hair, you could say something like, "*I am a beautiful human being.*" When you brush your teeth, "*I am creating the life I desire with my positive words.*" When you get dressed, "*I attract amazing things into my life.*" When you eat, "*I am so fit and healthy and nourish my body with good things.*" When you drive your car, "*I am on the path to success.*" When you go to bed at night, "*I am so richly blessed.*" These are simple yet highly powerful exercises that will rewire your thinking patterns.

Now it will take time and *consistency* to make your new statements become automatic responses. Habits take three to six weeks to form and three to six months to become automatic through the subconscious mind. The more consistent you are, the faster your brain will rewire to create these new positive thinking patterns. Therefore, at first, I encourage you to have your positive statements pop up on your electronic devices and/or to put them on sticky notes on your mirror, by your tooth brush, in your closet, car, refrigerator, desk, etc. until the statements become automatic "thought habits."

The ultimate goal is to use your autopilot settings to your advantage to create the life you WANT! The more you see these positive statements and repeat them, the more you will deactivate the old negative thought pathways and create new positive neural connections supporting these new statements. Thus, you will in time turn these new statements into *beliefs*.

When you BELIEVE something, you will ALLOW it to happen in your life.

When you do not believe something, your mind will not allow it to happen. Right now, your subconscious mind believes all the negative statements you have been telling it. Therefore, it is critical that you say your new positive statements over and over again. Envision yourself in *full possession* of what you are saying while *feeling* gratitude and happiness. With time and *consistency*, you *will* believe these statements as true (and then the "shift" will happen!). How exciting that you can literally resculpt, rewire and reprogram your brain for what you truly WANT!

Congrats! You are now ready to be a VICTOR and go conquer your negative and sabotaging self-beliefs. Whenever the negative thought, word or emotion comes to you, immediately say "*NO*" or "*STOP*," and quote the new positive statement. Negative thoughts are like weeds, they must be uprooted, not just plucked. With *consistency* you will uproot these bad thinking habits or as I like to call them, "*Stinkin Thinkin.*"

Choose to put a conscious end to the weeds that are sabotaging your efforts to move your life forward by **THINKING HAPPY THOUGHTS!** AND keep identifying your negative beliefs, rewriting them as positives and eliminating them from your life. These positive statements are not only powerful weed killers but also seeds to produce an amazing harvest in your life. Remember, your life is a garden—what you sow will grow!

Again, put these Top Ten Positive Statements where you will see them. Smile and repeat them DAILY! I have also included a printable PDF of this positive statements exercise at www.trainyourbrainworkbook.com. Use this exercise frequently. Whenever life gets you down, print out this exercise, and write ten ways you are overcoming whatever circumstances you are facing. My husband and I have used this exercise when facing some really tough situations and obstacles. Together, we write down our ten new positive statements about our situation, read them out loud, and hang them on our bedroom mirror. Over and over, it has made a huge difference in our attitudes and our outcomes!

It's time for you to see yourself as the victor and overcomer you were born to be! Shake yourself from the dust of the earth. You are not a worm anymore. It's time to FLY!

Now say out loud,

"I AM happy, healthy, wealthy and wise! I AM a VICTOR!"

Don't forget! Take two minutes at breakfast to look at your goal task(s) today. Add any other tasks that MUST be completed today (meal planning, repairs, shopping, cleaning, kissing your loved ones, etc.). Then visualize yourself completing these tasks with *total ease.* Your life just keeps getting better and better!

If you have a minute, go to Day 16: *Water Crystal Experiment (Dr. Emoto)* at www.trainyourbrainworkbook.com and watch how words, thoughts and emotions change water crystals. It is quit astounding. While there are skeptics who say these crystals were not produced in an adequately controlled environment, I still believe this experiment is food for thought. Your body is made of 60-80% water.

Now go be the VICTOR you were born to be!
THINK HAPPY THOUGHTS TODAY! They are your secret to success!

Day 17: What and Why Wednesday

Today we will look at your WHATs and WHYs as we again work on your top core values. Think back over the last week. Did you truly honor your core values with your actions? If you did, you will have a sense of fulfillment. If not, a feeling of imbalance.

Below is the list of "DOING" and "BEING" values again. I encourage you to re-evaluate the core values you chose last week. Maybe you chose values that are really your family's values and not truly yours. Maybe you felt guilty for choosing career or recognition or winning. However, you must decide for yourself what your core values are—what is truly important to YOU. Your values define who you are and where you are going in life. Your values reveal where to direct your time, energy and focus. Also, your values create passion in your life that will push you to achieve your goals and dreams. Your values are part of your WHATs and WHYs that make you want to BE more and DO more.

Therefore, what is truly important to you? What drives you? What gets you excited? What makes you feel alive? What values most resonate with you? I want you to be really honest with yourself and what you truly want in life. Read through this list carefully. Then again choose or create your top five Doing Values and Being Values. It's time to solidify these values as they are foundational to your life's success. (You will write your values at the end of this lesson.)

DOING VALUES

Serving, Helping, Giving, Teaching, Training, Equipping, Protecting, Empowering, Advising, Assisting, Solving, Pursuing, Entertaining, Performing, Ministering, Communicating, Mentoring, Inspiring, Influencing, Leading, Directing, Impacting, Excelling, Advancing, Promoting, Creating, Planning, Designing, Building, Beautifying, Collaborating, Organizing, Participating, Discovering, Exploring, Guiding, Nurturing, Growing, Connecting with Others, Honoring Family, Supporting Community, Improving Marriage, Developing Career, Making Money, Spiritual Growth, Love of Learning, Being a Role Model, Working Hard, Excellence in Service, Self-Development, Self-Discipline, Mastery, Expertise, Relaxation, Having Fun, Being in Nature, Playing Sports, Dancing, Developing Musical Skills, Competing, Winning, Being Successful, Being Challenged, Acting with Speed and Precision, Experiencing Pleasure, Intimacy, Upholding Spiritual Principles, Worshipping, Physically Disciplined, Obedience, Performance, Personal Power, Physical Vitality, Being Healthy, Productivity, Quality, Recognition, Respect for Life, Respect for People, Respect for the Environment, Risk Taking, Excitement, Tongue Control, Generating New Ideas, Playing, Good Decision Making, Good Listener, Ensuring Security, Becoming Famous, Being Goal Oriented

BEING VALUES

Integrity, Joy, Happiness, Love, Peace, Abundance, Balance, Truth, Uniqueness, Purity, Harmony, Loyalty, Empathy, Achievement, Spirituality, Authenticity, Godliness, Beauty, Flow, Energy, Transcendence, Unity, Accomplishment, Affirmation, Ambition, Attractiveness, Healthy, Caution, Compassion, Competence, Clarity, Creativity, Freedom, Organized, Orderly, Spontaneous, Determination, Diligence, Dependability, Devoutness, Discipline, Success, Efficiency, Elegance, Encouragement, Excellence, Enlightenment, Awareness, Excitement, Faithfulness, Forgiveness, Future Oriented, Freedom, Frugality, Fulfillment, Generosity, Gratitude, Grace, Gentleness, Genuineness, Good Taste, Honesty, Humility, Humor, Knowledgeable, Independence, Influence, Inspiration, Intelligence, Nurturing, Lack of Pretense, Patience, Perfection, Respectful, Reliable, Self-esteem, Originality, Intuition, Self-Expression, Sensitivity, Servanthood, Sincerity, Skilled, Detail-Oriented, Solitude, Stability, Temperance, Tolerance, Tranquility, Trust, Wisdom

Setting Boundaries According to Your Values

Our habits reveal not only our true values but also our boundaries. According to Dr. Henry Cloud in his fabulous book *The One-Life Solution,*[xxiv] saying *"yes"* or *"no"* is how we honor and dishonor our values as well as set the boundaries of our lives. For example, we may say our core value is family, and yet we can never say *"no"* to commitments that take away valuable time with our family. These poor habits result in ineffective boundaries, and boundaries are meant to protect our values. Healthy boundaries allow us to decide where we put our time, energy and focus. Our *"yes"* and *"no"* are powerful boundary setters that will allow us to determine the direction of our lives.

According to Dr. Cloud, what you say *"yes"* to will define where you are headed. Therefore, you must take time to stop and assess your life. Are you saying *"yes"* to things that support your core values? Are you saying *"yes"* to things that support your vision for the life you desire? Sometimes you must say *"yes"* to something that may be difficult or that you do not necessarily want to do, but you know in saying *"yes"* that you are moving closer to your goals and living out your true values. And sometimes you must say *"no"* to things that are not supporting your values and goals. Either way, it is always wise to take a step back and determine if saying *"yes"* or *"no"* is in alignment with your values and goals.

Now I am not suggesting that you selfishly turn down doing anything that isn't about YOU and your goals. What I am saying is to think things through, especially to those commitments that are very time-consuming. Determine if this time-consuming activity (and it may be one that you LOVE) is moving you toward your dreams or whether it is simply taking time and focus away from what really needs to be accomplished.

What can be Trimmed in Your Life?

When a company has a very clear mission for growth in a specific direction, they will take time to analyze what parts of the company need to be trimmed. Otherwise, these excess "parts" will continue to take time, energy and focus away from the company's primary goal (and thus growth). Let me ask you a question. What happens when a tree is trimmed or pruned? Cutting out the old, dead excess allows the tree to put its energy toward new growth instead of constantly repairing the unnecessary old parts. Even as a tree needs to be routinely pruned, so too, our lives need to be routinely trimmed. Trimming creates fruitfulness.

Now let me note that balance is key. For example, you could assume that saying *"yes"* to a commitment for recreation is taking away from your primary goal. However, that recreational activity could be a very important and needed way to refresh and reinvigorate your mind and body to give you the energy and focus needed to pursue that primary goal. Nevertheless, if the recreational commitment begins taking over your life, then it could be a distraction and begin to compromise your values and goals.

You only have so much time and energy for each day. There is only one you to go around. Decide where you want to spend your time, energy and focus and then make your boundaries clear. Establishing clear boundaries helps to keep you focused and on task. Take a moment to think about how you use your time in any given day. Where is your time, energy and focus being spent? Is it honoring your values?

The 80/20 Rule

Maybe you've heard of the 80/20 Rule, also known as the Pareto principle, which states that 80% of results come from 20% of the action. In other words, 80% of your productivity comes from only 20% of your efforts—or a fifth of your day produces the majority of your results. The other 80% of your time is spent producing only 20% of your results—or you waste most of your day being busy but not actually accomplishing much toward true productivity.

Why is this? As I mentioned early, if most people truly focused 100% at their job, they could quite possibly do all their work in half the time. Most people spend a good portion of their day being distracted by useless tasks, non-pertinent emails, calls and texts as well as disorganization, daydreaming and idle conversations. (I know this has never happened to you!)

But wait! It doesn't stop just at work. We do it in our private lives as well. We are always so busy running here and there and doing this and that and yet 80% of our busyness accomplishes very little (20% of our results). Therefore, we have to begin to look at the 80% of our time that is consuming our lives and yet producing so little toward our goals and values—our priorities—and then determine what we can cut out.

> *"In life, you will get what you tolerate. Period."*
>
> ~Dr. Henry Cloud

Otherwise, what we tolerate will remain in our lives. Are there things in your life that you tolerate even though they consume your time/energy or go against your core values? Are there responsibilities that you could delegate to others? Could you hire someone to run errands, make phone calls, market your business or clean your house? Are there activities or relationships that are taking over your life that need to be trimmed?

Here's a hard question. Are you too afraid to say "*no*" when people ask for your time or help? If you don't know how to answer when someone asks you for a commitment, take time to think about it. Don't allow anyone to bully you into committing to something that you're not sure about.

And saying "*no*" doesn't have to be rude. If you don't want to give an absolute "*no,*" just politely thank the person(s) for the invitation but then inform him or her that "*AT THIS TIME,*" you have other obligations (priorities) that you must attend to. He or she does not need to know all the details—this is none of his or her business. This is about you standing by your priorities. By saying "*not at this time,*" you allow others to see that your answer is not an absolute "*no*" (as this may be something you might want to do in the future), and it is not an absolute "*yes*" (locking you into a commitment).

However, choosing to live by your values will mean that at times you must give a very firm "*no*" and not feel guilty about it. At other times, it will mean speaking what is really on your mind and heart instead of just answering on autopilot trying to appease everyone. And sometimes, it will mean saying "*yes*" and meaning "*yes*" and following through. This is about setting your boundaries of what you will and will not do. Until your values and priorities are clear, you cannot clearly define and establish your boundaries.

What you do and do not commit to reveals your true current values.

If you recognize that you are not upholding your true values, then you must also recognize that your boundaries or commitments need to be re-evaluated. According to Dr. Cloud, the way you start this process of boundary setting is by deciding what you will and will not do and effectively communicating this to others. When other people begin to see your boundary lines, they will then understand them, learn to respect them, and finally learn to follow them.

For example, if a boss has a sales team that's very dysfunctional, it is because the boss has allowed the sales team to become this way. The sales team is a reflection of the boss's poor boundary setting because he has not clearly established his values, goals and rules for the sales team. A church is a reflection of the pastor's established values, vision and boundaries. Students are a reflection of a teacher's communicated and enforced boundaries and values.

Children are often a very clear reflection of parents' true values and boundaries as kids typically do what parents "do" versus what they "say." I highly encourage parents to establish clear *family* values and boundaries and to clearly communicate these to their children. Even better, have a family meeting to create family values (i.e. respect, honesty, kindness, etc.), clear boundaries (rules and expectations) and to define the repercussions of not following these expectations. Otherwise, you really can't get mad at kids (or adults) for not following rules that are unclear or rarely enforced. Values and boundaries create clear guidelines which brings understanding, peace and security.

In evaluating your current boundaries and commitments, it is important for you to determine whether you are saying "*yes*" out of guilt. Often, when we respond out of guilt, we are actually enabling others to use and abuse us. Sometimes that "*yes*" hinders the other person's growth and progress. For example, what a parent may say "*yes*" to when a child is five years old may be completely inappropriate to say to that child at age 20. By age 20, that parent may be enabling this "kid" to avoid responsibility and maintain dependence.

> "You teach people how to treat you by what you ALLOW, what you STOP, and what you REINFORCE."
>
> ~Tony Gaskins

Or, if you own/run a business/organization (or are in sales) and do not set clear boundaries of when you are available to your customers/employees and when you're not, don't be surprised when your clients/employees need you at *all* hours of the day or night. Most business owners who come to me for coaching are burned out because they do not take time for themselves. It is CRUCIAL that you set times when are you <u>not</u> available. Determine and uphold when you will take time for yourself and time with your family or friends. Let your clients/employees know that you are *not* available at these times. And don't worry that you will lose sales or clients. In fact, the vast majority of people will have no problem with it (and some may respect you more for it!). Further, a few lost sales is far better than a heart attack or stroke.

**Allowing yourself to be overworked is simply robbing yourself
of your health, relationships, peace and joy.**

If you don't have a lot of control over your schedule, then begin to speak how your situation is changing (define what you WANT). For example, my husband was working for a great company, but he was also working 60 to 70 hours a week. This demanding schedule was taking a toll on his health as well as our family unity. Therefore, he began to focus on obtaining quality sales versus quantity. He visualized the great sales he wanted to close and then repeatedly spoke, *"I AM working less and making more."* That year he worked 30% less time and made 30% more money. However, it began by him establishing his boundaries and expectations and focusing on what he wanted to happen so that he could honor his values.

As a life and career coach, I typically don't take on coaching clients in the evening hours when I have four children to attend to. Therefore, I do offer group coaching sessions several nights a week for those who are only available in the evenings. If someone wants to work one on one with me, they must either choose to make their schedule work with mine or find another coach whose hours better suit them. However, rarely has this been an issue.

> "The difference between successful people and really successful people is that really successful people say 'NO' to almost everything."
>
> ~Warren Buffett

If you can't say *"no"* because you are so fearful of losing money or people not liking you, then you must begin to take a look at yourself, your true motives and whether you are upholding the values that are of significance to you. Saying *"yes"* out of guilt is not doing you any good. Too often we respond to others' requests by simply answering on autopilot. We tend to uphold the patterns we have used in the past whether the results were beneficial or not. We have programmed our minds to think this way. We think that by telling someone *"no"* that we are being selfish. However, selfishness and establishing boundaries are two different things. If you are not in control of your life, you will *not* feel happy.

Locus of Control Theory

The "Locus of Control Theory" proves that successful people have an *internal locus of control*. An *internal locus of control* is when you feel in charge of your life: in charge of your decisions, your thoughts and your actions. You accept that your results are of your own doing. You believe that you can influence the events and outcomes of your life. Thus, you feel more powerful, more confident and happier. You become vastly more productive toward what you WANT. You set and achieve much greater goals as you see yourself as the creator and owner of your destiny.

However, those who have an *external locus of control* see themselves as helpless. An *external locus of control* causes people to view themselves as a victim of their circumstances: a victim of their job, family, health, heredity, childhood, neighborhood, finances, "bad luck" and so on. Outside forces are *always* to blame. Happiness is thus contingent on external sources and events. Those with an external locus of control see themselves as a boat with no rudder simply being tossed around in a merciless sea. This lack of control leads to anxiety, frustration, anger and even depression which is then vented in blame, excuses and ultimately hatred of one's own life. Failure, misfortune, hardship and unhappiness are thus inevitable.

I often find that many spiritual people fall into the *external locus of control* category as they want to fully surrender their lives to God but then allow themselves to be tossed around by every situation and circumstance because it must be "God's will" or "fate."

Listen close. You weren't put on this earth to be a helpless victim or a "consequence" of circumstances. You were put on this planet to be a CAUSE for good things! You were put on this earth to be an OVERCOMER, a VICTOR in this life! You were created to be God's (the Universe's) hands and feet in this earth to carry out amazing purposes, not just blown around by the winds of circumstance. You're not a worm anymore. You were created to soar *above* the circumstances and situations and to live a truly abundant and balanced life.

Choose to take control of your life which begins by upholding your values (priorities). If your current boundaries do not uphold your true values (priorities), you need to reestablish what you will and will not do. The goal here is for you to begin to define your boundaries so that you are in control of your life versus everyone and everything else controlling you—this is where true FREEDOM is found. Taking control of your life is the FOUNDATION to happiness, success and fulfillment.

Questions to Ask Yourself:

- Do I commit to things that do not come in alignment with my core values?

- When someone asks me to commit to something, do I go on autopilot mode and automatically say *"yes"*?

- Am I saying *"yes"* to commitments that are taking away from what really matters to me?

- Am I saying *"yes"* out of guilt?

- What can I cut out of my life to give more time to my true priorities/values?

- What are the long-term (versus short-term) consequences of my *"yes"* or *"no"* answers?

- Am I actually enabling others by saying *"yes"* and further hindering their growth?

It's time to take back the 80% of your life that is not producing much toward what you really want. Taking time to think how you can politely and properly use *"yes"* and *"no"* to define your boundaries, set limits and uphold your true values is essential to taking back control of your life. Remember, the highly successful continually *optimize* their lives by *daily* identifying what needs to be trimmed and also what needs attention/focus to produce growth for a better tomorrow.

This is a lot of food for thought. To learn more about boundary setting, I highly recommend Dr. Henry Cloud's book, *The One-Life Solution: Reclaim Your Personal Life While Achieving Greater Professional Success*.

Here is your chance to live by your values (priorities) by establishing healthy boundaries. Did you honor your core values with your actions and decisions this week?

My "DOING" Core Values   **Did I honor them?**

1.   Yes   No

2.   Yes   No

3.   Yes   No

4.   Yes   No

5.   Yes   No

My "BEING" Core Values   **Did I honor them?**

1.   Yes   No

2.   Yes   No

3.   Yes   No

4.   Yes   No

5.   Yes   No

How can I better honor my values this coming week? (What boundaries do I need to establish or uphold?)

1.

2.

3.

4.

5.

Now say out loud,

"I will live by my core values. I will set healthy boundaries.
I will live a fulfilled, productive and balanced life!"

Don't forget! Take two minutes at breakfast to look at your goal task(s) today. Add any other tasks that MUST be completed today (shopping, phone calls, going to gym, etc.).

Now go live by your values and be the amazing
and victorious person you were created to be!

Day 18: Thankful Thursday

On Tuesday, we focused on positive words and thoughts and their impact on our lives. Thinking and speaking positively really boils down to learning to *appreciate* yourself and your life. It is about learning to focus on the good that you want to see come forth in yourself, in your life and in the world around you. We also learned that positive thinking and talking leads to positive emotions, and positive emotions are more powerful than you may realize!

I have a question for you. Does success result in happiness, or does happiness result in success? Surprisingly, studies[xxv] show that positive emotions are not the result of success but actually PRECEDE and PREDICT success!

Did you catch that?

HAPPINESS CREATES SUCCESS, NOT SUCCESS CREATES HAPPINESS!

And here's another shocker: **Happiness is a decision**—a chosen state of mind where you DECIDE to FOCUS on good things. Happiness is taking control of your thoughts and choosing to focus on the things in your life that you are grateful for (instead of focusing on the negative).

Unfortunately, many people hold the false belief that they will *"only"* be happy *"once"* they obtain success and riches. Or *"when"* they obtain their goals, *"then"* they will finally be happy. And it's just not true. You can have all the success and "stuff" you could ever want and still be unhappy. You see, if you are never thankful for what you have now and only compare yourself, your success and your belongings to others ("keeping up with the Joneses"), you will never find happiness. Now this doesn't mean that you should not dream about having more. It means that you must learn to be happy with what you have in life NOW.

If you're not happy <u>now</u>, you certainly won't be happy <u>then</u>!

Also, when you are truly grateful for what you have now, you will be a good steward of it, take care of it, and treat it with respect….whether it is physical possessions, relationships, money, work/career or your *OWN SELF*! What it all boils down to is actually quite simple. You are not grateful because you are happy; you are happy BECAUSE you are grateful!

Learning to be grateful in the "little things" of everyday life is where true happiness begins. Even in the midst of turmoil and bad situations, there are always positive things to focus on and appreciate. You see, gratitude not only brings joy into your life but also sets you up for bigger and better things down the road. Global studies[xxvi] have shown that people who can find joy in the simple pleasures of life will be the most successful in life.

> ### Insight
>
> What if you woke up tomorrow with ONLY the things you truly appreciate?
>
> Look around you. Now look beyond just material belongings.
>
> You have more wealth than you ever imagined. You are *already* wealthy, and you didn't even know it!

Did you catch that?

**Global studies have shown that people who can find joy
in the simple pleasures of life will be the most successful in life.**[xxvii]

According to the broaden-and-build theory of positive emotion,[xxviii] positive emotions help to bring out the best in people because they produce optimism about the future. Positive emotions help people to create their desired outcomes by helping them to think bigger and to see many more possibilities as to how to develop the resources needed to deal with life's numerous challenges. Latitudinal and longitudinal studies[xxix] have found that happier people create the tools needed to produce such things as financial success, supportive relationships and good health.

How amazing that when you begin to find joy in the simple, daily pleasures of life (by deciding to be grateful), you will begin to find love, happiness, curiosity, awe, serenity, inspiration, etc. that will then cause your brain to think bigger, more creatively and to see from varying perspectives. These positive emotions then stimulate the brain to grow, to function at peak capacity, to think more creatively and reflectively; to be more flexible, open minded, empathetic, resilient and solution focused; and to actually **neutralize negativity**! Plus, it is these positive emotions that decrease the stress hormone cortisol while producing "feel good" hormones/neurotransmitters such as serotonin and dopamine, thus creating a sense of well-being.

> "Gratitude can transform common days into thanksgivings, turn routine jobs into joy, and change ordinary opportunities into blessings."
>
> ~William Author Ward

Think about little children; they are so happy and positive about life and the future. You ask them to come up with possibilities, and they will create a big, long list. Ask an adult, and they can only think of a few. Happy emotions cause you to think "big" and creatively like a child—to see possibilities instead of rationalizing them away. It's time to see the world from a child's perspective—a world full of endless possibilities and opportunities.

Insight

"Act how you want to feel and the feelings will follow." You have probably heard this statement before, but science has proven it true! Put a smile on your face as you think about all you have to be thankful for, and just watch how your day changes for the better! Incredibly, the physical act of a great smile (which involves the eye muscles that create "crow's feet," also known as a "Duchenne smile") stimulates the brain activity associated with positive emotion. Go ahead, try it!

Also, did you know that fear and excitement have the same physiological response? This means your body doesn't know the difference between the two. Therefore, when you are about to do something new and feel nervous or afraid, change your perspective by telling yourself that you are EXCITED! Smile and see everything going well, and just watch what happens!

Today choose to stop being so serious and to SMILE MORE! Learn to laugh and take pleasure in the simple things of life. Let the child within you come alive. Create your life to be AMAZING!

On the other hand, negative emotions like anxiety, worry, fear, frustration or anger decrease brain functioning by narrowing attention, cognition, coping skills, and the brain's creative ability to devise new options and solutions because these emotions trigger the survival response. The mind constricts to acutely focus on the "threat," thus greatly limiting the ability to comprehend or be "open" to new ideas and to building resources and relationships.[xxx]

In other words, when your focus is only on the "lack" and "stress" in your life as you try to *just make it through another day in this awful, grueling world where everyone and everything is against you,"* it will be very difficult for you to create the life you desire. In this anxious and self-focused "survival mode," your brain will greatly limit you. In fact, an incredible opportunity could be right in front of you but you will be unable to see it (<u>as your brain will literally filter it out</u>) because of your limiting, negative focus and subconscious beliefs.

> *"Be thankful for what you have, and you'll end up having more. If you concentrate on what you don't have, you will never, ever have enough."*
>
> ~*Oprah Winfrey*

So, in a nutshell, studies[xxxi] show that emotional happiness is based on what we FOCUS ON (think about, talk about, give attention to) and which DIRECTLY predicts our health, wealth, relationships, longevity and success. Positive emotions (created by focusing on the positive and by acknowledging and appreciating life's simple pleasures) create the ability to find the resources and solutions needed to build a better life. These resources then offer new opportunities for happiness, success and even more resource-building, thus feeding a cycle of lifelong growth, happiness and success![xxxii]

As you can see, the easiest way to bring joy and positive emotion into your life is by thinking thankful thoughts. Even when things don't seem to go your way, find something to be thankful for. As you do, you will begin to shift your whole day in a new positive direction. Positive thoughts/words = Positive emotions = Creating the solutions and resources needed to bring more happiness and success into your life! Remember, your brain wires the way you think, so think happy and thankful thoughts!

Thankfulness = Joy = Finding Resources = Success

Assignment:

Studies[xxxiii] show that unhappy people continually compare themselves to others instead of being thankful for who they are and what they have. However, when people are grateful for who they are, their self-worth dramatically increases. Therefore, on the following page (or in your journal/notebook), please list 10 things about YOU that you are thankful for (your attributes, strengths, talents, values, accomplishments, successes, what others most admire about you, and so on). I hope you've learned a few new things about yourself through our journey together.

Ten Things I am Thankful for About Myself:

1.

2.

3.

4.

5.

6.

7.

8.

9.

10.

You are AMAZING! Be thankful for who you are and be proud of it!

NEXT…I want you to find two people to encourage today. Say or write (email, text) a kind word or compliment to show your gratitude toward them. Even better, go find someone you don't even like and encourage them!

Don't forget! Take two minutes at breakfast to look at your goal task(s) today. Add any other tasks that MUST be completed today (giving your spouse a big compliment, hugging your kids, setting up appointments, doing repairs, shopping, de-cluttering, going to the gym, etc.) and see yourself completing these tasks quickly, easily and efficiently. Your life is becoming more amazing with each new day!

"Always remember, you are braver than you believe, stronger than you seem and smarter than you think."

~A.A. Milne, author of Winnie the Pooh

You are amazing! You are capable! You are getting closer and closer to your dreams and goals! Begin to find joy in the simple things of life. Now go be thankful and begin to draw success to you!

Day 19: Fearless Friday

What fears and obstacles did you face this week? (Look back at the list of fears and obstacles from last week if needed.) Did you overcome these fears and obstacles, or did they overcome you? How can you better deal with these fears and obstacles in the future?

Now let's talk about a fear that often lies in our subconscious mind. Have you ever heard the saying, *"A chain is only as strong as its weakest link"*? While you want to focus on your positive strengths and keep developing them, your subconscious mind will still try to hold on to the fears and limitations of your weaknesses. While you do not want to dwell on your weaknesses, it would be unwise not to develop and strengthen them. We want to increase both ends of the spectrum, moving our strengths and weaknesses to higher levels of success.

Focusing on increasing your strengths will give you a great boost in confidence in your capabilities. In fact, when your strengths shine so brightly, few will even notice your weaknesses. However, how much more confidence would you gain if you could positively strengthen your weaknesses? Now please note that some weaknesses are innate, some have developed out of bad habits, and some are a result of lack of attention in developing a particular skill or trait. While I cannot promise that you will eliminate your greatest weaknesses—especially those that are innate to your specific personality—you can most definitely improve them, learn how to work around them, and/or gradually reduce their effects in your life. All the highly successful possess weaknesses as well; however, they have learned to overcome or work around them. Therefore, don't let your weaknesses be an excuse to keep you from attaining your dreams.

Take a moment and identify your greatest strength and your greatest weakness. You may need to look back at your personality assessment. (Go to your personality report from Day 1, re-read your 4-Letter Personality type and look at the strengths and weaknesses section).

> *Decide today that your weaknesses will no longer hold you back!*

Maybe you have a weakness in listening or in communication. Maybe you become easily obsessive, unfocused, impatient or angry. Maybe you are terrified of speaking in front of groups. Maybe you are a serious procrastinator. Maybe it's hard for you to finish what you start. Maybe you have poor self-esteem, are easily hurt or intimidated, or are unable to take initiative. Maybe you are too sensitive to others' opinions and criticisms or let perfectionism hold you back from stepping out. Maybe you're an extrovert and are always so busy talking that you never stop and truly listen. Maybe you're an introvert and have a hard time thinking of what to say when meeting new people and this is hindering your relationships or your ability to grow your business.

In the next exercise, you will write your greatest strength and weakness, and then identify ways you can help strengthen both.

Example:

Here is one of my personal weaknesses that I have learned to overcome (as I am an introverted personality type).

My Weakness: Difficulty in thinking of what to say when meeting new people, especially in business networking situations. (Overcoming fear of the unknown, feeling nervous, intimidated, shy, incompetent and not good enough).

Ways to Improve this Weakness: Create a dialogue model to follow.

1. Before event, repeatedly visualize my conversations going extremely well.

    - **Use visualization to overcome ANY FEAR** such as fear of public speaking, interviews, important meetings, flying, heights, small spaces, crowds, athletic competitions and so on. Visualize the situation in detail, and see everything going smoothly. Repeat visualization until **confidence** is built.

2. Day of event, right before walking into event:

    - Hold picture in my mind of everything going well.
    - Take a deep breath, and allow my entire body and mind to relax.
    - Trick my mind to change my feelings of fear into excitement by shifting what I tell myself. Change *"I'm so nervous!"* to *"I am so excited to do this! I've got this!"*
    - Stand tall with confidence and good posture. Use a **high power pose** to build **confidence**. (The most well–known high power pose is called *"The Wonder Woman."* This is where you simply stand tall with your chest out and hands on your hips, thus expanding your body space and dominance level versus hunching over or tightly clinging your arms to your body which are low power poses, or fear-based body language. Hold pose for a minute or two. To learn more, please watch Day 19: *The Power of Power Posing* at www.trainyourbrainworkbook.com.)

3. Walk into event. Smile BIG. Happily introduce myself while shaking hands. Say a nice compliment if possible. Keep good eye contact and posture. KEEP SMILING!

4. Follow the **FORM model**. Ask about the person's **F**amily, **O**ccupation, **R**ecreation, and then finally share my **M**essage. (In formal settings, ask first about occupation.)

    - **Message** meaning what I want to convey about myself. AFTER I have listened to THEIR NEEDS, I let them know what I can specifically offer them such as my business expertise, a possible business opportunity or a business referral. (Be laid back and personal, not a pushy "sales person.")
    - Memorize my points of what I have to offer backward and forward.
    - Make my **elevator speech/pitch** irresistible, and practice it every day. (Here is my current elevator speech: *"I help motivated people to train their brains for success using proven techniques from neuroscience, psychology and life coaching."* A good elevator pitch will stimulate curiosity and more questions…just what you want!)

      Elevator Pitch Formula: "I help (who) to do (what) by (what means).

5. Exchange contact information. (Give person my business card and ask for his/hers—or write down person's contact information if they don't have a card. I never know when this contact might come in handy, whether for personal or business reasons.)

6. Thank person for talking with me.

7. Pat myself on the back for overcoming my weakness/fear! "*Good job me!*"

8. After event, send a quick thank you note/email to those I collected business cards from.

Now it's your turn!

My Greatest Strength:

Ways to Improve this Strength:

1.

2.

3.

4.

5.

My Greatest Weakness:

Ways to Improve this Weakness:

1.

2.

3.

4.

5.

"Picture a limit as simply a possibility in hiding."

~Josiah Cullen (autistic child)

Insight

To be successful, you must NETWORK, NETWORK, NETWORK!!

Don't expect success to come knocking on your door while you're sitting at home watching television. Get your name out there (in person, through social media, phone calls, etc.). Let others know what you do. BUT FIRST! RELAX! If you feel desperate, others will pick on it and will not be interested in what you have to offer. People reflect back to you what you are communicating verbally, nonverbally and subconsciously. Pay attention to how people react to you as it will give you great insight into what you are actually communicating—which is really your subconscious beliefs. For instance, if internally you feel confident, you will outwardly convey confidence, and people will more than likely buy from you.

A good example is when my husband has gone on selling streaks for months straight, literally selling hundreds of contracts without one single *"no"* for an answer. In contrast, he has also gone for months with absolutely NO SALES, not one solitary *"yes."* What was the difference? During his selling streaks, he felt confident in himself, got himself on a good "roll" (good positive energy and focus) and became unstoppable. He "saw" in his mind the sale completed before he even walked through the door. He then walked in with a laidback, relaxed confidence in HIMSELF. (In sales, you are not really selling a product or service; you are selling "yourself.") Because my husband keeps such a friendly and laid back disposition, people feel comfortable around him. He also talks to prospects (potential clients) as real people—not as customers he could care less about as he just wants their money. He gets to know prospects, which requires him to be truly interested in them. He listens and learns how he can best help them (look again at the FORM model). He is also very honest, which prospects appreciate. If he doesn't feel his services are a good fit for a particular prospect, he will tell them. If prospects like him, feel that they can trust him (because he truly has their best interest in mind), they will buy from him even if he is much more expensive than the competitors.

In contrast, when he got on that really bad streak, it all started when he had a few things go wrong which shook his confidence, put his focus on the negative and got those negative energies flowing. This may come as a big surprise, but people respond negatively to negative energy. With each *"no,"* he felt more and more defeated and created more inner desperation. Thus, a bad cycle began to perpetuate itself. However, now when a bad cycle tries to start, he knows to shift his focus and energy and to see/speak everything working out in his favor. He also realizes that a *"no"* doesn't mean *"never,"* but merely *"not now."* He is simply the messenger, and as he consistently plants good seeds, a good harvest will come in due time.

Therefore, begin working on YOURSELF. Use visualization exercises to visualize confidence…a laidback and relaxed belief that things are working in your favor. Further, create belief by seeing yourself helping others solve their problems through what you are marketing. (Visualize clients being incredibly happy with their results.) If you convey belief, others will receive belief. If you convey doubt, others will receive doubt. They will mirror you! Also, learn to "let go" as trying to "strangle" sales and success will only make things much more difficult. Don't try to force anything on anyone, or you will only cause resistance. Force creates a fear response (fight, flight or paralysis). Instead, learn effective "closing techniques" to gently GUIDE your prospects to clearly see how they are improving their lives by making the decision to work with YOU.

Also, begin to flood yourself with so much positive thinking and positive vision that your mind is no longer bothered by a *"no"* or by the negative situations and circumstances that may surround you. Positive thoughts and energy will create positive results…if not immediately, then down the road. Further, remove desperation by seeing yourself as simply spreading good seed—and be sure to water the seed by "following up" and "cultivating" the relationship. Sales is all about creating relationships. If prospects feel they can trust you, they will befriend you, do business with you, refer you and overall associate with you. Be sincere. Sell "yourself," not just your product, service or business. If others feel that you truly have their best interest in mind, they will buy from you and/or refer you to others—no matter what you are selling!

I would highly encourage you to make developing BOTH your strengths and weaknesses a priority over the next 12 months by adding them to your Top Ten Goals List. And please note that developing both strengths and weaknesses is a progressive work. For example, when you have conquered one weakness or feel as if it is not holding you back as it did before, identify another major weakness, and work on it. Refuse to allow weaknesses to subconsciously hold you back anymore.

Remember, when you are aware of something, you can give it conscious attention for change. Ignoring it does not make it go away. In recognizing your weaknesses, be sure to remember that everyone has weaknesses. There is no perfect person on this earth. Criticizing yourself for your weaknesses is when you become your biggest enemy and often the biggest obstacle in your own life. Choose instead to be your own best friend. Love yourself for being uniquely you (weaknesses included). Treat yourself with respect, and your dreams will come true sooner than you ever thought possible!

AGAIN, it is important to note that you must NEVER give your weaknesses negative attention! Do not focus on them as hindrances but as a way to make you better. Focusing on the negative only draws more negative energy to it and causes it to grow. You must choose to focus on the *positive solutions*. Remember, it is about turning those negative thoughts and energies into positive ones—turning your lemons into lemonade!

Insight

Do you want to hear something that is going to blow the walls off your preconceived ideas about obstacles, limits and weaknesses? Did you know that everyone has a distinct speaking voice? There is no one else with a voice exactly like yours. However, did you know that everyone also has a beautiful and distinct singing voice? You may say, *"Well, you sure haven't heard me sing!"* Actually, everyone has an amazing singing voice, but they may not know it IF they are using improper singing techniques. Many celebrity singing experts have proven that once these obstacles (improper techniques) are removed and correct/proper techniques are employed, a person's unique and beautiful singing voice comes through. There is a beautiful song inside of you, and you may not even know it! What obstacles and limitations have you created for your life? Today begin to see possibilities instead of just limitations.

Let your weaknesses become stepping stones and blessings in disguise. See your weaknesses not in a negative light but in a positive as they will allow you to learn, grow and develop in new and exciting ways! Your weaknesses will make you strong. Your past will make you wise. Your failures will make you an overcomer. Your strengths will make you rise to the top! Keep improving both your strengths and weaknesses, and watch yourself begin to soar up your mountain of success!

Positive Affirmation Statement: (Read Aloud)

Every day, my strengths are opening new doors of opportunity for me.
Every day, I turn my weaknesses into amazing stepping stones to a better life.
Every day, the weakness of _____ is improving and giving me the skills and knowledge needed to attain my dreams and goals.

Visualization

Take a moment and see yourself a year from now, realizing that your most hindering weakness is not even an issue anymore. How are you different? Look around you. What do you see? Now feel a sense of relief as your weakness has seemed to disappear. You have improved it. You have found ways to work around it. And your strengths shine so bright that the weakness is not even an issue anymore. Breathe in your sense of relief, happiness, confidence and positivity toward the future. You did it! You have overcome your greatest obstacle!

Don't forget! Take two minutes at breakfast to look at your goal task(s) today. Add any other tasks that must be completed today (scheduling a date with your partner, finishing a work project, shopping, cleaning your car, organizing the garage, getting a haircut, etc.). Then visualize yourself completing these tasks with total *EASE*. Your life is getting easier by the day!

P.S. Create an **elevator pitch/speech** if you haven't already; this will give you a big boost of confidence too! Formula: "*I help (who) to do (what) by (what means).*"

> "I am strong because I have been weak.
>
> I am fearless because I have been afraid.
>
> I am wise because I have been foolish.
>
> I can laugh because I have known pain.
>
> I am a lover because I have known loss.
>
> I am beautiful because I know my flaws.
>
> I am unstoppable because I know my potential."
>
> ~Unknown

Now go conquer your weaknesses! You are rising to higher levels! You are becoming "more" as you make yourself stronger to climb up your mountain of success! Your weaknesses are becoming stepping stones to an amazing future! Your strengths are continually opening new doors of opportunity for you. You are rising to the TOP!

Day 20: Celebrate Saturday

Today is Celebrate Saturday! Take two minutes at breakfast to look at your task list for today. This is also your day to catch up if you missed an assignment this week. Add any other tasks that MUST be completed today (shopping, cleaning, repairs, etc.).

Next, reflect on your **AWESOME** accomplishments for the week. I have dished out much to you this week as we worked on breaking old, limiting habits and mindsets. I pushed you in facing procrastination by "Eating Your Frog;" in rewiring your thinking patterns; in creating gratitude to fuel positive emotions and success; in establishing your true values and boundaries; in facing your weaknesses, fears and obstacles; and in allowing yourself to truly BE YOU! These are not easy tasks. You are well on your way to becoming a better, more positive, productive and happier you! You are climbing your mountain to success! So job well done! Not only are you breaking old, limiting habits but also creating new success habits to build a new, amazing life!

Therefore, today I want to take a minute and talk about habit formation—the brain's ability to cause you to do something automatically and with little effort. The whole goal of this program is to help you create new, positive and healthy habits for life because ultimately it is your on-going habits that determine the direction of your life.

Creating Healthy Habits for Life

Habits typically take three to six weeks to form; however, they can take three to six months to become instinctual—or performed automatically and with little effort by the subconscious mind. This means that if you are on day 24 of your new eating pattern and go to Grandma's house for Thanksgiving dinner, you had better have a plan of action before setting foot in her house. Otherwise, this inconsistent action (breaking your new eating habit) could give you a flat tire in terms of motivation and momentum.

However, if you do end up binging at Grandma's, make a committed effort to not give up. Many people defeat themselves because of the guilt of "failure" and go right back to old habits. Therefore, you must choose to keep going with your new habit and not lose momentum. It is after three to six months of consistent action that habits become effortless because they are well established through strong neural reinforcement.

So, back to Grandma's delicious dinner and turning a dangerous situation into a plan. Maybe that dinner can be your special reward for the week. You will plan ahead to indulge and not feel guilty about it. However, be prepared that the next few days after the indulgence will be challenging to get back into the rhythm of the new eating pattern. Nevertheless, it is in knowing this that you can prepare, press through and get back on track. Maybe the best plan of action is to have someone else fix your plate with only healthy foods (or bring your own food) and to ask for everyone to be committed to not letting you eat anything unhealthy (accountability). Being mentally prepared ahead of time will help you to maintain momentum when faced with set-backs, obstacles and temptations.

Maybe your plan of action for when your favorite bag of potato chips or chocolate chip cookies starts calling your name is to "wake" yourself up out of autopilot by stopping and asking yourself, *"Why am I eating? Am I hungry or just bored? Is there a better and healthier option? Is this really worth the long-term consequences? I respect my body and choose healthy habits."* Maybe putting these statements on a note card and taping them to the cabinet, pantry door or bag of chips or cookies would be helpful to begin to train your brain to wake up and make a rational decision instead of acting on impulse.

Maybe your new habit involves overcoming an angry temper. Maybe your plan includes limiting exposure to those things that get you really upset and also being prepared with steps or a protocol of what to do when you become extremely angered. Maybe this protocol involves stepping away from the situation, taking three to five deep breaths, asking yourself why you are angry, seeing from the other person's perspective and then thinking about long-term consequences of your actions. *This plan of action allows the powerful and emotional limbic system (subconscious mind) to calm down and for the conscious, rational mind (prefrontal cortex) to begin to take control again.*

Now let me remind you that the subconscious mind is a powerful force behind habits, and it is focused on NOW, not long-term planning. Also, as a survival response, the subconscious is designed to move *toward* pleasure and *away* from pain and suffering. This is why the rational, conscious mind can design a 30-day diet plan while the subconscious mind screams in the background, *"Give me that donut now!"* The subconscious mind wants *instant gratification.*

This primitive, emotional brain is impulsive, self-focused, and it wants things NOW, not later.

This is why it is willing to take risks *if* it knows it can get the immediate gratification it seeks (which is really a dopamine fix/adrenaline rush). This is why people jump out of airplanes—for the instant "adrenaline rush." Or why others roll the dice at the casino—for that "winning rush" of dopamine. Food, drugs, alcohol, anger and even a shopping spree can release these powerful hormones/neurotransmitters that activate the reward centers of the brain. This rush of pleasure chemicals is the REWARD the selfish subconscious mind seeks. Eating that donut is much more rewarding to the brain than not eating it. <u>Can you now see how the subconscious mind tries to sabotage long-term goals as it is focused on pleasure and immediate gratification</u>?

Therefore, your subconscious mind can either be your biggest enemy or your greatest ally…and the way you program it decides which it will be. You see, your own selfish, impulsive, "primitive" nature will rob you of your dreams and goals over and over and over…*IF* you let it. "In the moment" is where the battle is lost and won. Every day, you must make choices "in the moment." And those seemingly small and insignificant choices actually determine the direction of your life as they either form habits to the road to success or habits to the road of the status quo where you stay locked in repeating cycles.

You see, "in the moment," it will always be much more *pleasurable* to buy those expensive shoes than to save money toward retirement. In the moment, it's much more *enjoyable* to stay in bed than to get up and go to the gym. In the moment, it's more *exciting* to go hang out with friends than to finish that project that's due. In the moment, it's more *pleasing* to watch television than to work on improving yourself through self-development. In the moment, it's more *gratifying* to angrily scream, rant and rave than to humbly close your mouth, consider the other person's perspective and then respectfully and kindly respond.

However, it is your decisions "in the moment" that accumulate over time and define you and the direction of your life. A good marriage is not magically created overnight but is built moment by moment, choice by choice, action by action. Divorce is not produced in a day but moment by moment. Olympic champions are not born overnight but are fashioned moment by grueling moment. A business is grown or destroyed decision by decision. Health and obesity are created choice by choice. Wealth and poverty are formed action by action. Success and failure are molded one decision at a time.

Therefore, our impulsive and self-centered nature that seeks instant gratification must be trained, disciplined and *refocused* to create the life we desire. Look at a little child. Young children are usually quite self-focused, strong-willed, and stubborn and will typically throw a few angered temper tantrums to get their way. Delayed gratification is not something that comes easily for them. If the child is not properly trained, these tendencies will continue. (I think we all know a few adults who fit this description!) However, with proper training, the child can reroute and REFOCUS these strong and powerful emotional energies toward positive outcomes. The same force that can destroy you through negative, self-destructive behaviors and addictions is the same force that can push you to build empires, create revolutionary inventions, discover life-changing cures, win Olympic medals, mobilize the masses for positive change and achieve every dream and goal imaginable as you push the limits of personal potential.

You see, when you show your brain what you really want and begin to believe that you can have it (are in full possession of it "now"), that selfish subconscious mind is transformed. Instead of being impulsive toward temporary pleasure, it now "sees" the pleasure it truly wants and runs toward it with stubborn, uncompromising passion. This is why you need to repeatedly "see" your desired future to keep the subconscious mind FOCUSED and MOTIVATED. Motivation is very emotionally driven. When you find something you feel passionate about, excited about, grateful and happy about, *your emotionally driven subconscious mind will become a driving force to intuitively and creatively guide you to success.*

In fact, your brain is very motivated by pleasure and creates habits based around this pleasure. Your brain is literally wired to get you addicted to learning and exploring by releasing pleasure hormones (such as dopamine) when you do something new or fun. Because you like the way you feel, your brain then helps you to repeat the behavior by beginning to wire your brain to remember what you did that produced those pleasurable feelings. Your brain then begins to seek out ways to <u>manipulate</u> your behavior to achieve that gratifying outcome over and over. This is how habits, addictions and autopilot settings all form as strong reinforcement loops (neural connections) are created in the brain. When the subconscious mind finds a reward (those pleasurable feelings), it wants to keep repeating the behavior…whether the behavior it is reinforcing is healthy <u>or</u> destructive. This is why anger is so addictive but so is gratitude.

Habits and addictions run your life whether you realize it or not. From the food you eat, to the way you respond in relationships, to how you spend your money, to the time you set aside to achieve your goals, these are all habits that you have chosen "in the moment." Day after day, you make your choices, and then the primitive brain keeps you locked in these repeating patterns as it is programmed to create efficient pathways (or habit reinforcement loops).

Either you form habits to the road to success or habits to the road of mediocrity.

Therefore, in terms of breaking bad habits, the reinforcement loop must begin to be interrupted. We do this by having a simple "plan of action" that will help shift control from the impulsive, emotional brain back to the rational, logical mind. By simply becoming aware of your automatic actions (habits), you begin to wake up your brain out of autopilot. You can then ask yourself, *"Why am I doing this? Is this helping me obtain my goals? What would be a better choice?"* This disturbance begins to break the habit reinforcement loop and is the same principle used in breaking negative thinking patterns: becoming aware of them, replacing them with new positive thoughts, and eventually deactivating old, negative neural pathways with non-use.

In contrast, those positive habits we want to create, we reward, thus feeding the selfish subconscious mind (through a dopamine "fix") and causing it to work in our favor. Since the subconscious mind craves dopamine and uses it to create habit reinforcement loops, let's take a look at some of the many positive and healthy ways to release this rewarding, "feel good" hormone all while developing new fabulous success habits!

Healthy Sources of Dopamine

The following may also release other "happy hormones" such as serotonin (the well-being hormone), oxytocin (the love hormone) and endorphins (the pain-blocking hormones).

- ✓ Exercise
- ✓ Meditation/Prayer
- ✓ Gratitude
- ✓ Acts of Kindness
- ✓ Positive, Uplifting Music
- ✓ Physical Affection (i.e. touching, hugging, kissing and spending time with loved ones)
- ✓ Relaxing Activities (i.e. getting a massage, taking a bubble bath, journaling)
- ✓ Creative or Playful Hobbies and Activities
- ✓ Problem-Solving
- ✓ Exploring (outdoor exploration in the sunlight boosts serotonin and dopamine levels)
- ✓ Learning Something New
- ✓ Working on Projects that Inspire You
- ✓ Using your Natural Strengths and Talents
- ✓ GOAL ACHIEVEMENT (even just reflecting on your successes and/or anticipating your achievements are so rewarding to the brain!)

Congrats! By simply accomplishing small, daily tasks toward your goals, you have given yourself a *healthy* dose of dopamine to positively feed that selfish subconscious mind! With repetition, you will create a new and wonderful success habit! How exciting!

Plus, dopamine is called the "motivation molecule," and it puts a little skip in your step as it **increases your drive, focus, memory, energy, concentration, creativity, ability to learn and that "can do" attitude.** This is why when you work on something that inspires you, you begin to enter into that "flow state" of amazing creativity and focus. This is also why exercising first thing in the morning helps you feel more driven and focused to make your whole day more productive. (Exercise also promotes the growth of new brain cell receptors, slows aging and releases serotonin and pain-killing endorphins!).

Can you now see how the highly successful use simple,

daily habits to make their lives so AMAZING?!

Your subconscious mind is a powerful force in habit formation—and thus the direction of your life—and how you use it is completely up to you! You are truly a creature of habit! Therefore, decide to create amazing habits that will build the amazing future you desire! Again, you do this by taking control of your brain and rewarding the behaviors you desire and changing/replacing the behaviors you want to eliminate. This takes a plan of action. Since the subconscious mind wants instant gratification and is highly regulated by rewards, a great way to change behavior/habits is to follow the THREE Rs.

The Three Rs: Replace, Remove, Reward

1. Replace the undesired behavior, food or activity with something positive.

> Replace your craving for ice cream with a protein shake, fruit smoothie, yogurt, bowl of fruit, herbal tea or another activity. The goal is to replace it with something that will allow you to not feel deprived. Remember, the subconscious mind wants instant gratification and is very powerful in convincing you to reward it *now*. Simply resisting the temptation without replacing it creates a war inside you that you will more than likely lose. Don't fight with yourself. Begin to change habits by replacing them with new and healthier habits. Extreme diets produce only temporary results because, in the end, you go back to your old eating habits. You must replace old habits with new, *sustainable* healthy habits.

2. Remove yourself from the undesirables.

> Remove all ice cream from your house or remove yourself by staying out of the kitchen during "temptation times." (At first, it may be helpful to *distract* your brain with another activity such as taking a walk, doing a puzzle, reviewing your goals, looking at pictures of your ideal body.)

3. Reward yourself.

> If you go all week without eating ice cream, treat yourself to a movie night, massage, bubble bath or a fun night with friends. Rewarding positive behavior is crucial to conditioning the subconscious mind.

Choose to make your life AMAZING by creating fantastic new habits! The beginning is always the hardest in creating change because you have to take initiative (which may require a little sacrifice), clarify *focus* (the direction you want to go) and then create a plan of action. However, once you begin to set these new actions in motion, they will begin to create *momentum* and lead you almost *"effortlessly"* to new and amazing places you never thought possible. You will have programmed your subconscious mind to become an unstoppable force to make your dreams come true.

Since rewards are powerful in creating new positive behavior, take a minute and think about what you already do in a normal day that you could use as rewards for creating new habits. For example, one of the best life-long habits you can form is setting aside a few minutes every day for self-development. So, if you *love* your morning coffee, you could create a "plan of action" where you drink your coffee only during your self-development time. Or if you *love* to watch your favorite television show at bedtime, you could create a "plan of action" where you only watch the show after you complete your self-development. You will be surprised how small and "normal" rewards can act as big motivators in your life.

What habits do you need to change or create? Decide your plan of action, be prepared, and then go do it. Remember, habits take three to six weeks to form and three to six months to become automatic through the subconscious mind. AND choose to stop fighting with yourself by replacing bad habits with new good habits. It's simple—you are a creature of habit, and you must accept this fact, and choose to use it for your good.

Choose to create an amazing life of WONDERFUL HABITS!

Insight

Can you now see why rewarding your new positive behavior is so important? Do you see why long-term planning goes beyond the scope of the subconscious mind's understanding? Can you now see why the long-term *must* be mapped out into small, <u>daily</u> doable steps in order for the subconscious mind to embrace it? Do you see how each time you accomplish your small, daily tasks, you feel a sense of pride and accomplishment which releases dopamine that then further encourages your brain to make you repeat the behavior? Can you also see how visualizing your perfect future brings this future into the "now" with strong and pleasurable positive feelings that feed the selfish subconscious mind's desire for instant gratification? Do you see how these pleasurable feelings are like "drugs" to the brain, and the brain will keep looking for ways to get that "high" again and again, and thus will begin to subconsciously manipulate your behavior to make your dreams a reality?! Your brain is a powerful force in creating your dream life, so choose to use it wisely!

Support and Accountability

It is also important to remember that we are relational creatures. We all need other people—especially when we are trying to create major change in our lives. This is why life coaching is so effective; it provides the accountability and positive support needed to create lasting change.

This is why you need to find others who will support you, motivate you, hold you accountable, encourage you and cheer you on toward your goals so that you can create life-long success.

Right now, think about how you can find your support system. Is it with family, friends, co-workers, a personal trainer, a local support group or even a private Facebook group? Find like-minded people who want the same kind of change you do, and join them, or create your own new group. I have participated in many online group challenges for exercise, photography and life coaching that took me to the "next level" as we (all the participants) held each other accountable and pushed one another to do more and become better.

Maybe you could agree to pay a friend or co-worker $100 if you don't meet your goal deadline. (I bet you would meet it with time to spare!). Maybe a friend could call you at a clearly specified time once a week to check-in on your progress from the past week and your new commitment for the coming week—just be sure to find a positive friend who will lift you up and not push you down. There are many creative ways to create your own support system. I'm sure you already have some ideas in mind. Don't be a bone on your own. Find a way to keep yourself supported and accountable.

Concerning my new habit of _____,

my plan of action is to_____

_____,

and I will find support and accountability by _____

_____.

Signature _____ **Date** _____

Accountability is hard…that selfish subconscious mind doesn't like it. Were you tempted to skip filling in the blanks? Creating new habits not only takes consistent, daily effort but also requires us to recognize that we need others' support and encouragement. Change is hard stuff, but look at all you've accomplished. You should be really proud of yourself, and I mean it! You are now way ahead of the pack! I'm sure proud of you! So go ahead and give yourself a big pat on the back, and say "*GO ME!*"

Now go CELEBRATE and REWARD yourself for your hard work this week!

Remember to associate the reward with this week's accomplishments in order for your brain to make the connection. Do not skip this exercise! You must reward yourself so that your mind will begin to establish these new behaviors as habits. So, go relax in the sun, go out with friends, go to a movie, the beach, or for a long walk or bike ride. Treat yourself to your favorite dinner or dessert, sleep in, take a nap, play your favorite sport, take a long bath, read your favorite book, go to a sports game...whatever is FUN to YOU (and within your budget), go do it!

Now go have some fun! YOU DESERVE IT!

Day 21: See It Sunday

Today is SEE IT SUNDAY! It's time to *literally* SEE your future coming closer to you. We will do this by putting your perfect life on paper so that you can start looking at it with your own two eyes. So, what does success look like to YOU? Only you can answer this question for yourself. What did your perfect life look like when you did the visualization exercise last week? (I highly encourage you to listen to a visualization exercise every Sunday, or create your own audio.)

Today I want you to start a **Vision Board** (also known as a Dream Board). This may sound trivial, but it is POWERFUL! A vision board is a tool used to help clarify, concentrate and maintain FOCUS on specific life goals. It involves simply finding and cutting out pictures and words that represent the life you are trying to move toward (i.e. career, family, home, ministry, finances, health, fitness, relationships, spirituality, recreation, vacations, etc.) and attaching (gluing, taping, stapling or pinning) them to a poster board.

When you make a vision board and put it where you can see it daily, your brain becomes familiar with the images and begins to accept these images as REAL. (Remember, the subconscious prefers familiarity.) Daily, as you look on these images, you begin to see yourself within the world of these places and situations. This dream world begins to come *alive* as it becomes a part of your brain's current "reality," and thus your brain accepts the belief that you can indeed have this reality.

Daily, these words and images remind you of your goals and become motivation for change because a vision board clearly shows your subconscious mind what you WANT. The more you FOCUS (with positive emotion) on what you truly want, the more you will feed that selfish subconscious mind which will then create a "burning desire"[xxxiv] to have what you are showing it. Think of a little child who sees a toy he/she wants. The child becomes fixated on obtaining the toy. However, if the child doesn't SEE the toy for a period of time, that motivation wanes. Daily SEEING a vision board creates *focus* to generate *desire* to *motivate* you to obtain your dreams.

Plus, vision boards are fun! My vision board has pictures of houses, cars, vacations and physical fitness levels I want to obtain. I've also added words such as "abundance," "intelligent mind," "spiritual devotion," "financial freedom," "loving and thriving relationships," "inner happiness" and the dollar amounts I want to obtain and give away to good causes. Over time, I've further added pictures of office buildings, investment properties, and outreach/ministry organizations I want to buy or start. With time, my vision has increased, and so will yours. Therefore, it is wise to periodically update your vision board or even yearly create a whole new board. It may be helpful to create multiple boards such as a personal, career and/or fitness board. (Pinterest is also a great place to create dream boards, but you must make time to look at them.)

As my vision has now increased even more, I have added words and pictures such as "Best-Selling Author," "Coach Trainer," "World

> "The people who THINK they are crazy enough to change the world are the ones who do."
>
> ~Steve Jobs

Changer," "Creator of One Million Millionaires," "Public Speaker in Seminars, Radio and Television," and "$100 Million Net Worth." At first, your words and pictures will seem ridiculous, even ludicrous; but give them time, they will become more real than you ever imagined!

If your dreams don't scare you, they aren't *BIG* enough!

Remember, small thinking is no longer a part of you. Big dreams precede the accomplishment of big goals! Decide to believe for the impossible. Decide to be a world changer in your sphere of influence. Whether you are a teacher, a student, a doctor, an artist, a sales person, a police officer, an accountant, a fitness instructor, a manager, an entrepreneur, a stay-at-home mom and so on, you can do incredible things with your life. You can make a dynamic impact in the world around you. You were created to do BIG things. Are you ready? Let's do this!

> "Don't let 'reality' or 'false wisdom' rob you of your dreams. There is nothing too out of the box, nothing you can't afford, nothing too unrealistic, nothing too silly—when you dream. When it comes to vision—if it doesn't make you a little nervous, it's not from God."
>
> ~Lance Wallnau

Assignment.

Today begin to look through magazines or online for pictures that represent your desired ideal life. Dream BIG! Cut out or print at least one picture for your vision board.

Now see yourself in the picture. **Visualize yourself already in possession of what you desire while feeling the strong emotions of gratitude and happiness**. Soak in and breathe in these positive emotions. Do this often so that seeing these images will begin to create <u>automatic</u> feelings of happiness, peace and gratitude. You are reprogramming your autopilot settings for success as you literally create new neural connections and habit reinforcement loops to "manipulate" your behavior to obtain your dreams. Also, remember, the brain cannot distinguish between what is real and what is imagined. When the image(s) is combined with strong emotion, this new reality is sealed into your subconscious mind. Creating a new belief system starts by targeting the subconscious mind; thus, vision boards and visualization exercises are powerful and effective toward this goal!

USE YOUR VISION BOARD TO "SEE" YOUR FUTURE AS REALITY!

This week, set your tasks to pick up some sort of poster board or display board for your new vision board(s) (Walmart, Dollar Store or any craft store will have them). Also, please listen to the "Day 21" visualization exercise at **trainyourbrainworkbook.com.**

NEXT....Either Sunday evening or first thing Monday morning, look at your Key Goal and some of your secondary goals. Decide on your focus for this week, and decide on five specific tasks for your key goal and five specific tasks for your secondary goal to be completed Monday through Friday. This is now two tasks per day (I am not asking for hours spent on each task, even giving five to 10 minutes of focused time will keep you moving forward). If two tasks seem overwhelming right now, then just stick with your one goal task for each day. However, if you are up for the challenge, add that second task. Write down (in your calendar, phone task list, the Weekly Goal Setting Template, etc.) these specific tasks/actions that will support your goals.

VERY IMPORTANT!
Your Key Goal MUST hold your main focus.

Taking on too many things at once will cause you to lose focus and fizzle out. Do NOT exceed THREE GOAL TASKS per day...remember, laser focus. Also, only gently add more goal tasks as you know you have enough time, energy and focus to complete them. Being too ambitious will only set you up for failure. While highly creative personality types often flourish with three goal tasks per day (as they get bored quickly), other personality types may feel overwhelmed and confused by more than one goal task per day. Do what feels right to YOU. You know yourself the best. Find the pace that creates the best momentum for YOU.

I find that I am most productive when I am busier. Starting out, I focused on one main goal per week with only one goal task per day. However, with time, I've built momentum and now focus on three main goals per week such as my coaching business, writing this book and my photography business. If I find that my secondary goal tasks are taking away from my Key Goal, then I scale them back so that I do not hinder my primary focus and impede my timelines/deadlines. Also, if you prefer variety, you can always, for example, focus on your Key Goal on Mondays, Wednesdays and Fridays and then on secondary goal(s) on Tuesdays and Thursdays. Mix it up all you want; just make sure your Key Goal stays as your priority, or it will quickly become <u>forgotten</u>. Either way, start slowly and build momentum with time. Remember, slow and steady wins the race!

Example:

My **Main Focus** this Week (KEY GOAL): Career—Create my website
My **Secondary Focus** this Week: Health—Drink 10 glasses of water (I feel confident in my water drinking, so I am adding two days of exercise.)

Monday: Key Goal: Career—Research websites offering similar services
Secondary Goal: Health—Drink 10 glasses of water

Tuesday: Key Goal: Career—Create the "Home" page of my new website
Secondary Goal: Health—Drink 10 glasses of water, 20 minutes of exercises

Wednesday: Key Goal: Career— Create my "Services and Fees" page
Secondary Goal: Health—Drink 10 glasses of water

Thursday: Key Goal: Career—Create a "Blog" page, and write a short article for this blog
Secondary Goal: Health—Drink 10 glasses of water, 20 minutes of exercises

Friday: Key Goal: Career—Create the "About" page of my website, finalize site, publish
Secondary Goal: Health—Drink 10 glasses of water

Now it's your turn!

My Main Focus This Week (KEY GOAL):

My Secondary Focus this Week:

Monday
Key Goal:
Secondary Goal:
General Tasks:

Tuesday
Key Goal:
Secondary Goal:
General Tasks:

Wednesday
Key Goal:
Secondary Goal:
General Tasks:

Thursday
Key Goal:
Secondary Goal:
General Tasks:

Friday
Key Goal:
Secondary Goal:
General Tasks:

Saturday
Goals: Make-up day for any tasks not completed
General Tasks:

Now take 60 seconds and visualize yourself *easily* completing each of these goal tasks.

SEE IT, and BELIEVE IT! You are on your way to a better life!

Week 4: Rewriting Your Blueprint for Success

This week is about taking focused action to rewrite your conscious and subconscious mind's blueprint for success. Your life is simply a reflection of your internal thinking patterns and belief systems. Therefore, daily we will take specific action steps to rewrite your internal programming so that success can't help but come to you!

Remember, your life is a garden—what is growing in it is up to you. Doesn't a wise gardener create a blueprint for what and how he wants to sow and reap? Right now, your garden grows what you have sown (your prior thoughts, actions and habits) whether you like what you have sown or not. Therefore, wouldn't it be wise to write a blueprint that will create the life you desire? Without a well-designed blueprint, you will continue to plant weeds and wonder why you're not growing beautiful apple trees. If you want an incredible harvest, you must take clearly designed *action* steps to plant good seeds, nurture them to properly grow, pluck the weeds and be patient for the plants to mature. However, with consistency of *focused, intentional action*, your harvest will become more and more fruitful (and your dreams will become more and more real!).

Decide today if you will live your dreams or just settle for the status quo. Your dreams—your harvest—await you. Will you take *action* to make your dreams come true...to live an extraordinary life? You are the author of your destiny!

Week Overview:

Day 22: Motivated Monday: Determining Action for the Week, Reverse Engineering

Day 23: Thoughtful Tuesday: Law of Attraction, Achievement Priming

Day 24: What and Why Wednesday: Your Calling, WHYs, Mission Statement

Day 25: Thankful Thursday: Emotional Intelligence

Day 26: Fearless Friday: Identifying Energy Drainers

Day 27: Celebrate Saturday: Celebrating Your Achievements, Developing Grit

Day 28: See It Sunday: Achieving the Impossible, Vision Board

> *"Only those who attempt the absurd can achieve the impossible."*
>
> **~Albert Einstein**

Day 22: Motivated Monday

Today is the day to get motivated to DREAM BIG! Don't hold back. What is the big dream in your heart? Maybe your big dream is another 20 years away; maybe it's 10, five or even just one or two years away. However, don't let your big dreams die or part of you will die. (I know firsthand as I let this happen to me years ago when I became a busy stay-at-home mom and began to "lose myself," my identity and my big dreams). Therefore, it's time to awaken your BIG dreams by getting them down on paper. Over time, they may change, be tweaked or completely re-written. However, let's start by mapping out your biggest dream today!

Today you will **Reverse Engineer** the greatest dream of your heart.

What is the greatest dream you have for your life? If you could do anything, be anything, accomplish anything, what would it be? Close your eyes, and imagine this dream come true. Look around you. What do you see? How do you feel? This is about following your heart, your passion. This is about walking in your greater purposes.

If you are having a hard time determining your greatest dream, then decide where you want to be in the next five, 10 or even 20 years. What kind of life do you see for yourself? Until you have some sort of vision of where you want to go, you will not be able to figure out how to get there. This exercise is to get you thinking and planning for the long term.

If nothing else, think about who you are the most jealous of. What is it they have (or do) that you really want? Maybe you've heard the phrase *"follow your jealousy."* This means to follow those who inspire you (or who you want to be like) and then do what they do! It is important to find someone who has already achieved a similar goal as yours who can serve as your inspiration, role model and idea generator. Don't waste your time reinventing the wheel. Use others' successes and failures to build on. Study these successful people, and find out the steps they took to get where they are now. And don't worry about being a copycat. You can build on the groundwork they've laid and create your own version of it. A piano has only 88 keys and yet think of the unlimited songs that can be written! Write your own song! Your song will resonate and touch people differently than other people's songs.

If you don't know anyone personally whom you can ask, then research those who have achieved your goal. There is so much information at your fingertips...online, books, magazines, articles, seminars and online programs. There are amazing bloggers, authors, speakers and YouTube gurus from whom you can learn. And who knows, if you kindly wrote to them for assistance, they just mind respond or at least direct you to a program that could help you!

However, you must decide to start somewhere. Often, when we start on a grand journey, it can seem overwhelming to figure out how to get from here to there. We are quickly confused, overwhelmed, disappointed and give up before we have even given our dream a chance. However, by starting at your end point and working backward, you can more easily figure out how to achieve this grand goal.

Reverse Engineering

Reverse Engineering is simply defining where you ideally want to be and then figuring out how to get from there to where you are now. It is easier for the mind to step back one step at a time from a *clearly defined destination* than to try to start at the beginning and figure out all the in-betweens. Further, reverse engineering begins with research, research and more research. Here are a few questions to get you started.

Reverse Engineering

What is my ultimate goal? (Clearly define it.)
What will I need to do to accomplish this goal?
What skills will I need?
What do I need to know?
What obstacles could I face?
What resources will I need?
What support or connections will I need?
Who do I need to talk to who can help me and give me insight (an expert)?
Who has done this before that I can learn from (books, articles, websites)?
What are the pros and cons of achieving this goal?
Are there multiple paths to obtaining this goal and which one works best for me?
What specific steps/most important tasks do I need to do to make this goal happen?
What is my contingency plan if my method fails? (Contingency plans are important as your mind now sees less risk and FEAR because you have a clear and thought-through backup plan.)

Once you have all your information gathered, you can then map out a basic timeline of goal achievements. Start from the end point and work backward asking yourself, *"If I was here, what step would precede this?"* Then in each step, ask yourself, *"What actions must I take now? What finances would I need? Who could help me?"* And so on.

Whether you realize it or not, reverse engineering is something you use on almost a daily basis whether it's planning a meal, a social event or a vacation.

Let's take a vacation for example. You decide that it's been a long winter and you want to go somewhere tropical for an extended weekend getaway. FIRST, you must decide exactly **where** you want to go, **when** you want to go, **how much** you want to spend, and **who** you want to work with (who can give you the best deal). NEXT, you must book your trip, buy your plane tickets, and arrange for transportation to and from the airport. FINALLY, you must buy items needed for the trip, pack your bags, make sure everything is safe at home and then hop in the car for a fun getaway!

Did you see how we started at the end and worked our way backward? Without starting at the end, we would not have gotten far...literally! We would have no idea where we were going, when we were going, what it would cost, what would be needed and so on. We would have our bags packed (with things we may or may not need) sitting in our driveway going nowhere fast! Ever feel this way?

Let's take another example. What if you wanted to open your own fitness studio in the next three years? FIRST, let's think about where you are going, when you want to get there, how much it will cost, and who you want to work with.

Where are you going, or what kind of studio and services do you want to offer? What is your purpose? (Visualize your studio and determine what it looks like and what it offers.)

When do you want to be up and running? (Research and set a timeline.)

How much is it going to cost? (What is the average cost of getting a business like this up and running?) Also, how much money do you want to ultimately earn per year?

Who do you *want* to work with? Who do you *want* to come to your studio? Who would you LOVE to work with? (Determine your ideal client.)

Next, what needs to happen before all of this? (Arranging and booking your flight.)

What does your market look like? What makes your business different from your competitors? What is your niche? What specific services do your ideal clients want and how will you create these services? What equipment, supplies and staff do you need? Will you rent or buy a building? What is the average amount of time before a company in your industry breaks even and begins to make a profit? How much money should you have set aside to cover your business until it makes an adequate profit? Who is making the kind of money you want to make whom you can learn from? Who can help you in your business planning and marketing? Do you want someone to invest in your business to offset costs (a business partner)? What will you name your company? How will you establish your business with the state, register your trade name, and create your logo, brand and website? How will you create marketing strategies to target your ideal clients? How will you locate and secure available properties to rent/purchase? How will you locate and secure distributor(s) for products you want to sell? How will you find and buy equipment? How will you hire and train staff? How many hours do you want to work a week, and how will you make this happen?

Finally, what's in your suitcase, is your home secure, and who can drive you to the airport?

What skills, training and certifications do you need to run this kind of business? Are you and your family in a good place in life to do this (or what is required to get you/them to a good place)? Do you have or can you develop the kind of support system needed to run this kind of business? How will you find the kind of resources needed to make this all happen? What obstacles might you face? Who could help you? What is your contingency plan if all this fails?

Now you can begin setting timelines for exactly what needs to be done to get you from the final destination to now. In other words, visualize the business in its awesome flourishing state and then take a step back in thinking about how you would get to that ideal state. If possible, find someone who is already *successfully* doing "your dream" and ask for their advice as this can save you a lot of time and research. Just ask for 20 minutes of their time to give an overview of the main steps they took to get where they are today. (However, I do not suggest going to your direct competitor because you are essentially asking them to teach you how to steal their customers/clients. There are also many business-building courses available online.)

Let me show you how reverse engineering helped me. My original goal was to become a life coach and to work in companies. In reverse engineering, I realized that to get hired by companies, I had better have some sort of amazing program to offer. To have an amazing program, I had better have clients to verify that my program is amazing. This led me to obtain a good education (training/master's degree), work one-on-one with coaching clients and create the foundational program that this book is based on.

I then began to increase my vision and saw myself hosting my own seminars and trainings around the world and on television. So, how in the world would I ever do that? Well, when I reverse engineered, I saw that those who have gone before me had written best-selling books. And to sell best-selling books, they had expert knowledge in their field that led them to write a book to help others. By reverse engineering, I could see that to become a sought after speaker, I should write a really helpful book that is based on the expert knowledge I have gained. So how do I gain expert knowledge? Through continual study, research, practice and experience.

As you can see, my original goal was not to write a life coaching book—it wasn't even on the radar! However, since I had already created a foundational program, a book was a *natural* direction to move toward. Plus, writing a book has been a dream of mine since I was a little girl. I have absolutely LOVED every minute that I have sown into this book over the last two years. Just writing and publishing a book that can help others is an absolute dream come true, and it motivates me to take the NEXT STEP!

Can you now see how I *naturally* began to move toward my inner dreams once I began to step out? Make your vision clear, and you will *intuitively* take steps toward it. As your vision becomes bigger, reverse engineering will become your best friend. Take the short cut, and reverse engineer!

Eliminate RISK by Reverse Engineering.

Making your dreams a reality involves risk. However, it should involve calculated risk, not irresponsible risk. Every highly successful person has taken a risk to get where they are today; however, it was a risk with a plan of action. For example, to quit your job tomorrow to start your new business when you do not have the resources in place to properly run your business and to financially support yourself is plain irresponsible. This would be an unnecessary risk that could be disastrous. I know firsthand the consequences of uncalculated risk, as early in my marriage, my husband jumped enthusiastically into a business opportunity without a definite plan of action and the results were not good—it took a blow to our finances and pride. However, it was a good lesson learned.

Reverse engineering reveals the resources needed, the time-line needed, the support needed, the skills needed and so on. Therefore, for now, keep your day job until you know you have a calculated plan in place to truly make your dreams a reality. Slow and steady is a good piece of advice here. If you want to start your own business, work at your normal job during the day and gradually work on creating your own business on nights and weekends. Once the new business is generating enough income for you to step away from your day job, you have found the right time to turn in your resignation. Calculated risk is key to making your dreams a reality.

Further, in eliminating risk, try to imagine the worst thing that could happen when you try to achieve your goal. Then create an action plan of what you would do in this worst case scenario. Now your mind sees that this goal is not so scary after all because you have a plan even in the absolute worst situation!

Reverse Engineering reveals that you must INVEST in YOURSELF.

Maybe you've heard it said, "*Work hard on your job to make a good living, but work hard to invest in yourself and make a fortune.*" The absolute best thing that you can invest in is yourself. If you want to improve your career, marriage, family or recreational life, then invest in developing skills to improve these areas. Don't expect others to invest in you. You must decide to invest in yourself (skills, knowledge, experience, etc.). This is also about finding a mentor who can take you to the "next level." While there is a multitude of free information out there, do not be afraid to hire someone who knows what they are doing.

For example, when I wanted to learn photography, I hired an amazing photographer (who I wanted to emulate) to teach me. When I decided to become a Life Coach, I hired those (in the form of a master's degree and other professional training) who could teach me the expert knowledge I needed and who would push me to excel. Now that I am writing this book, I need guidance to become a best-selling author. Since I don't personally know anyone who is a best-selling author, I hired a mentor through an online program to teach me exactly what to do to achieve this goal. (And while I can't guarantee this book will become a best seller, I know that the knowledge gained from investing in myself will make me a best-selling author at some point in time). I've also invested in courses to teach me how to properly market my business.

Don't be afraid to invest in yourself. Whatever the investment (schooling, mentoring, online programs, coaching, etc.), choose wisely knowing that every penny invested will reap a good harvest. It's time to start investing in yourself and your future. You are so worth it!

Assignment.

Today find your mentor to learn from and begin to reverse engineer your "BIG DREAM" timeline. To find a mentor, think of or research a person whom you can learn from who is an expert in your field (or has at some point accomplished your goal or a similar goal). If you don't know where to start, search online for articles, blogs, books and websites relating to your subject. Maybe someone has even posted a video on YouTube with some great tips about how to achieve your goal. Begin to "follow" those who have had great success. Also, consider taking a shortcut and hiring an expert to coach you.

Even if you feel like you know your plan backward and forward, there are always better, easier and newer ways of achieving goals. Therefore, stay open to new ideas and be creative. Everything you need for your goal achievement is already available…you just have to go get it!

My Mentor:

Reverse Engineering Ideas (Imagine your dream in action)

Where do I want to go? (Create a clear picture.)

When do I want to get there? (Timeline)

How much will it cost? How much do I want to earn?

Who do I want to work with? (Who are my ideal clients?)

Arrange and book my flight. (What do I need to research, buy, and get set in place?)

What's in my suitcase? (What skills, schooling, training, certifications are needed?)

Is my home secure? (What about my family, support system?)

Who can drive me to the airport? (Who can help me?)

Don't forget! Take two minutes at breakfast to look at your goal tasks for today. (If you haven't decided your action for the week, go back to yesterday's exercise.) Add any other tasks that MUST be completed today (**picking up a poster board or display board for your VISION BOARD**, doing laundry, grocery shopping, complimenting your spouse and/or loved ones).

Congrats! You are creating the resources needed to achieve your dreams!
How exciting! I knew you could do it!

Day 23: Thoughtful Tuesday

Last Tuesday we learned just how powerful your thoughts are in creating the life you desire. Maybe you've heard the phrase "*As a man thinks in his heart, so is he*" (Proverbs 23:7). You are the sum of your thoughts, as your thoughts form your character, your circumstances and your level of success. We've already studied how thoughts are scientifically found to affect health, happiness and success. Therefore, today we are going to look at the molecular level of thoughts as we jump into the world of quantum physics.

I have previously covered a little on how positive thoughts are positive energy, and negative thoughts are negative energy. Did you know that quantum physics shows us that everything in the universe is made up of energy, but just in different forms or what we call "matter"? Does $E = mc^2$ ring a bell? Albert Einstein determined that energy equals mass (matter) times the speed of light squared. Or energy equals mass in motion. These two elements (energy and mass) change back and forth between the two "forms," and they are always equally proportional. For example, water changes from solid (ice, snow) to liquid (water, dew) to vapor (gas, cloud, fog) and yet it is still always H_2O.

We live in a sea of energy. The air we breathe is made of molecules that are comprised of energy. Sound is made of waves that are energy. The light we see is energy from the sun. The food we eat is broken down into its energy form. When we smell the fragrance of a flower, we breathe in the molecular energy through our nose, and it causes chemical/energy reactions within our brains. Our brains use energy in the form of electrical pulses to form brain waves.

Everything is ENERGY.

> The world around you is a reflection of your past and present thinking.

This means that even your thoughts have measurable energy. Therefore, at some point, your thoughts will begin to "materialize" into what we see as "matter." At some point in time, your thoughts (words, emotions) will manifest in your life. The world around you is the product of your thinking and your decisions. This means you have a lot more control over the world around you than you ever thought possible!

Do you remember how we've discussed that our thoughts <u>become</u> our decisions, which <u>become</u> our actions, which <u>become</u> our habits, which <u>become</u> our reality/destiny? Our thoughts simply manifest as we direct them! Again, we know that we cannot control others. Manipulating others is not the goal here. The only person we can control is ourselves. However, by choosing to control and change our thoughts and decisions, we can cause a chain reaction in whatever direction we begin to change.

Therefore, let's look at Newton's first law of motion, the law of inertia, which states that objects in motion tend to stay in motion with the SAME speed and the SAME direction UNLESS acted upon by an unbalanced force. Let me try to break this down for you.

If, for example, you see yourself as inferior, you will act inferior, you will see others as seeing you as inferior, and you will see your work and relational styles as inferior. Guess what? You have just successfully created a self-fulfilling prophecy! It is not the fault of others that they respond to you as being inferior. They respond this way because you have CAUSED THEM TO!

You are generating negative energy that is moving you continually in the same negative direction and at a constant speed. You have created the world around you because others pick up on and respond to your inner beliefs, thought patterns, emotions, decisions and actions (all energy). If you have an inner transformation (a CHANGE in energy and motion) and go back to work feeling confident, worthy and capable of accomplishing great things, people will begin to respond to you DIFFERENTLY. Possibly with shock and disbelief! However, with time, they will accept this change and respect it.

Here's another example. If you are so fearful that your spouse or children are going to do something "bad," you will keep replaying these bad scenarios over and over in your mind. Guess what? At some point you are going to begin to react to your loved ones based on these on-going thoughts. You will treat your loved ones as if they are already guilty, and you may even begin to control and manipulate them to keep them from these wrong doings. Therefore, don't be surprised when your loved ones actually do these "bad" things out of rebellion toward your control and manipulation. The very thing that you feared and were "trying to prevent" ends up happening! The negative energy of your thoughts caused you to react in ways that made this energy manifest into its "material" form.

Let me ask you a question. Have you ever not wanted to go to an event and thought, "*If I was sick, then I wouldn't have to go?*" I know I have entertained these ugly thoughts, and guess what? I ended up sick every time! What I focused on manifested in my life.

We are the creators of our "world."

Now I am <u>not</u> saying that you should start blaming yourself or feeling guilty for all the bad actions of those around you. Each person in your life is accountable for his/her own decisions and actions. This book is about EMPOWERING <u>YOU</u> to take personal responsibility to change your world for the better by realizing that your on-going thoughts, beliefs and resulting actions create a chain reaction as to how others respond to you.

So, let's start using this chain reaction for good! This is why the highly successful seem to just keep climbing the ladder higher and higher while the naysayers who call themselves *"unlucky"* keep digging their ditches deeper and deeper. Taking personal responsibility for the world you have created around you—understanding that it ALL begins with YOUR thoughts, emotions and attitudes—is the ONLY way you will create true success in your life.

> **Each person has created his own world (mass) by his own thoughts, emotions, words and actions (energy). Energy and mass change "forms" as they are directed by YOU.**

Law of Vibration

> "If you want to find the secrets of the universe, think in terms of energy, frequency and vibration."
>
> ~Nikola Tesla

Now let's take a really close look at quantum physics. Matter (mass) is simply energy in motion or $M=e/c^2$. At the sub-atomic level, you will not find true "matter" but energy vibrating at specific frequencies to form this "matter" that we see, touch and taste. However, it is the frequency of the energy's vibrations that determines the form of the matter. A strawberry's vibrational frequency is different from that of a potato or a pine tree.

Well, guess what? People have vibrations too. Have you ever heard someone say, "*She is such a downer,*" or "*He has a bad vibe*"? Or maybe a sports team has gotten on a losing streak, and you say they need to get their "*good vibe*" back. Vibe is a vibration. You were picking up on the person's or team's vibration!

What determines our own vibration? Again, energy is measured in vibrations and the rate of the vibration determines the frequency. If everything in the universe has a measurable vibration, this means that our thoughts, words, emotions and inner beliefs are what define what kind of vibrational frequency we are sending out. Also, unlike a strawberry with a set frequency, our frequency can constantly change. For example, our vibrational frequency goes up when we are excited and happy (our energy increases), and our frequency goes down when we are sad or disappointed (our energy decreases). Think about this: why does happy, upbeat music energize us and make us want to tap our feet or dance? Those positive musical "vibes" affect our bodies!

Further, quantum physics shows us that *"like" vibrations attract one another*. You can see this when you strike a string on a guitar. If there is another guitar nearby, the same string or note on that guitar will begin to vibrate—they *resonate*. Also, when you choose the frequency on a radio, it picks up the radio station that is set to that same frequency. Vibrational frequencies attract like vibrational frequencies.

The law of vibration and the law of attraction are one and the same!

Therefore, positive thoughts, words and emotions have positive energy. Positive energy has a high frequency which attracts other things at those same high frequencies. While negative words, thoughts and emotions have negative energy. Negative energy has a low frequency and attracts other things with low frequencies. This is the law of attraction. You get more of what you think about (good or bad). You also attract to you other people who are operating at your same frequency because your frequency resonates with their frequency. To *resonate* means to share mutual emotions, thoughts or beliefs with another person. Maybe you've commented how someone's statement strongly "resonated" with you. Birds of a feather truly do flock together!

If you don't like what and who you are attracting, then change your frequency.

You alone control your thoughts, emotions and beliefs. I used to think I was a pretty positive person until I began learning the principles of this book. Negativity sneaks in, and we don't even recognize it. (And remember, energy will keep moving in the same direction unless an outside force changes it.) Our thoughts are like a slippery slope. It is easy to get the negative ones rolling and to just keep going with the strong negative energy force that is created. Negativity quickly attracts low frequency emotions such as worry, anxiety, discouragement, frustration, irritability, jealousy, bitterness, rejection, anger, vengefulness, pride, arrogance, selfishness, hatred, despair, depression, helplessness and even sickness.

Negative energy is always rooted in FEAR as it protects and defends itself at ALL costs. Fear is based out of the limbic (primitive) part of the brain. Fear ignites the "fight-or-flight' response, making the limbic system become highly emotional, reactive, irrational, unreasonable, self-focused and lacking in empathy for others. When you find yourself in this highly reactive and out of control limbic state, recognize that your brain is controlling you, instead of you controlling it.

Either your thoughts and emotions will control you,
or you will choose to control them.

In contrast, **positive energy is rooted in LOVE** as it is focused on helping others, giving, kindness, selflessness, thankfulness, forgiveness, humility, patience, generosity, gentleness, peacefulness, faithfulness, encouragement, joy and so on. Love attracts more love. Your acts of love, with consistency, will begin to attract acts of love toward you!

Remember, the only person in the world that you can change is YOU. You cannot force anyone else into true change. However, your consistent acts of genuine love (a kind word, a helping hand, forgiveness, refusing to be negative or critical) will cause a chain reaction that will eventually create a new world around you as others begin to respond differently toward you. It may not happen overnight, but it will happen. As you plant your seeds of love, water and nurture them, a harvest will come in time.

You reap what you sow, or some call it karma. What you sow grows. What you send out comes back to you. You alone choose how and where your energy will go, and it is determined by your FOCUS. Choose to stop focusing on the negatives of your current reality, or you will just continue to attract more of what you don't want. You attract what you focus on (as you attract the type of energy or vibrational frequency you are sending out). Whatever you focus on, you will *frequently* think about which will then create your emotions, beliefs and thus frequency.

Frequent Focus = Frequency

This is why focusing on what you want (seeing yourself in full possession of it) while maintaining 100% faith and 0% doubt should be your primary goal. Again, what you focus on (*frequently* think about) creates your emotions and beliefs which creates your frequency. Your frequency then causes those beliefs to manifest and grow as they attract other things and people operating at those same frequencies.

What you FOCUS on will increase and GROW.
What do you want to grow in your life?

Insight

Growing a Healthy Marriage

Your marriage is like a garden. What you nurture will grow and flourish, but what you neglect and treat poorly will die. Choose to nurture your relationship by focusing on your spouse's positive attributes, and you will draw them out. If you focus on the negative, not only will you stay annoyed and irritated, but you will also keep drawing out and intensify these negative qualities. What you focus on will grow. Therefore, choose to focus on what made you fall in love with him/her. Focus on what you admire about him/her. Focus on what you are thankful for in him/her.

See your spouse as that wonderful mate he/she is capable of being, and act as if he/she is that NOW!

I can say all this because I have lived it. Years ago, I used to complain constantly to myself about my husband and our marriage. However, when I made a conscious decision to stop the negative talk/thinking and to start focusing on the positive, things began to dramatically CHANGE. As I began rooting out the negative (i.e. complaining) and began complimenting him, thanking him and overall just being more grateful for him, our whole marriage transformed! I am now more in love than ever with a man who is my perfect match. We are now a team instead of working against each other. I now see his good qualities, instead of taking them for granted—and these good qualities have even increased! AND those annoying traits that once irritated me to no end don't seem so annoying anymore—they even seem trivial as they have either diminished, or I have just "let them go." Why fret over things we can't change? The only person that we can change is OURSELF. Focusing on the good brings about amazing results, BUT it is a choice—a lifestyle—that takes practice and practice and more practice.

I must also add that understanding your spouse's personality type is extremely helpful in creating a healthier relationship. While we are naturally attracted to those who are similar to us in values and beliefs, we marry our opposites in terms of personality type. Opposites make a good team. For example, if you are putting together a football team, would you want all quarterbacks? Of course not. Each player's specific skills combined together make a team that can win. The same is true in marriage; differing personality types complement each other. For example, one spouse is typically an introvert and the other an extravert. One is often more logical/fact-oriented and the other more people-oriented. One spouse is usually a spender and the other a saver. Together, they make a balanced team.

Having your spouse take the online personality test (Day 1) is really important. Read through the descriptions about his/her personality traits, strengths, weaknesses, relationship and parenting styles. I can almost guarantee that as you read these descriptions, a "light bulb" will go off in your mind as you will begin to understand that your spouse is "programmed" to be the way he/she is. Understanding then allows you to know how to make your "style" and his/her "style" work together. Learn to complement each other, not contradict and oppose each other. You are a team, not enemies. (Note: This is not an excuse to ignore unhealthy negative traits, behaviors or addictions. Your spouse may need professional help.)

Stay positive and create positive experiences for your relationship and just watch things change! Remember, you attract what you focus on (frequently think about)! So begin to attract what you want in your life! Your life is what YOU make it. Today decide what kind of person you want to be and what kind of relationship you want to have; then choose to focus in that direction. (I highly recommend the books *Why Don't We Listen Better?* by Dr. James C. Petersen and *The Five Love Languages* by Gary Chapman.)

Choose to make your today and your tomorrow beautiful!

WHAT Are You Focusing On?

You will move toward whatever you focus on. You will also draw to you whatever you focus on. Where does the majority of your focus go? More than likely you've been sending out mixed messages (frequencies) as your thoughts, emotions and inner beliefs have not all been in sync. Your thoughts can "seem" focused on the good things you want for your life, but your inner beliefs may still be fear-based and be telling you that you are not really worthy of having these good things. It's one thing to know something in your "head" and another to know it in your "heart." It is ultimately your inner beliefs that have the dominating affect, and this is where most people get "stuck" as they wonder why they are not attracting what they really want. If internally you don't truly believe that you can have something, you will in fact never have it.

However, be encouraged! I have a great technique that is going to help your brain (especially your subconscious mind that controls your inner beliefs) to accept moving toward the life you desire. Both the conscious and subconscious mind respond to and are transformed by positive emotion. What creates positive emotion? Acts of love, meditation, gratitude and even focused attention on positive things STRENGTHEN the activity of the left prefrontal cortex (which controls positive emotion or the "happy brain") and also REDUCE the activity of the right prefrontal cortex (which controls negative emotions) bringing greater personal well-being.

So, let's learn how to stimulate your left prefrontal cortex! (Bet no one has ever said that to you before!) I am going to teach you a technique called **Achievement Priming.** It is extremely complicated. Are you ready??? It requires you to repeatedly focus on or meditate on a word or statement. Do you think you can handle this very difficult task?

Not so hard, now is it? But, don't underestimate it! It is powerful to the subconscious mind. Giving full focus and concentration to something specific begins to change how the brain functions. Studies[xxxv] show that achievement priming is effective because when a person repeatedly gives focus to a positive word such as "achievement" or "success," they activate networks in the brain that trigger goals outside of their awareness (the subconscious mind). Remember, the subconscious mind is said to be over 30,000 times more powerful than the conscious mind. This now "subconscious goal" is extremely powerful as it creates strong mental and emotional motivation to achieve this new goal.

Subconsciously, you experience much greater <u>expectancy of achievement</u> for new tasks and goals because you are rewriting your subconscious mind's "blueprint" for success!

Research[xxxvi] shows that the priming stimulus (the word) increases idea generation, improves cognition and creativity, creates expectancy toward achievement, and **influences <u>BEHAVIORS</u>, <u>ATTITUDES</u> and <u>BELIEFS</u> toward that achievement**! This is the same principle that makes the vision board and visualization exercises such powerful techniques. Priming the subconscious mind for achievement is especially important because it begins to reprogram your mind to accept and attract those things in life that you really want. A very clear *focus* on the positive things you desire will trigger positive emotions which will create beliefs, attitudes and behaviors to move you toward what you want to achieve! Priming is powerful as it creates *concentrated focus* on what you really want so that you can't help but move toward it!

If you think priming is something new, think again. Every time you watch television, you see commercials that "prime" your brain with messages to buy their products. And it works! How many times have you seen a commercial advertising some delicious looking food and soon found yourself snacking? This is the subconscious mind at work! Learn to use it to your advantage! Are you ready to prime your brain for success and begin attracting what you truly want into your life?

Assignment:

Write down the words "Success," "Achievement," "Happiness," "Love," "Peace," "Abundance," "Integrity," or whatever keyword, goal, core value, money amount, number amount, job title, fitness level, etc. that you want to work toward.

Now put these priming words on your Vision Board, on sticky notes around your house, in your car, and/or have them daily pop up on your mobile device. Put them anywhere and everywhere that will get your attention. You must FOCUS on these words every day. The highly successful already know this. Many have reported looking at their goal statements or key words every morning when they wake up and every night before they go to sleep. Why? So that the goals/words can get into their subconscious minds all day and all night long.

Earlier, I mentioned how the statement *"I love my life. I am so blessed. Good things come to me."* transformed my life. (I also used the phrase *"I attract abundance, abundance, exceeding abundance."*) Can you now see why these phrases were so effective? These positive phrases literally reprogrammed my entire life and belief system by my consistently focusing on them multiple times throughout the day.

And listen to this! Research [xxxvii] shows that the longer you concentrate on positive words, the more you affect other brain areas in charge of creating the perception of yourself and reality. Concentrated focus on positive words creates a positive view of yourself which then creates an internal positive "bias" that helps you to see the good in others and in life. Positive words are powerful in creating a positive life full of happiness, success and abundance!

Don't forget! Take two minutes at breakfast to look at your goal tasks today. Add any other tasks that MUST be completed today (i.e. **picking up a POSTER BOARD for your VISION BOARD).**

"Fix your thoughts on what is true, and honorable, and right, and pure, and lovely, and admirable. Think about things that are excellent and worthy of praise."

~Philippians 4:8

The Focus Funnel

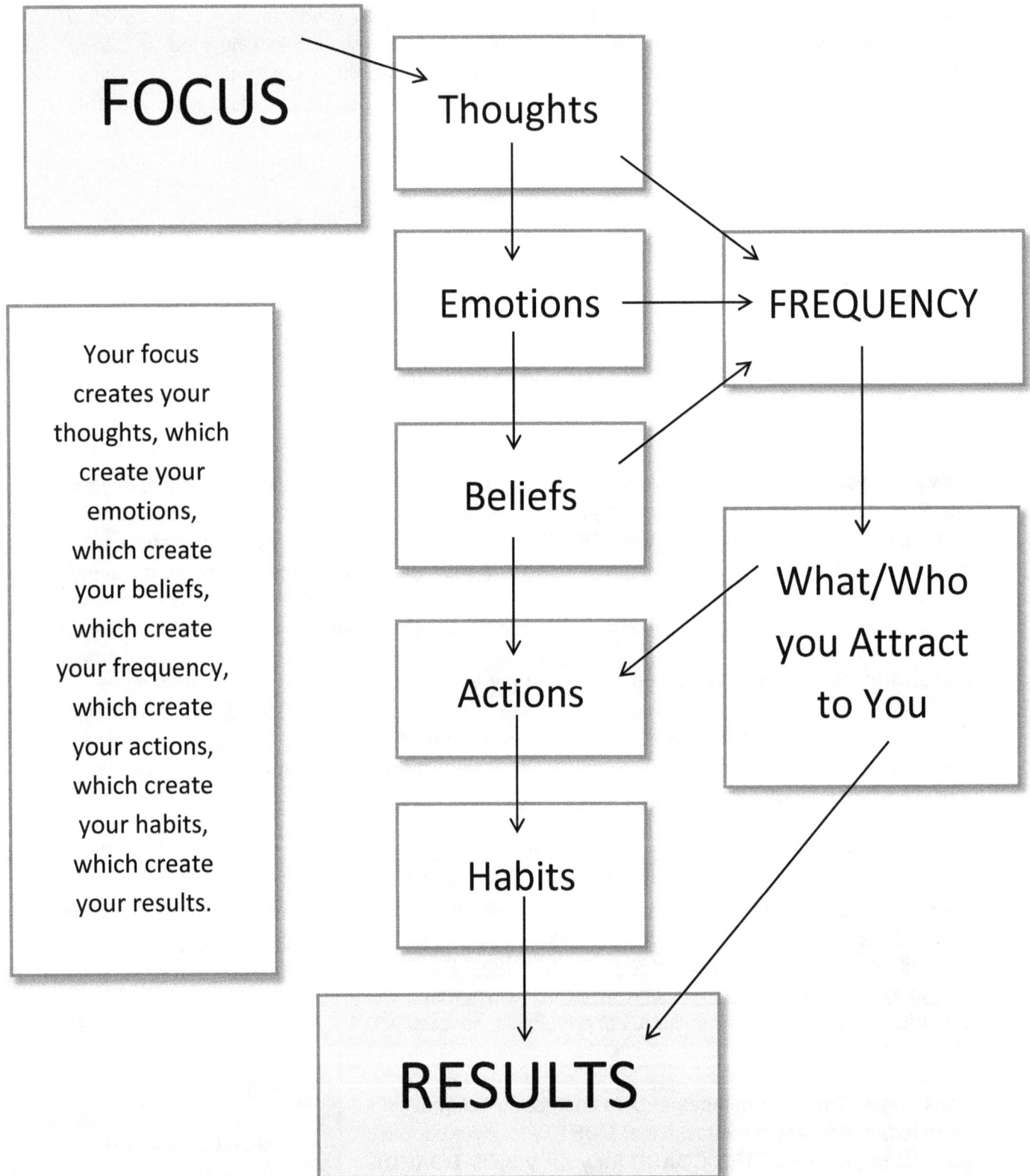

FOCUS

Thoughts

Emotions

Beliefs

Actions

Habits

FREQUENCY

What/Who you Attract to You

RESULTS

Your focus creates your thoughts, which create your emotions, which create your beliefs, which create your frequency, which create your actions, which create your habits, which create your results.

Insight

Vibrational Frequency of Emotion Scale

Your emotions are made of energy vibrating at varying frequencies. Even the Earth has a frequency called the Schumann Resonance. The following information is not meant to provide exact emotional frequencies but is a simplified explanation based on a scale of 0 to 1000. Most people average a value of 200 or below because of fears, negative subconscious beliefs and self-defeating thinking patterns. They live in a stressed (fight-or-flight) mindset that allows fear to control their lives. They thus keep themselves stuck in a worm's perspective and continue to attract others (relationships, clients, etc.) operating at those same low frequencies. For example, if a person has a belief that he/she is not worthy of love, then he/she will simply attract those who will uphold and fulfill this belief. If someone believes that he/she doesn't deserve to make more money, he/she will simply attract clients who do not have the money to pay more. However, FAITH, HOPE and LOVE are the door keepers to an abundant life as you must 1) **BELIEVE** that you CAN have good things and 2) **LOVE** yourself (and others) enough to feel worthy to RECEIVE these good things into your life. Higher frequencies also allow you to easily manifest abundance as they are life-giving energies (and are powerful in increasing lower frequencies). Therefore, choose to FOCUS on GOOD things, on life-giving energies such as faith, love and gratitude! *(To learn more, visit the works of Dr. David R. Hawkins, MD, PhD.)*

1000+   **GOD CONSCIOUSNESS/God's Infinite Love and Glory** ("I am intimately known and loved by God. I radiate God's love, glory and light. I am co-creator with God.")

900   **GRATITUDE, Freedom, Empowerment** ("Life is a gift. I am incredibly blessed in every way. I give thanks in all things. I live in abundance. I walk in freedom and purpose. I am victorious in this life!")

700   **ENLIGHTENMENT, Inspiration** ("I seek truth. I can see from a higher perspective.")

600   **PEACE, Harmony, Serenity** ("Everything is as it should be. I rest secure in the hands of my Creator.")

540   **JOY, Bliss, Enthusiasm, Happiness** ("Life is beautiful. I love my life. My life overflows with joy.")

500   **<u>LOVE</u>, Purity of Motive, Reverence, Generosity, Compassion** ("I love/respect myself/others.")

470   **<u>FAITH</u>, <u>HOPE</u>, Optimism, Belief** ("Everything will work out. All things are possible.")

400   **UNDERSTANDING, Empathetic** ("What can I learn from this?")

350   **ACCEPTANCE, Forgiveness, Grace** ("I accept what is. I forgive and move on.")

310   **WILLINGNESS, Trust, Readiness, Surrendering** ("I let go. We can do this.")

200   **COURAGE, Boldness, Nervousness** ("I think I can do this.")

175   **PRIDE, Vanity, Scornful, Frustration, Irritation, Entitlement** ("I have all the answers.")

150   **HATRED, Anger, Rage, Revenge, Unforgiveness** ("I hate this. I will not forgive.")

125   **JEALOUSY, Greed, Selfishness, Disappointment** ("I have to have it. I have to have more.")

100   **FEAR, Anxiety, Worry, Doubt, Withdrawal** ("I'm afraid that... I worry that... I doubt that...")

75   **GRIEF, Sadness, Regret, Depression** ("I should have... I wish I had... It's too late.")

50   **APATHY, Helplessness, Hopelessness** ("I can't. No one can help me. I can't ever get ahead.")

30   **GUILT, Victim, Blame, Self-Loathing** ("It's all my fault. I deserve to be miserable.")

20   **SHAME, Worthlessness, Powerlessness, Despair, Humiliation** ("I'm not good enough.")

0   **DEATH**

Create your life to be AMAZING! An abundant life is yours for the taking!

Day 24: What and Why Wednesday

Today we will look at our WHATs and WHYs of life again. When we live by our values, we feel peace in our lives and a sense of fulfillment because we are living according to what is most important to us. These values are part of our calling. Our calling is about living out our potential, our purpose on this earth. Don't let success *only* be about money, fame or personal glory; instead, let it be about living your dream, fulfilling your potential, and making this world a better place. When it all comes down to it, money will not bring happiness and neither will fame or glory. Success should be tied in with your true core values, or it will not feel like success at all.

When you are walking in your calling—using your specific skills, abilities and talents to make this world a better place—you will be the happiest and feel the most fulfilled. When you walk in your calling—living out your potential, living by your values—your life will touch those around you. You will become a blessing everywhere you go because you are giving back your contribution to this world. You will feel a sense of purpose as you serve others using your gifts, abilities and amazing potential.

A job is what you are trained to do, but a calling is what you are BORN to do!

However, when you are not walking in your calling, you will feel miserable and will try to make others miserable with you. Further, it is easy to become jealous of others as they fulfill their dreams while you feel so far away from your goals. Jealousy is a negative energy and a dream killer. Life is not a competition. Your dream is not someone else's dream, and their dream is not exactly your dream either. Don't be discouraged by others' success. Instead, be encouraged that others have found the path to success to live out their dreams—this means that there is a path for you too! If they can do it, you can do it! Always remember, no one person is better than another. We are all human beings. Each of us has unlimited potential within us. Therefore, stop seeing others as better than you. Choose to believe in yourself, and be the BEST YOU POSSIBLE. There are many unlikely and unqualified people who have tapped into huge success. Why can't you tap into huge success too? You were created to walk with purpose and unlimited potential. Be determined to push through to live out your calling in this earth.

What are your WHYs in life?

Both success and failure are based on what you focus on. Clearly defining your WHYs gives you FOCUS which motivates and pushes you to the next levels of success (walking in your calling). Therefore, let's define your WHYs by determining what motivates you. WHY are you even reading this book? What are the WHYs that motivate you to do more, be more and have more? What are the WHYs that make you cry? Search deep. Your WHYs will begin to give you clear FOCUS, so that you can move toward them and attract them to you. Your WHYs will also create a fire inside of you—a passion to pursue your calling, an unquenchable desire to fulfill your greater purpose in this earth, and an unstoppable quest to be the best you possible.

WHYs are *different* for *different* people as we all have *different* goals, visions and motivators. Even so, our WHYs are typically a mix of materialistic and altruistic motives. Therefore, maybe your WHYs involve having a nicer home, cars, clothes, school, neighborhood, the ability to travel to amazing places or to create a better life for you and your family. Maybe your WHYs are getting in peak physical shape, creating amazing relationships, getting promoted or becoming debt free. Maybe your WHYs are in creating time and financial freedom with a lifestyle that allows you to work when you want instead of having to clock into a 9-to-5 job. Maybe your WHYs involve building business empires, being a positive leader and mentor, or becoming an accomplished writer, speaker, musician, artist, politician or athlete. Maybe your WHYs are in helping and serving others by using your gifts and talents. Maybe your WHYs are in creating or supporting good causes or giving to charities and helping organizations. Maybe your WHYs involve living a fulfilled life where you live out your purpose and potential as you make this world a better place. Maybe your WHYs are spiritually driven as you desire to please God or your Higher Power. Maybe your WHYs are ALL of the above!

Now define YOUR WHYs, and let them begin to drive you. Keep them in front of you to motivate you, especially when you want to quit. On Sunday we talked about creating a vision/dream board. This is where you want to put your WHYs. If your WHYs are clearly before you, they will motivate you to keep going even when everything in you wants to quit.

Let me ask you a question. If you clearly decided that your WHY is creating a better life for your family, but you had a terribly hard day/week and wanted to quit on your dream, would you be able to tell your family to their faces that you have given up on creating a better life for them? I hope not. I hope that big WHY called "your family" will keep you going when obstacles, rejections and hard times come. Your WHYs are what will motivate you to bring the change you desire in your life. I encourage you to search your heart and define your WHYs. This week, begin to search for pictures and words (through the internet, magazines, etc.) that represent your WHYs to put on your vision board on Sunday.

My WHYs...

(Which is your BIGGEST WHY? What WHY makes you cry?)

Now take your WHYs and use them to drive you forward.

See your goals and your WHYs so crystal clear that your mind truly believes you already possess them. Now instead of being jealous of others' success, you can finally accept that success is a reality for you too. Instead of being bitter from watching others succeed, you can choose to learn from others' success. Instead of being envious that others are attaining their dreams, you can be thankful that you have those who can help, encourage and/or motivate you to obtain YOUR DREAMS.

Insight

Jealousy can be a big success and wealth blocker. As we feel negative emotions about someone having more than us or having what we want for ourselves, we are imprinting on our subconscious mind that others *should* have more than us. The subconscious mind will do as it is told and will uphold this belief. It is important to remember that the subconscious mind is very literal; it does not understand sarcasm or joking. Whatever we repeatedly tell it (with strong emotion), it will believe and thus enforce.

However, when we begin to see the abundance and wealth within us that can help and serve others, we begin to show our subconscious mind that we are already wealthy and successful. Also, through visualization exercises, we show our mind that we are "currently" in "full possession" of those things we aspire to. Therefore, the subconscious mind accepts this "new reality" as real and enforces the belief.

Further, a key success habit is to not compare yourself with others. Learn to use others' success to motivate you instead of allowing comparison to breed envy and bitterness. It is also important to note that feeling negative emotions toward others simply impresses those negative emotions on your own mind and against your own self. If you feel ongoing resentment against someone, you are not only programming your subconscious mind to be resentful toward others but also toward yourself, which will only block what you really want. The good or evil you do to others, you are really doing to yourself! *"Love your neighbor,"* and *"Do unto others as you would have them to do to you"* is for your own good!

You are of great worth and have much to offer this world. Life is not a competition; it is a journey. And that journey is not to become "the BEST" but to become the best YOU possible. Now go be YOU!

Success breeds success. Hang around the successful, and be *happy* for them. Learn to "tap" into their positive flow of energy and into their wisdom and guidance. Copy their success habits. Decide to be encouraged and energized by those who have found success (whether they are in your life or on the pages of a book or internet source).

Also, let me give you a little warning. Don't expect those close to you to cheer you on as you set out to achieve great things. Often, our loved ones are our biggest critics and will always be there to remind us of our weaknesses. And remember that when others mock your dreams, it is a sign of their own jealousy—an expression of their own insecurities and disappointments. Don't let their mocking words get you down. Instead, let it energize you to be more and do more as you have now risen to a higher level of thinking and understanding! Shake the dust and dirt off you. You're not a worm anymore.

Your days of being a worm are over. It's time to SOAR!

Decide to set pettiness aside and be the bigger person (whether this involves cheering on those who are way ahead of you in success or in not allowing small-thinking people to pull you down). Further, reach out to help these jealous individuals begin to live their dreams too. An act of kindness sets in motion more acts of kindness. Be a spark for success to those around you.

However, don't be surprised by the lack of motivation and the fear of change you will begin to see in others. Change is hard. Living your dreams comes with a price; it takes effort, vision, persistence and unwavering determination. Therefore, decide to be a positive and encouraging role model to show others that success and happiness are possible.

Each person must own their own their life. Your race is your race, and you alone decide whether you will be a winner. Therefore, when you begin the path to live your dreams, you must see yourself already at the finish line. When you see yourself as a winner, it helps you to regroup and keep going forward after setbacks and discouragements...which will always come! Plus, true winners aren't jealous and insecure.

When you see yourself a winner, you don't mind if others become winners too!

When you see yourself a winner, you take on the attitude of gratitude and abundance—that there is more than enough for everyone to have their share. Helping others becomes a gift instead of a burden. When you are convinced that you are in possession of your dream (and your WHYs), it becomes easier to help others fulfill their dreams too. Choose to be a winner and a spark to inspire others. A small spark can set an entire forest on fire.

> *Choose to see success as something that flows to you and through you to others, not something you hoard for yourself.*

When you begin to live in the world of potential—seeing yourself already at the finish line—you begin to allow success to flow to you. However, you must also choose to allow it to flow through you—the law of abundance. (I explain more on the law of abundance later in this book, so keep going!) Holding success all for yourself is hoarding (a lack mindset) which plugs up the success channel and stops the flow. You must allow success to flow to you and through you to others.

In other words, help others, and you will, in turn, be helped. Sow into others, and others will sow into you. This is the law of sowing and reaping. Any highly successful person will tell you that if you want to be successful, go help others to become successful. What goes around comes around. Why? Because when you help others, you are stepping up to be a leader, a mentor, an educator, a giver, a servant, an encourager, a cheer leader! When you step up and "become more," you are then able to "have more." Also, these positive roles will draw positive energy, people and things to you! Ever heard of a magnetic personality? This is what you want!

Whatever you put out there will come back to you—some call it karma. If you are a person of integrity, people will respect you. If you are a sneaky liar, no one will trust you. If you put out ill-will toward others, guess what? That negative energy will just come back on you! (In fact, it probably never left you!) If you are a giver, you will find that people will want to give back to you!

> "For every **ACTION**, there is an equal and opposite **REACTION**."
>
> ~Newton's Third Law of Motion

The same law applies to success. Hoard success, and watch it wither. Help others become successful, and you will sow seeds and open new doors for your own success. For example, people think I'm crazy for "giving away" my best and most transformational information through this book, but I want EVERYONE to use this information to transform their lives!

Today choose to not only walk in your calling but to also be an encouragement to those around you. Help others on their path to success. You truly do reap what you sow. Therefore, chose to sow good seeds, and just watch a good harvest come back to you. As you sow into others, you are really sowing into yourself! Just try it, and see what happens!

Assignment:

Now it's time to think again about your WHATs and WHYs in life—your top core values. Name them, and think back over the past week. Did you honor these values with your actions? How can you better honor them?

My "DOING" Core Values	Did I honor them?	
1.	Yes	No
2.	Yes	No
3.	Yes	No
4.	Yes	No
5.	Yes	No
My "BEING" Core Values	**Did I honor them?**	
1.	Yes	No
2.	Yes	No
3.	Yes	No
4.	Yes	No
5.	Yes	No

How can I better honor my values this coming week?

1.

2.

3.

4.

5.

I trust by now that your values, dreams and goals are becoming clearer. Today I also want you to look back at your mission statement from Day 2 and begin to better finalize it. Rewrite it if needed. A mission statement is powerful as it makes you dig deep to find your calling. Your mission statement will more than likely change throughout the years as you mature and grow, but let's get a really good one nailed down today. Your mission statement should also go on your vision board. If you use a white board or chalk board for your goals, write this statement there as well. Your mission statement is empowering; therefore, put it where you will see it until it becomes a part of who are you. Then let your WHYs drive you to accomplish this mission.

Sample Mission Statements:

My mission is **to use** my gifts and talents **to assist** others in finding their best health so they can be free to live the amazing life they desire.

My mission is **to enable** others to feel positive **through** my writing and entertainment venues.

My mission is **to build** successful businesses **that will** have a positive impact on the world.

My mission is **to be** a role model to both adults and children **by** daily becoming a greater person of integrity, excellence, influence and wise counsel.

Here's my mission statement: My mission on this earth is **to empower** others to become all they are created to be **by educating** them through coaching and ministry settings.

Re-written/Finalized Mission Statement:

Don't forget! Take two minutes at breakfast to look at your goal tasks today. Add any other tasks that MUST be completed today (picking up a **POSTER BOARD** for your vision board, exercising, phone calls, etc.). Visualize yourself completing these tasks quickly and *easily*.

> "Be who you were created to be
> and you will set the world on fire."
>
> **~St. Catherine of Serbia**

Great job! You are living your life with purpose!
You are living out your mission on this earth!
Now go set the world on FIRE!

Day 25: Thankful Thursday

Today is Thankful Thursday. Have you found yourself more thankful in your daily life? Are you going to bed each night thinking about what you are grateful for? Would creating a gratitude journal and keeping it by your bed help you remember to be more thankful?

Now I want to discuss **Emotional Intelligence (EI)** and how it relates to gratitude. It is said that 80% of the world's most successful people score high in Emotional Intelligence. Also, those with high EI outperform those with high IQ by leaps and bounds as Emotional Intelligence is the strongest predictor of performance and success.

> Emotional Intelligence ultimately has to do with personal and social awareness and is an essential KEY to SUCCESS.

So, what is Emotional Intelligence? EI really comes down to being in touch with your own emotions (self-awareness) and being able to relate to others (social awareness and empathy).

Wikipedia defines Emotional Intelligence as:

 the *"ability to recognize one's own and other people's emotions, to discriminate between different feelings and label them appropriately, and to use emotional information to guide thinking and behavior…. Studies have shown that people with high EI have greater mental health, exemplary job performance, and more potent leadership skills."*

Let's, therefore, take a look at the top 15 behaviors of Emotional Intelligence. Check off the ones that are easy for you, and circle (or write down) those you need to work on:

1. You have an extensive **EMOTIONAL VOCABULARY** to label and describe exactly how you are feeling so that you can figure out what's wrong and find solutions. (You change *"I'm having a bad day"* to *"I feel disappointed because…"*. You allow yourself to process situations, which may involve negative emotions. However, as you process these negative emotions, you acknowledge that you have the choice to release them as you understand the situation is only temporary, and you will find solutions.)

2. You are **CURIOUS** about people because you truly care about others and want to help them. (High empathy—the ability to see from another's perspective—is the keystone to high Emotional Intelligence. You honor others and respect their opinions and differences.)

3. You are **SELF-AWARE**. (You know how to use your strengths to your full advantage while keeping your weaknesses from holding you back. You know your values and ethical beliefs and choose to uphold them instead of responding on "autopilot.")

4. You **APPRECIATE** what you have. (Daily, you cultivate an attitude of GRATITUDE, thus improving your mood, energy and physical well-being. You appreciate yourself and your relationships.)

5. You genuinely enjoy **CONNECTING WITH OTHERS**. (People feel comfortable around you and are able to openly share with you. Others know that you are not judging them but are there to truly LISTEN and help—empathy. You build strong relationships because you are constantly thinking about how to help and serve others. You win friends and influence people!).

6. You are able to **READ OTHERS** well. You are a good judge of character and are, therefore, **DIFFICULT TO OFFEND**. (Instead of quickly judging others, you have the ability to know why they are the way they are—empathy. You are self-confident, open-minded and able to distinguish between humor and insult. You do not let other people's opinions define you.)

7. You know how to set **HEALTHY BOUNDARIES** and aren't afraid to say *"No."* (Self-control and respecting your own boundaries is a powerful skill. Taking on more than you can handle only leads to stress which can cause your limbic system to act impulsively, irrationally and selfishly instead of empathetically.)

8. You **FOCUS ON THE FUTURE,** and choose to let go of past mistakes. (You do not dwell on past failures, but accept them as part of life, and choose to learn, grow and advance by using these "lessons learned" as building blocks and stepping stones. When you fall down, you pick yourself up knowing that you have just gained a wealth of new information to help you on your journey.)

9. You have learned how to **FORGIVE** and let go. (You recognize that the offender may not deserve your forgiveness but you deserve to be free from this negativity. You let go, and release the stress and negative memory instead of allowing your mind to re-live the situation over and over which only puts you into fight-or-flight mode. Remember how powerful visualization exercises are and how your brain can't decipher between what is real and what is imagined.)

10. You surround yourself with **POSITIVE PEOPLE,** and limit interactions with toxic people. (You stay close to positive, like-minded and supportive people. You approach negative, toxic, low-frequency, dream-killing people with caution. You also keep your own emotions in check. Out of empathy, you consider these difficult people's standpoint and are able to find solutions and common ground.)

11. You are **MOTIVATED** but not a perfectionist. (You celebrate what you have achieved instead of dwelling on imperfections and shortcomings. You don't compare yourself with others but instead focus on becoming a better version of yourself day by day and step by step.)

12. You are **BALANCED** and **MINDFUL**. (Despite your busy schedule, you take time to disconnect and enjoy the moment—being "mindful." Taking time to be mindful allows you to stop life's chaos and to be fully present in that moment. You pause, take a step back, take a breather and begin to see life from a new perspective. You are then able to relax, regroup, reduce stress, feel peace and to truly enjoy the present moment. Mindfulness also increases awareness of your habitual thinking/behavior patterns as you are able to "reflect" on life. In addition, being mindful involves taking time to turn off all electronics.)

13. You focus on **POSTIVE THOUGHTS** and stop negative self-talk in its tracks. (Instead of giving energy toward the problem, you are energized by finding and focusing on the solution.)

14. You **EMBRACE CHANGE** as you are flexible and constantly able to adapt. (You do not fear change but create a plan of action should change occur.)

15. You won't let anyone take away your **HAPPINESS**. (You alone control and own your emotions. You recognize that you will not feel happy 100% of the time. However, your identity, future and joy are not based on others' opinions or temporary circumstances. You are motivated from within—your dreams and goals—and find joy through appreciating life itself. You do not allow anyone to take away your freedom of owning your emotions, attitudes and destiny.)

Which of the 15 behaviors are the easiest for you?

Which behaviors are the hardest?

You may want to add some of these Emotional Intelligence behaviors as goals under your Top Ten goals list (especially the ones you need to work on). We have actually covered most of these behaviors in our journey together. You have become a more emotionally intelligent person, and you didn't even know it! Go YOU!

Today we are going to practice the Emotional Intelligence behavior of gratitude by recognizing those people in our lives for whom we are most thankful. Think about the two closest people in your life, and name at least three qualities about them for which you are thankful.

Name:

Three qualities I am thankful for:

1.

2.

3.

Name:

Three qualities I am thankful for:

1.

2.

3.

Insight

Win Friends and Influence People

If you want to become a person of influence, you must do as Dale Carnegie says and learn *"How to Win Friends and Influence People"* which starts by honoring and respecting all you meet. Choose to treat others as the special, unique and wonderful creations they are. Learn to make friends everywhere you go and with all you meet. Compliment, encourage and be genuinely interested in others (whether they are strangers, work in your office or live in your own home). Also, learn to listen. One of the greatest gifts you can give another is to genuinely listen to what he/she is saying—whether it interests you or not. Learn to listen without interrupting. Stop your thoughts, look them in the eye, and truly listen to hear what they are sharing. Many hear but few listen. Many act but few truly care. Many speak but few influence. Become a person of influence by learning to love people. See the beauty and worth in each and every individual, and you will never leave a life untouched by your influence. Daily, begin to say, *"I love people, and people love me!"*

Tahni Cullen is mother to Josiah Cullen, a severely autistic child, and author of *Josiah's Fire: Autism Stole His Words, God Gave Him a Voice.* I have included a few of Josiah's incredible quotes in this book. Tahni said the following as a way for us to understand and love better as every human life is of highest significance:

"It was a beautiful day and Joe, Josiah and I went to look for a park to go to. We really wanted one that was mostly empty so we could all just relax and Josiah could play. Josiah has this loud vocalization he has been doing as he's really "exploring the space" with a loud scream here and there. It's a show-stopper, and kids talk. We got to a park, and then people started showing up. I decided as kids and parents arrived that I would just go right up to them really upbeat and say, *'Hi, I'm Tahni and this is my son Josiah. He doesn't yet speak with his mouth, and though he might make a loud sound you might hear, he's actually just really, really happy to be here right now. He understands everything, but just doesn't talk. He likes playing at the park like you guys. It's really a nice day to play at the park, huh?'* It broke the ice on the front end, and everybody was actually really cool with it. It also took the pressure off of me because I knew everyone was told and understood.

Then, guess what happens? A young man who was in his 20s shows up with his mom, brother and niece. He likely had a number of diagnoses (possibly autism being one), including that physically his head fell forward and neck was bowed. I introduced myself and pointed over to my husband and Josiah and said my statement, and his mom said, *'This is Clark. He's nonverbal. We get it.'* I chatted with her a little and then saw Clark by himself standing under the slide and moving and looking at his hand in front of his face. I went over to him, and I just started complimenting him and talking to him like I would talk to any 20 something (just always assume age level intelligence and talk normally). I then put my hand up like his and looked at my hand in the same way, and I said, *'Hands are pretty cool to look at aren't they? It can really be calming to look at your hand.'* And then I said, *'Clark, I just have to tell you, from the second I saw you come to the park, I thought, I bet that guy brings joy to people wherever he goes. I know I feel joy just by meeting you and seeing you here. You don't have to worry if you can't reply back. I know you understand what I'm saying and that I truly appreciate you.'*

I kid you not—he lifted up his heavy head that was in downward looking posture and his blue eyes locked with mine and he smiled. I said, *'Wow, what a smile you have! Do you feel like I do, the breeze on your face? It feels so good to get out in the sun and feel the wind after a long winter. Clark, you bring joy to the park! Thank you!'* He slipped his hand in mine—on his own, and held it tight! We connected in minutes! It was beautiful. I wonder how many people with disabilities that affect their speech and socialization have many people aside from family and therapists that ever just come up and just say anything to them. Just anything, without needing one thing back, not even an acknowledgment? It would have been okay if he would have done nothing, but I won't soon forget Clark. He lifted up his heavy head, and we connected with indescribable joy between us.

It was a learning experience—from me not wanting my son to cause a disruption to others…to me realizing that I need to pay attention myself to those who have no voice. We all should have the same spaces to be human beings together. It's not just about not staring or just not saying anything. It's about getting in there and making them feel so welcome in this space—whatever and wherever that space is, not just because it's the right thing for us to release to them, but because they have so much also to release to us! This is the lesson of worth—everyone is worthy. Everyone."

Next, let's practice both gratitude and empathy. (Empathy is learning to see from another person's perspective and is the hallmark of Emotional Intelligence). Please name someone whom you don't always get along with, agree with, or like, and answer the following.

Name:

Why does he/she act the way he/she does? (Begin to see from his/her perspective—this is empathy. Does he/she have low self-esteem, past hurts, disappointments, limited mindsets, sabotaging subconscious beliefs, depression, anxiety, fear, poor role models, a hard life, abuse, self-hatred, fear of rejection, need to be right, bitterness, desperation for love and attention...?)

What is one thing you can be thankful for or admire about this person?

How can you be a positive influence in his/her life? (Also, visualize sending love and forgiveness to him/her.)

Today be sure to tell at least one of the individuals on your list how thankful you are for them (maybe even do something special for them). Remember, being thankful stimulates the happy side of your brain. This stimulation helps your brain to think bigger, more creatively, more *empathetically*, and to see from varying viewpoints, thus allowing you to generate new and better resources and solutions to create your desired life. During your grateful thoughts, breath in the positive emotions associated with them. Begin today to be an emotionally intelligent and successful person!

Don't forget! Take two minutes at breakfast to look at your goal tasks today. Add any other tasks that MUST be completed today (picking up a **POSTER BOARD**, preparing for a work meeting, scheduling appointments, shopping, cleaning, meal planning, etc.). Then visualize yourself completing these tasks *with total ease.* Your life is incredibly amazing!

(To learn more about Emotional Intelligence, check out Daniel Goleman's *Emotional Intelligence: Why It Can Matter More Than IQ*, as well as *Emotional Intelligence 2.0* by Travis Bradberry and Jean Greaves.)

> "Tonight, give thanks to those who have done you wrong.
> They've unknowingly made you strong."
>
> **~Unknown**

Today's lesson provides a powerful list of behaviors to help you lead a happy and successful life. Decide to be a person of high Emotional Intelligence as it is a key to your success! I know you can do it!

Day 26: Fearless Friday

What fears and obstacles did you face this week? Did you find ways to overcome them, or did they overcome you? How can you better overcome these fears and obstacles in the future? Daily, most of us face obstacles called "energy drainers"—those people, things and situations that pull us down and hinder us from moving our lives forward. Take a moment, and think about any energy drainers you need to remove, neutralize or limit from your life.

Energy-Draining People?
Energy-Draining Emotions?
Energy Drainers at Work?
Energy Drainers at Home?
Energy Drainers (other)?

Energy drainers dwell among us. Let me remind you again that your friends and family will probably not give you a big party to celebrate the amazing dreams you set out to achieve. In fact, they will more than likely criticize you and your "extraordinary" plans as they point out all your weaknesses, flaws and past failures. Therefore, be careful with whom you share the dreams of your heart (stay with like-minded people).

Unfortunately, for some of you, your greatest energy drainer may be the person you're married to or a family member or roommate with whom you live. Your worst energy drainer may be someone whom you work with day in and day out, and there is simply no way to limit your exposure to this person. Let's face it; you can't live your life in a bubble! In these cases, your job is to keep your positivity level so high that your strong positive frequency increases their low frequency.

Think how quickly the energy of a room can change when a highly excited or an extremely angry person walks in. Emotions have powerful energy. In fact, the HeartMath Institute (www.HeartMath.org) found that the electromagnetic signal (a carrier of emotion) from your heart is registered in the brain waves of those around you! Your emotions show up in others' brain waves (because the brain is really a vibratory instrument). Emotions are *literally* contagious.[xxxviii]

> *"Spread love everywhere you go. Let no one ever come to you without leaving happier."*
>
> ~Mother Teresa

Therefore, your overall goal should always be to increase the atmosphere of positive energy (vibration) everywhere you go. When others are around you, they should feel energized as they bask in your positive energy flow of love, optimism, faith, thankfulness and joy in the little things! Positivity is food for the soul. And positivity and enthusiasm are *contagious*! Therefore, make it a goal to be a catalyst for positive change in the world around you. Remember, we create the world around us by our thoughts...so let's make it a great one by radiating positivity everywhere we go and to all we meet.

Therefore, if you create the world around you by your thoughts, then many of your energy drainers may have been created by YOU! If your life is out of control, it is because you have allowed it to become out of control. If your children are completely disrespectful to you, it is because you have allowed them to become disrespectful to you. If you are overworked and under-appreciated on your job, it is because you have allowed this to happen to you. If you are in a romantic relationship that is abusive, recognize that you have attracted and allowed this bad situation into your life.

Begin to dig deep and identify your underlying subconscious beliefs (the lies that tell you that "*you're not good enough*" or "*not worthy of love or of being respected*"). Choose to change these inner thoughts and beliefs, and the world around you will soon change. For example, in the abusive relationship, your inner change may cause the abuser to leave, to change for the better, or it may cause you to seek help or stand tall with dignity and leave the relationship.

If you're attracting all the wrong kinds of friends and romantic partners (or lack thereof), you must stop and ask yourself "*Why? What inner beliefs do I have that are sending out the wrong frequency?*" No matter the situation, decide today to become the author of your destiny. No, you cannot control and manipulate others. You can only control yourself. But remember, your thoughts, decisions and actions have a domino effect in all the directions of your life. Either you will play the victim in the movie called "*Your Life*," or you will be the victor. The choice is always yours.

Law of Social Attraction

Now let's take a quick look at the law of social attraction. I'm sure you've heard the saying, "*Birds of a feather flock together*." It's true, like-minded people stick together. People who spend time together also "rub off" on one another. You become like those you spend the most time with. Why is this? It is thought to be caused by *mirror neurons in your brain that mimic others' feelings*.

Insight

We all have energy-draining people in our lives. However, you alone decide how others' opinions define you. Either you allow negative opinions to soak in and affect you, or you choose to define who you are despite what others say. Remember, opinions are just that, opinions—they are not facts.

Let me ask you a question. Does one criticism make you feel completely unloved or incompetent? If one negative statement can crumble your life, then you may have an ALL or NOTHING mentality—meaning you are EITHER "amazingly beautiful" OR "completely ugly." You are either "totally competent" or "completely stupid." You are either a "perfect success" or an "utter failure." This kind of attitude only sets you up for a rollercoaster of emotions. If you look at your family's responses to criticism, you will probably recognize that you respond similarly.

Don't let criticism eat away at you… and it will if you allow it! Judge the criticism for what it is worth and who it came from. Determine the motive. Is this constructive criticism based out of love and concern, or is it destructive criticism based out of jealousy? Either way, ask yourself what you can learn from it to become better. See it as a stepping stone not a stumbling block. You will always have critics, and the more successful you become, the more critics you will have! However, the more you LIKE yourself, the less criticism with affect you.

Think through how you will respond to criticism in order to keep yourself moving up in life instead of allowing others' opinions to pull you down and ruin your day, week or life! It's your life, not theirs. So keep your chin up, and keep going! It's time to FLY!

For example, when someone smiles, the part of your brain responsible for smiling will also light up. When others are happy and optimistic, it reinforces happiness and optimism in your brain. When others are compassionate, it reinforces compassion in your brain. Even more, when you repeatedly hear the same phrases, either positive or negative, these words and feelings are *reinforced in your own brain*! You **literally** begin to think and feel like those you spend the most time with!

WHO do you hang around?

Who are your five closest associations? What are their lives like? What are their habits? How do they talk? How much money do they make? Do they hold the success that you desire? If you desire financial freedom and prosperity, is hanging out with those who are broke going to help you? If you desire to improve your marriage, is spending a lot of time with those either divorced or miserable in their marriages going to benefit you?

No, of course not! It seems so simple, and yet many of us do spend large quantities of time with others who are energy drainers, dream killers and accepters of mediocrity. Our friends, family and co-workers would be hurt if we called them such; however, this is often the hard truth. Therefore, limit your time with these people, and seek out those who will lift you up and encourage your dreams. Seek out those who have obtained the success you desire and observe them. Study them. Ask them questions. Listen to how they talk, how they think about their future, and how they react to failure and criticism.

Thankfully, the more committed you are to your dreams, the more you will find that you will attract other like-minded individuals to yourself. Why? Because that positive frequency you are sending out will attract those at similar frequencies. Maybe you've heard it said, "*Your vibe will attract your tribe.*" I definitely know this to be true in my own life. Once I shifted my thinking (and thus my frequency), I've had many timely connections with amazing and inspiring people who have been integral to my own personal and professional development and success.

What if you can't get away from these energy-draining "friends"?

For those associations who are limiting you, you can certainly try to have a positive impact on their lives, but remember you cannot change anyone. It is only by creating change in YOU that change will begin to occur around you. It just might happen that your positivity will begin to rub off on them! Use those mirror neurons to your advantage! Remember, your kind smile will cause their brain to light up smiling too!

Also, be on guard to quickly change the subject when negativity begins. And you can certainly try to *kindly* show others how to be more positive, but know that they may not be as open as you would expect (maybe recommend this workbook to them!) Therefore, don't argue with negative friends, family, neighbors, co-workers and such. Simply limit your exposure to their negative words and limiting beliefs so that they do not become **reinforced in your own brain**.

Think of the powerful effects of verbal abuse on people's lives. Words either *build or destroy*. Literally. Negativity in equals negativity out! Therefore, try your best to turn off the negativity (which sometimes may involve social media, television, news, radio, music, literature and such). You are not a trash can. You deserve to fill your life with good things, not garbage.

However, if you must spend time with these energy-drainers, stay positive, speak positive and think positive. (A little positivity can overcome any negativity. Light always dispels darkness). Remember that these people's negativity stems from their own self-limiting beliefs, fears and unhappiness. Just don't let their negativity soak in! You may even need to walk away from some conversations and literally brush yourself off from all the negativity. Too much time with these low frequency, energy-sucking associations and you will find it hard to fight against the strong, downward pull. Remember, your goal is to move up in life, not be pulled down. Choose your associations wisely. Who will you spend your time with? Who will you limit (or eliminate) your time with? The choice is yours. Just remember, you become like those you most associate with!

Assignment:

Create a positive affirmation for overcoming your greatest energy drainer.

Examples:

Energy Drainer—Criticizing People:
- I will be me. I alone define who I am and where I am going. I will forgive that person who criticized me. I realize that their criticism stems from their own feelings of inadequacy and past failures. (Note: Unforgiveness is a major energy drainer, while forgiveness instantly removes blocks in your life. Forgiveness is a powerful energy giver. As is love. Forgiveness is based out of love. Choose to forgive the person, forgive yourself, let go and move on.)

Energy Drainer—Negative Words:
- I will limit my time with (person) and choose to not accept his/her negative words in my life, but will immediately restate these words (in my mind) as positives.

Energy Drainer—Negative Feelings:
- When I begin to feel depressed at work (or after being with my co-worker), I will begin to focus on the things and people I do like and how I am daily becoming better and attracting good things to me.

Energy Drainer—Past Negative Memory:
- When this past memory tries to defeat me, I choose to tell it that it is powerless in my life. I choose to believe that I am worthy of the great future I desire. I am full of joy knowing that anything is possible to those who believe. My present and future are AMAZING!

Positive Affirmation Statement:

Now repeat your statement **out loud**. Then write your statement on a note (i.e. sticky note), and put it somewhere you will see daily (bathroom mirror, car, refrigerator, desk, vision board).

Stone Throw Exercise

The Stone Throw Exercise is a very powerful activity that will bring you to the next level of life. You must let go of the old to make room for the new. As you have been learning to overcome your fears, obstacles, weakness, energy-drainers and negative self-sabotaging beliefs, you have been letting go of those things that have been hindering you to make room for the new life you desire.

Remember, the brain cannot tell the difference between what is imagined and what is real. When we dwell on negative past memories, our brains think we are reliving these memories—which affects us body, mind and spirit. We must throw these past hurts and traumas into the "sea of forgetfulness." This exercise is powerful and therapeutic, and I encourage you to do it.

Directions:

Go to an open field, into the woods, find a pond or lake, or go to the ocean. Find stones and name each stone according to your fears, obstacles, weaknesses, energy-drainers, failures, stressors, hurts, negative beliefs, lies, past memories and any other hindrance in your life. Then throw each stone, one by one, as far as you can into the woods or water.

As you throw each stone, you can say something like, *"I release _____,"* or *"_____, you are gone from my life,"* or *"_____, I choose to let you go, you are not a part of me anymore,"* or *"_____, I am free from you! You are defeated as a hindrance in my life! I choose to be FREE!"*

Yell, scream, cry, whatever is needed to release the pain, hurt and memories. You have carried these heavy burdens too long, and it is now time to physically, mentally, emotionally and spiritually release them. There may be someone whom you need to forgive and release. (While this person may not deserve your forgiveness, you deserve to be free. Name that stone, and throw it into the sea of forgetfulness.) Maybe you need to forgive yourself. Maybe you've held guilt, shame and blame in your heart. It's time to be free. Lean on your High Power during this very powerful and therapeutic activity. You should feel a heavy weight begin to lift off your shoulders while completing this exercise.

As you throw the stones into the "sea of forgetfulness," you choose to no longer dwell on the negative feelings of these past traumas and memories. You will not re-live these traumas anymore. They are not a part of who you are now. Begin to see the memory becoming a beautiful stepping stone to your incredible future. Feel empowered as your past is becoming an incredible story that will not only help you create an amazing life but will also empower others to do the same! Become <u>THANKFUL</u> for all you have experienced as it has made you a better and stronger person. Now focus on the marvelous future that awaits you, that wants to come to you!

(Note: You can also do this exercise using pieces of paper. Write the "name" of what you want to release on each piece of paper, and then throw it into a trash can.)

The Stone Throw Exercise is an activity that we should all do periodically. We all need to cast off our cares and heavy burdens; they are doing us no good and only serve to hold us back. By releasing these weights and chains, we create freedom within us. We release the old to make room for the new. We are then able to attract success, love and joy because we have removed the hindrances that have blocked the good things we desire from coming into our lives. We launch ourselves into higher levels of personal potential so that we can BE more and thus HAVE more!

Congratulations. You are becoming an incredible person who chooses to walk in freedom. You choose to be FREE so that you can attract the life you truly desire and deserve.

> *"Success is something you attract by the person you become."*
>
> *~Jim Rohn*

Another great exercise for releasing old-baggage, memories, stress and worry is the Day 28: *Releasing and Embracing* visualization at www.trainyourbrainworkbook.com. This exercise is very powerful. I use it anytime I feel a block in my life that is hindering me from moving forward such as when I face rejection or realize I am harboring bitterness in my heart concerning a past or present occurrence.

Choose today to live a life of FREEDOM. You deserve it!

Don't forget!

Take two minutes at breakfast to look at your goal tasks today. Add any other tasks that MUST be completed today (**picking up a POSTER BOARD for your VISION BOARD,** repairs, shopping, cleaning, scheduling a date night, getting a haircut, sending out invitations, meal planning, etc.). Now visualize completing your tasks quickly, efficiently and with *total ease*. Life keeps getting easier and easier for you!

> "When something bad happens, you have three choices.
> You can either let it define you, let it destroy you,
> or you can let it strengthen you."
>
> **~Unknown**

Today is your day to be SET FREE from hindrances that have held you back. It's time to let go of the old to make room for the new. You are an OVERCOMER! You were born to be a VICTOR!

Day 27: Celebrate Saturday

It's Celebrate Saturday! First, take two minutes at breakfast to look at your task list for today. This is also your day to catch up if you missed any assignments this week. Add any other tasks that MUST be completed today (shopping, cleaning, repairs, etc.).

Next, reflect on your AWESOME accomplishments for the week. This week you truly took focused action to reprogram your mind for success through reverse engineering your greatest dream, learning achievement priming (looking at a word to create subconscious goals), and understanding the power of your thoughts and emotions on what you attract into your life through the principles of quantum physics. You also evaluated your core values, determined your WHYs, finalized your mission statement, learned Emotional Intelligence, and identified how to overcome your energy-drainers. Wow! What an incredible week! I'm so proud of you!

In addition, you have been developing what psychologists[xxxix] define as "grit." Grit is what makes some individuals more successful than others. The personal trait of grit (perseverance, passion, and stamina) has been highly linked to achievement of long-term goals and far outweighs IQ. Grit is about the ability to keep going despite setbacks and disappointments.

Grit is about seeing life as a marathon instead of a sprint.

What creates grit? **Thinking, seeing and believing** that you are in possession of your greatest desire. Grit is what the late and great Paul J. Meyer called a *"dogged determination to follow through on your plans despite obstacles, criticism, circumstances or what others might say, think or do."*[xl] Isn't this what you have accomplished over the last four weeks? You are still here which means you have developed a dogged determination to PUSH through!

Congratulations, you are getting GRITTY!

Remember, if we only see life as a sprint instead of a marathon, we will quickly fizzle out and lose vision. How many people do you know who have worked day and night in preparation for running some big athletic race, only to go back to lying on the couch and eating junk once the race was over? I know a few! This is because they saw getting in shape as only a temporary fix and not a long-term goal or vision. Or how many people have worked themselves into the ground to quickly obtain wealth, only to spend the wealth as fast as they gained it? Again, they saw success as a sprint instead of seeing the long run or big picture.

Life is a marathon, and endurance (grit) is key. When you see the big picture, you will want to invest in the long run—your future. We've all heard that it's wise to invest toward our future financial security, but what about investing in the long run for our health, marriage, relationships, career, spirituality, skills and our greatest dreams?

What will you begin to do today and continue to do tomorrow to invest toward your future?

Take a step back. Take a view from above (the eagle's perspective), not from below (the worm's). See the big picture from high above—instead of getting caught up in "temporary fixes," (extreme diets, extreme risks, extreme schedules) because you are seeing from ground level.

At ground level it is also difficult to see the many paths that can lead you to your goal. However, with a higher perspective you know that when you hit a "dead-end," you can either find a new path or even create your own path. Seeing from above (the big picture) helps you in your decision making so that you can keep going when others would have quit. With a higher perspective, it becomes easier to reroute and even completely shift your vision if needed. There may be times when you need to "reinvent" yourself as you see things from this new, higher perspective and realize that what you thought you wanted isn't the best option and that there is a better goal. Seeing the big picture keeps you flexible and adaptable so that you are able to keep going when life throws its hardest punches at you.

Seeing the big picture gives you vision for tomorrow and strength for today. Having vision of your finish line keeps you going when you would have otherwise given up. Never lose sight of your finish line. When you get knocked down, take a deep breath, breathe out feelings of defeat, and breathe in victory. <u>Turn those powerful emotional energies of frustration, anger and disappointment into positive energies of passion and motivation to PUSH you on to victory</u>!

Becoming the best you possible means seeing life as a marathon—a race of endurance for the long haul. Thus, set your mind on the goal. Set your mind on seeing everything working out for your good. Remind yourself that your race is YOURS! It belongs to YOU! So just keep going! It doesn't matter the speed you go, just keep maintaining a steady and healthy pace. It doesn't matter how old you are or how young you are, just keep going! Keep fighting the good fight. It is through the *struggle* that you will become *strong*, so keep *pushing* through until the end. Never give up. Be all that you are capable of. If you accomplish all your goals, create new ones. It's not over until it's over. Never stop dreaming! Never stop moving forward! Never stop believing!

CONGRATULATIONS! You are still here! You are determined to win your race in life, and I know you will! Now go do something special to celebrate and reward yourself! You really do deserve it. I know this has been a challenging program that has pushed you above and beyond!

I will reward myself by:

Now go have some fun! YOU DESERVE IT! CHEERS to YOU!

You are amazing! You could have quit, but you are still here!
You are moving closer and closer to your dreams and goals!
You are becoming like the "gritty" highly successful. Keep going!

Day 28: See It Sunday

By now your brain has created many new neural pathways because of your actions over the last 28 days. New habits do not happen overnight but come with repeated and consistent action. Remember from week one: *"Your thoughts determine your behavior, your behavior determines your habits, and your habits determine your destiny"* (Napoleon Hill, *Think and Grow Rich*).

Positive thinking and focus will help you to establish new habits for success to keep you moving toward your bright future. You will continue to become "more," meaning you will feel worthy of your desired future as you become more of the person you've always wanted to be. Also, you will use the law of attraction to your advantage as you keep increasing your positive frequency which will increase the frequency of what and who you attract into your life. Good things will come to you in greater and greater proportions.

Vision Board

Now it's time to SEE your desired future so you can bring it toward you. Did you pick up your poster board? Today you will find more pictures and words (from magazines, online or created by you) that represent your ideal life to paste (tape, staple, pin) to your vision board. Are you ready? Let's get your creative and inspirational juices flowing!

1. **What does your ideal life look like?** (Think about what you saw/envisioned when you did the visualization exercises of your perfect life and your perfect day. Think about what your life would look like if you dramatically improved all the main areas: health, relationships, career, finances, self-development, spirituality, community, environment and leisure/fun.)

2. **What are your WHYs?** (Think back to your WHYs from Wednesday. It is your WHYs that will inspire and motivate you to press through and to keep moving forward. Your WHYs may involve having a nicer home, neighborhood, cars, clothes, school or vacations to create a better life for you and your family. They may include getting in peak physical shape, creating amazing relationships, becoming debt free, getting promoted or creating time and financial freedom. Your WHYs might involve building business empires, being a positive leader and mentor, serving others by using your gifts/talents, creating/supporting good causes, making this world a better place, living out your full potential, or pleasing God/Higher Power.)

3. **What is your Mission Statement, Values and Key Goal? What are your BIGGEST Life-Long Dreams/Goals? What Dollar Amounts, Sales Totals or Titles do you want to obtain?** (How can you include these on your board in either written or picture form?)

4. **What inspiring words describe the life you desire?** (Words such as *"Abundance," "Success," "Joy," "Health," "Love," "Favor," "Wisdom," "Generosity," "Time Freedom," "Integrity."*) **What words reflect how you want to FEEL?** (Words such as "Amazing," "Happy," "Peaceful," "Loving," "Energetic," "Powerful," "Thankful," "Inspired," "Balanced" "Thriving," "Free," "Fearless.") **What "I Am" statements do you want to include?** (Statements such as *"I am Financially Free," "I am Strong, Lean and Fit," "I am Making a Difference," "I am Happy, Healthy, Wealthy and Wise," "I am Worthy of an Amazing Life!"*)

In pasting the words and images on the board, be sure that the board doesn't become so cluttered that you cannot read the words or see the images. Keep the board neat and easily readable. Create multiple boards if needed such as a health, wealth and career board. (You could then put the career board in your office, the health board in your kitchen or pantry, and the wealth board in your bedroom. You could even create a board specifically to your Key Goal.) Be creative and do what works for you! This is all to motivate you so your dreams become a reality!

Once completed, you will hang your vision board in a place where you will SEE it DAILY. This is *very important*! Your brain *needs* to see these images/words—remember how powerful visualization and achievement priming are to the subconscious mind! I then want you to take a few minutes to look at your vision board and begin to daydream about your desired future. Have fun with it! Enjoy every moment of this daydreaming as it puts your brain in a relaxed and receptive state. Soak in the wonderful *emotions* as emotions are very powerful in activating the subconscious mind to go to work for you.

Do you remember how the subconscious mind wants instant gratification? With repeated exposure, the brain will see these positive images and words as REAL, will begin to "believe" them, and will become *fixated on possessing them*. As these pictures and words representing your ideal life are daily imprinted on your brain, you will become aware of the resources and opportunities around you that can make your dreams a reality. You will begin to step out almost effortlessly as your subconscious mind, in its quest to possess what you are showing it, will allow you to move toward this desired life with ease *as resistance is now removed*. You will have brought the future into the "now" so that the subconscious mind can comprehend it, believe it, and run toward it with unyielding passion and endurance.

Therefore, make it a goal to look at your vision board daily. Look at it throughout the day (and also preferably upon rising and going to bed when your brain is in a more relaxed and receptive state). Be sure to soak in the positive feelings, so that with time, you will instantly associate your dream life with these positive emotions. Look at your board, breath in a deep breath, and smile as you see yourself in the pictures and as you repeat the positive statements. Feel a deep sense of gratitude as you believe what you see is *already* yours. See yourself happily in *full possession* of this amazing life.

As you begin to believe that you can have this amazing life, you will begin to conquer those thoughts of being unworthy (or other self-sabotaging beliefs). Be consistent. Otherwise, *your old belief system will only hinder these good things from coming to you (or your being able to keep these good things).* Mediate day and night on the vision in your heart so that you will create a new belief system to support the life you desire. With <u>consistency</u>, your mind will begin to not only accept your new belief system but also reject outside information that disagrees with your new positive beliefs. How exciting that visualization exercises combined with happy emotions are incredibly powerful for reprogramming your mind, beliefs and frequency for success, happiness and abundance!

It's time to Dream BIG, and turn the impossible into the <u>POSSIBLE</u>!

Assignment.

Work on your vision board. Your Vision Board is a reflection of YOU! So have fun, and begin to inspire yourself! Don't worry about the "HOWs" of getting to your perfect future. Just begin to see this future, and your mind will find ways to make your dreams a reality. No more excuses. No more delays. It's time for YOU to *DREAM BIG!*

I hope this program has become easier with time as your new positive behaviors are becoming habits. Either tonight or first thing Monday morning, please look at your Key Goal and some of your secondary goals. Decide on your focus for this week, and then decide on five specific tasks for your Key Goal and five specific tasks for your Secondary Goal to be completed Monday through Friday. This is two goal tasks per day (I am not asking for hours spent on each task, even giving ten minutes of focused time will keep you moving forward). If two tasks seem overwhelming right now, then just stick with your one goal task for each day. But, if you are up for the challenge, add that second (or even third) <u>small</u> goal task!

My Main Focus This Week:

Monday:
Key Goal:
Secondary Goal:
General Tasks:

Tuesday:
Key Goal:
Secondary Goal:
General Tasks:

Wednesday:
Key Goal:
Secondary Goal:
General Tasks:

Thursday:
Key Goal:
Secondary Goal:
General Tasks:

Friday:
Key Goal:
Secondary Goal:
General Tasks:

Saturday:
Goals: Make-up day for any tasks not completed
General Tasks:

IMPORTANT!

<u>It's best **not** to exceed **THREE** goal tasks per day</u>. Overwhelming yourself sets you up for failure. You also want to keep your **total daily tasks** (goal tasks **and** general tasks) to no more than five or six per day for maximum productivity. Having a list of a dozen daily tasks will only overwhelm you. Completing one task well is better than poorly completely 12—or even worse, feeling so overwhelmed that you don't complete any!

Remember, slow and steady wins the race. Keep your eyes on the prize, and *steadily* work toward your goal(s) instead of trying to go in 100 directions at once. Go after your dreams with laser focus. Doing "less" but doing it *well* will give you the ability to pick up momentum because you will be putting your time, energy and focus toward what you really want. With time, you will be amazed at the momentum you will have created that is moving you steadily toward your dream life. Momentum begins to "set you on fire" and puts wind beneath your wings so that you can soar easily and quickly toward your wildest dreams. So, what are you waiting for? Your wildest dreams await you!

> "ONE LIFE.
> JUST ONE.
>
> Why aren't we soaring like we are on fire toward our wildest dreams?"
>
> ~Unknown

Now put in your calendar, mobile device task app, white board, Weekly Goal Setting Template (or whatever you prefer) these tasks (actions) that you are committing to complete this week. Then take 60 seconds and visualize yourself completing each of your goal tasks with total ease. See yourself climbing higher and higher up your mountain of success! How exciting! Success is closer than you ever thought possible.

AND congratulations! You have truly begun to rewire your brain for happiness, abundance and success! Can you notice any difference in how you now think and approach life? Are you now seeing how you weren't put on this earth to be ordinary; but instead, you were put on this earth to be EXTRAODINARY! Choose to live the extraordinary life you are capable of!

> *"To guarantee success,*
> *act as if it were impossible to fail."*
>
> *~Dorothea Brande*

Your potential is limitless! EXTRAORDINARY things are coming to you!
Believe for the impossible! Soar toward your dreams like you are ON FIRE!

Week 5: Maintaining Success Mindsets & Habits

This week is about learning to maintain new positive thinking patterns, mindsets, belief systems and habits for life. A truly abundant life is awaiting you...if you will just keep going! This means you must keep your vision so crisp and clear in front of you in order to *keep fanning the flame inside you.* No one and no thing can stop you, but YOU! Therefore, decide to keep up your good work and continue to set goals to create the life you desire, a life you LOVE!

Remember, studies[xli] show that goal setting dramatically increases your physical and mental effort toward that goal. Also, goals that are specific and challenging consistently lead to the highest performance, compared to goals that are too difficult or easy. Therefore, continue to set goals that are a good fit for YOU; goals that will create a passion and fire inside of you; goals that will not only positively change your life but also the world around you. Then decide to do the daily, *small* things to keep you moving forward. I know you can do it. I believe in you. You have come this far! You are AMAZING! You are EXTRAORDINARY! Success is YOURS!

Week Overview

Day 29: Motivated Monday: Staying Motivated, Creating Your Legacy

Day 30: Thoughtful Tuesday: Miraculous Faith, Abundant Health

A Final Word: Law of Attraction & Abundance

My Story: Overcoming Fear & Unworthiness

Now What?

The Toolbox: Suggested Book List, My Top Ten Rules to Live By, Weekly Goal Setting Template, Sample Positive Affirmations, Habits of the Highly Successful, Vibrational Frequency of Emotion Scale, The Focus Funnel, Declaration Cut Outs

> *"One of the most powerful forces on earth is the human soul on FIRE."*
> ~Unknown

You are on fire! You are the author of your destiny!
Keep up the good work!

Day 29: Motivated Monday

I hope by now that you can anticipate the daily name prompts (Motivated Monday, Thoughtful Tuesday, What and Why Wednesday, Thankful Thursday, Fearless Friday, Celebrate Saturday and See It Sunday). I also trust that you can associate what needs to be done on that day—if not, please look back through the past assignments. I have created this program in hopes that you will continue to remember and use the daily name prompts to maintain your progress toward your dreams, goals and success!

So, today go Eat Your Frog and keep working on your Reverse Engineering. Keep your goals in sight and stay motivated and focused. Remember, it is not about perfection, it's about progress. Also, keep the 80/20 Rule in mind by continually keeping an eye out for those things that are simply distractions to keep you "busy" and hinder your journey to live out your greater purpose.

Now I want to talk about getting motivated for the long run, which involves **keeping the new mindset** that you are developing and not allowing **excuses** to hinder you anymore. You see, this is what I have done for most of my life…allowed excuses to hold me back.

I mentioned earlier in this workbook that my husband and I have been mentored by a very successful business man, Darin Kidd, a protégé of the late and great Paul J. Meyer. Darin is one of the most sought after network marketing trainers in the world and has been featured on television, in books and in more magazines than I could ever count. He has stood on stage with some of "The Greats" like Tony Robbins, Sir Richard Branson and Eric Worre. It seems like every week he is in a different country speaking before multitudes.

My husband sat under Darin's inspiration for many years, and my husband's success as a six-figure income earner can greatly be attributed to what Darin sowed into my husband—a new mindset. While I sat under Darin's instruction here and there (I was usually home with the little ones), my husband took every opportunity to learn from Darin and began to allow Darin's words to take root in his mind and in his life. Few days went by that my husband didn't say a "Darinism" (quote Darin). When something went wrong, my husband would always take responsibility for it and then quote Darin. However, I did not have the same mindset. I really did not understand what my husband was saying and would typically just disagree with him. I was living by self-limiting mindsets that held me in a self-imposed cage—and I didn't even know it!

However, it was through writing this book that I began to finally have revelation to what Darin had been saying all these years. I could finally SEE this higher level of truth. My eyes were opened, and I now "*got it.*" I hope you are starting to "*get it*" too. I once was blind, but now I see! What an incredible GIFT!

Recently, Darin shared some very moving words. It had to do with being motivated to diligently press on to victory—which requires you to overcome your excuses. Darin said the following in a most passionate speech:

…It really fascinates me when people share with me how much they need to change their life and how bad things are and THEN say, "I could do something about it…IF and BUT and IF and BUT." Well, you know what?!? If IF's and BUT's were candies and nuts, we would all have a Merry Christmas! Show me someone who uses excuses as a reason why they can't do something, and I will show you someone who has a LOT BIGGER challenges and uses them as REASONS to fuel them!

The sky is not the limit, our VISION and MINDSET are. I had to get so dang disgusted with my life that I was determined to do whatever it took to fix it. When I was bankrupt, I borrowed audio programs from my grandmother like, "Psychology of Achievement" and many others and concentrated around the clock on working on me and my mindset. Insanity is doing the same thing over and over again and expecting different results. I knew for things to change, I had to change! To get something different, I needed to DO SOMETHING different! We can use our current situation and circumstances and be a VICTIM or a VICTOR, it's our choice!

Thank God I didn't wait until I felt like I was ready…I would have NEVER felt ready. I FOUGHT anyway! ACT the way you want to feel, and soon you will FEEL the way you act.

I'm finding that I'm starting to be allergic to excuses! Give me someone who everyone considers an "underdog," with no skills, no college education, no marketing background BUT who has an "I WILL NOT BE DENIED," "I WILL UNTIL," NO MATTER WHAT IT TAKES," "NO EXCUSES" attitude and I will help them change their life.

And Darin Kidd has impacted a multitude of lives because he took on the *"NO EXCUSE, NO MATTER WHAT"* attitude. Excuses are the greatest dream killer of all. Excuses are always based out of fear, and they only lead to procrastination, lack of motivation and stagnation. Choose to step beyond the fear because fear (unless it is protecting you from a real, life-threatening danger) is really just an illusion of your mind or **F**alse **E**vidence **A**ppearing **R**eal.

FEAR = <u>F</u>ALSE <u>E</u>VIDENCE <u>A</u>PPEARING <u>R</u>EAL

You alone must choose to step out beyond the fear and step into the new world of endless possibilities. Isn't this the mindset of the eagle…endless abundance?

Looking at my own life, I'm so glad that I didn't wait until I *FELT "READY"* to step out and be a life coach. I'm so glad I didn't wait until I FELT *"READY"* to be a career services director speaking in front of thousands of people. I'm so glad I didn't wait until I *FELT "READY"* to become a parent of four children, to go back to school in my 30's, to launch my businesses or to start writing a book that would transform my life. I could go on and on. If we wait until we *FEEL "READY,"* it will NEVER happen!

You will never FEEL 100% *"READY"* to do anything new. Why? Because perfection is not possible. Your skills, knowledge, image, brand or the book you are writing will never be PERFECT. Stop using this lack of perfection as an excuse to not move forward. I'm a total perfectionist. I could work on this book for the next ten years…and it still would not be perfect! I have to set a realistic deadline and then step out and publish it whether I FEEL "*READY*" or not!

If you need more skills, then get more skills. If you need a better degree, then go get the degree. If you need to better define your brand, then by all means, define your brand. If you don't know how to grow or market your business, then start studying from those who do know. Whatever change you need in your life, GO find the answer, and DO it. Take that FIRST STEP!

Just don't keep sitting on your hands waiting to magically FEEL "*READY*" or expecting things to mysteriously work out and fix themselves. Remember, the longer you wait to step out, the more time your mind has to convince you to not take action. So, what's the answer? Just STEP OUT! Every day choose to step out beyond how you *FEEL*. You can't move forward, unless you STEP OUT. Also, God and the Universe can't bless the works of your hands if there are no works to bless! (And don't forget, you can use visualization to conquer any fear and to build confidence!)

Do you want to know my biggest regrets? Not my mistakes and failures but all those times I DIDN'T step out. Or all those years I wasted before I finally did step out. Time after time, I was my own worst enemy. I can't tell you how many times I've held myself back because of my own self-criticism, insecurities and self-doubt. I can't tell you how many times I didn't step out to do something, say something, pick up the phone, respond to an opportunity, knock on a door or just show up! I allowed my fears and my perfectionism to hold me back over and over. I wish I could tell you I'm perfect…that I'm a perfect wife, mom, friend, business owner and overall person…that I always make perfect decisions, never mess up, never get upset, and always have a perfectly flawless home, perfectly behaved children and look picture perfect….but I can't! I have to accept and love myself and my life—FLAWS included. This doesn't mean I don't try to be better; it means that I must *choose to move forward DESPITE these imperfections.*

We must choose to stop judging ourselves and our abilities so harshly that we paralyze ourselves from moving forward. Or we create a self-fulfilling prophecy where others don't like or accept us because we don't like and accept ourselves. Perfection is not possible. Let go of the idea that you or your abilities must be "perfect" before you can step out. Accept the beauty and uniqueness of imperfection. You don't have to be "The Best." Just strive to be the BEST YOU.

You are full of incredible talents, abilities and POTENTIAL!

Are you your own worst enemy? Assuming that others will judge and reject you is really just an EXCUSE. You deserve to be YOU, imperfections and all. Make a choice to stop conforming to other people's ideas for you, and choose to be YOU! Forget about others' opinions because in the end, it's your opinion that matters. Strive to impress yourself, not others. Otherwise, you are only allowing fear and excuses to control your life as you will never feel "*good enough*" or "*ready enough.*" This program is designed for you to be the best possible YOU—not what other people want you to be and not a better version of someone else. You must CHOOSE to be uniquely YOU with all your imperfections—because after all that's what makes you special!

Step out and be YOU! The world needs you to be YOU!

Step out NOW with what you have, and THEN you will begin to attract to you what you need. Plus, stepping out will build your **CONFIDENCE** which will then allow you to step out into even greater things.

Let me ask you a question. Would you sit down at the piano for the very first time and expect to play Beethoven? Of course not! You start off with *"Mary Had a Little Lamb,"* and you practice and begin to build your confidence. Then you move on to something harder and gain confidence again. Then you move to something even harder and gain confidence yet again. Before you know it, you are playing Beethoven!

You may have heard the saying, *"Anything worth doing is worth doing poorly at first."*

You can't learn if you don't TRY! You have to start somewhere…even if that means not doing something very well. But listen, no one starts at the top. Everyone has to start SOMEWHERE! And it starts by taking that FIRST STEP.

Choose to say "NO" to FEAR and "YES" to your DREAMS.

Say *"yes"* to your dreams and start taking small steps that will build your confidence and destroy fear's hold on your life. Fear is only an illusion in your mind. If you step out and it's not the right time, you will know it, and as a result, you will recognize how to better prepare yourself for next time.

However, waiting until all the *"IF's," "WHEN's"* and *"BUTs"* perfectly align will only serve to hinder all that you really want. Therefore, the decision is yours. Say *"yes"* to your future. Say *"yes"* to your dreams. Darin Kidd chose to say *"yes"* to his future and dreams, and now he is creating a legacy of empowering others to change their lives for the better.

Insight

Do you want to be promoted?

If you desire to be promoted, step back and take a look at your life. Are you just sitting on your hands waiting for promotion to be handed to you on a silver platter, or are you taking planned action to obtain your goal?

Ask yourself: What am I doing NOW to prepare myself for this greater position? Have I acquired the skills and knowledge needed? Have I stepped up to the plate to show my leadership skills and commitment to the company? Am I faithful in the little things so that I can be trusted with greater responsibility? Do I treat the company as if it is my own? What qualities is my boss looking for, and can I meet these?

Now determine the future position(s) you want and then design a plan to make it happen (use reverse engineering).

And don't forget **CONFIDENCE**!

You sure don't feel like a million bucks dressed sloppily. Even if you work from home, ALWAYS get dressed nicely and neatly (if nothing else put on your shoes). Studies show that you have more confidence when you dress professionally, and it will come across not only in person, but also on the phone and in emails.

You are worth far more than a million bucks, so start ACTING like it! Begin to act like the kind of person you want to become. Act with confidence, courage, respect and integrity. See yourself as highly favored and excelling in all you do. Act as if you can't fail!

As Darin Kidd always says….***"Step out and ACT the part and soon the feelings will follow"***….along with the promotion!

(Stay motivated and connected with Darin by following him on his social media including Periscope and Facebook Live. You can also visit his site at www.SucceedWithDarin.com.)

What LEGACY are You Creating?

What will be said of you long after your days on this earth? Early in this book, we talked about legacies. Today clearly and boldly define your desired legacy. What does your heart long to be remembered for? (This will tie in with your passion, your mission statement, your values, your wildest dreams.) For me, I want to be remembered as a world-changer, a trailblazer who empowered others with vision for an abundant life so they could transform their lives and live out their God-given purpose and potential.

What is your desired Legacy?

(Add your legacy to your vision board.)

Now inscribe your legacy on your heart. Your legacy is what gives your life purpose, vision, passion, motivation and hope! Don't let go of it! Don't lose sight of it! Stay motivated by keeping your dreams and goals directly in front of you. Keep your WHAT's and WHY's in constant mind if you want to keep going despite setbacks and challenges....because difficult and disappointing times WILL come. Mean spirited-people will speak out against you. Friends may betray you. Unfair circumstances may take all that you have gained. Challenging days will come! SO WHAT!? Are you going to lie down and die? Are you going to give up and have a pity party because you are now a helpless victim?

What is your STRATEGY for when you want to QUIT?

What is your plan of action when life gets you so terribly down? Will you think and dwell on those negative thoughts and give them power, or will you envision yourself coming out of the situation better and stronger than ever? Either you will attack and conquer life, or life will attack and conquer you. Either you will be driven by fear or driven by faith. The GREATEST BREAKTHROUGHS often come after the worst failures, heartaches, hardships, tragedies and disappointments. BUT they come because of a choice to press on....a choice to create an incredible legacy. The choice is always YOURS.

Choose to see defeat as only temporary, not permanent. Choose to pick yourself back up and keep going because you have determined in your heart that you are a winner, and **YOU WILL UNTIL!** You WILL fulfill your purpose, your mission, your legacy in this earth. When troubles come, choose to shake yourself from the dust of the earth. You are not a worm anymore. You were born to fly! You were born to SOAR! **Say *"NEXT! I'm moving on!"***

Focus on what inspires you, draw from your spirituality to strengthen you, and never lose sight of YOUR PRIZE—it has your name on it! Get passionate about your dream, your mission on this earth, and it will take you to the finish line. No one can stop you but YOU! Choose to believe in YOU! You can do it! **Now GO DO IT!**

Insight

My life has become overflowing with amazing and divine connections. I wish I could tell you all the remarkable encounters and stories but allow me now to share about one that happened the other day as I was taking a little break at the beach. I met a mother who began to tell me about her son Chris Waddell and his incredible story of inner strength, courage and determination. Back in 1988, Chris was a ski racer at Middlebury College. However, in the middle of a turn, his ski popped off, causing him to fall and break two vertebrae and damage his spinal cord. He was left paralyzed from the waist down. For most people, this would have been the end of the road. But not for Chris...this was not a reason to quit but a reason to find new ways, new solutions and new beginnings.

Only two months later, Chris returned to college and within a year began monoskiing. Within two more years, he was named to the US Disabled Ski Team. He went on to win 12 Paralympic medals and became the most decorated male monoskier in history. But monoskiing wasn't Chris's only achievement. As a track athlete, he competed in four Winter Paralympics, winning 12 medals and three Summer Paralympics, winning a silver medal in the 200 meters in Sydney. In World Championship competition, Waddell won 9 total medals. Chris's drive to overcome any obstacle and to keep his vision of success crystal clear in his mind led him to be inducted into the US Ski and Snowboard Hall of Fame and the Paralympics Hall of Fame. Skiing Magazine placed him amongst the *"25 Greatest Skiers in North America."*

And it gets even better! Because of Chris's experiences, he became the founder of One Revolution Foundation, a foundation that creates programs to *"turn the perception of disability upside down."* His programs *"do not focus on disability, but rather the universal experience of challenge and the power of resilience."* Waddell speaks to audiences worldwide motivating them to be more and do more. The Dalai Lama honored Chris as an *"Unsung Hero of Compassion."* People Magazine named him one of the *"Fifty Most Beautiful People in the World."* Middlebury College presented him with a Doctorate in Humane Letters. National Public Radio (NPR) named his 2011 commencement address to Middlebury College as one of *"The Best Commencement Speeches, Ever."*

But it doesn't end there. In September of 2009, Waddell became the first nearly unassisted paraplegic to summit Mt. Kilimanjaro, the tallest mountain in Africa. The film documenting the climb has won awards throughout the world. Chris has appeared on Dateline, Oprah and 20/20. Chris's mother then told me that the reason he climbed that mountain was to prove his belief that *"It's not what happens to you. It's what you do with what happens to you."* So the next time you consider quitting or making excuses as to why you can't do something, I want you to think about Chris's story. I want you to remember the odds that he chose to overcome and the *"I WILL NOT BE DENIED," "I WILL UNTIL," "NO MATTER WHAT IT TAKES," "NO EXCUSES"* mindset and attitude Chris chose to uphold. I want you to think about the incredible LEGACY Chris has created. I want you to envision this paraplegic man named Chris Waddell pulling himself inch by inch by inch up that gigantic mountain, and then you can make your decision. I know I will.

Because, ***"It's not what happens to you. It's what you do with what happens to you."***
(Check out Chris's website at www.one-revolution.org.)

Congrats! You are designing your life! You are creating an incredible legacy! You could have quite, but you didn't! Daily, you are becoming more of who and what you were created to be! You are climbing up your mountain of success inch by inch by inch! Way to go! I knew you could do it!

Day 30: Thoughtful Tuesday

YOU DID IT! You are AWESOME! What an amazing journey! This was not an easy program but a boot camp for the brain that challenged you to literally rewire your thinking and YOUR LIFE! I required a lot of you, and you met the challenge. You should be so proud of yourself! Now take a moment and think back over the last 30 days. Has your thinking begun to change since Day 1 of the program?

The whole underlying purpose of this book has been to *empower* you to get into the driver's seat of your life so you can be set free from the mind-binding perceptions that have limited your potential. Over the last 30 days, you have learned that you are what you think about—your outer world is a reflection of your inner world as you attract what you focus on. What's going on inside of you determines your life outcomes.

Can you now see why you can desire an amazing life but *if* your inner thoughts and beliefs are stuck on old, limiting thought patterns and perceptions, you will never move forward? You may know the future you want, but if you don't really believe you can have this future, you will in fact never have it. As long as you allow these old negative thoughts and beliefs to remain in the deep places of your mind and heart, you will keep yourself stuck right where you are. For example, poverty thinking attracts more poverty. You may say you desire prosperity with your words, but your inner thoughts and beliefs say you will always have lack. You literally fear lack and that fear further creates energy to attract more lack to you and also creates a wall to block what you really want...prosperity!

Are you now realizing most people have this double-minded thinking? This is confusion of the mind as the mind receives constant mixed messages. What results will you receive from double-minded thinking? You receive more of the same that you've already been receiving! You go nowhere fast. You stay locked in repeating cycles. You create the world around you through your thinking and internal beliefs. Therefore, you must take a look at your current world as it is a reflection of what is going on inside YOU.

Further, this book, fundamentally, is about showing how you must walk in appreciation of what you have *now* while also seeing yourself in *full possession* of what you desire. At this point, you walk in peace and joy with both your now and your tomorrow. You are then able to open yourself up for abundance to flow to you and through you because no longer are you striving or fighting against your current situation. You walk in peace and full assurance (faith) that everything is working out (somehow) in your favor and for your good.

Again, to create the reality you desire, you must not only SEE this new reality and FEEL this new reality, you must also ACT this new reality. **You must act as if you are in full possession of this new reality NOW.** You must trick your mind to believe this reality is happening now. Whether it is a promotion, improved relationships, better health, obtaining a degree, building a business empire, buying a home, speaking to multitudes, winning awards and competitions, writing a book or making a billion dollars, you must visualize the completed result in your mind in great detail. The clearer you can see your desired reality, the more the mind will embrace it, believe it and create ways to move toward it.

Remember, the mind doesn't know what is real from what is imagined.

For example, when you watch an intense movie, doesn't your heart beat increase and you feel anxious? Why? Because at that moment, your brain thinks the movie is happening in real life. Plus, television activates "relaxed" alpha waves in your brain making your mind very "open" and "suggestible." Visualization and daydreaming do the same! Therefore, keep dreaming about your future. Keep seeing your desired future in your mind, so crystal clear, until your mind believes it as REAL, as happening "now."

Therefore, I want you to write down your top five personal affirmations for your desired reality, and write them as if they are happening **NOW**.

What are your personal affirmations?

I am a successful….
I am
I am
I am
I am

(Now go to a mirror, stand tall, look yourself in the eye, and confidently with conviction repeat these statements. Repeat again, but this time, clearly visualize yourself doing what you are saying. Next, change the statements to "I ALREADY am a [millionaire, world-changer, physically fit, wonderful spouse, etc.]")

STEPS of FAITH

You must believe these statements as NOW—present tense, not future tense. You must remove all doubt, worry and fear and believe your dream 100% as you walk in peace and full assurance that you possess what you desire. This is the definition of FAITH. Maybe you've heard the phrase, "*Faith is the substance of things HOPED for and the evidence of things not seen*" (Hebrews 11:1). Faith is an energy, a real substance. Faith is the unseen fore-runner (energy) to the materialized reality (matter). And energy and mass are always changing "forms."

What does your faith level look like? Either you walk in FAITH or you walk in FEAR and DOUBT. Do you believe that faith can move mountains? I do! Faith enables miracles to happen. What is a miracle? Simply believing with all that you are that something WILL happen. Now please note that I am <u>not</u> talking about "believing" for someone to fall in love with you or give you a million dollars—this is manipulative. Miracles, *based on noble purposes and LOVE*, are created when faith is put into ACTION—meaning that as you STEP out in FAITH, you cause your faith to manifest (the MIRACLE).

A MIRACLE is a REACTION and MANIFESTATION
of someone's STEPs of FAITH.

I want to live a life of MIRACLES! I want to see lives transformed, restored, healed and raised up to greatness! I want to see the poor, lost, broken and homeless walking in victory. In my life time, I want to raise up one million millionaires to positively impact this world. I want to train and equip WORLD CHANGERS! Would these all require some *serious* miracles?! Yes, yes and YES! It takes incredible FAITH IN ACTION to produce major results. Faith without action goes nowhere, but faith with action moves mountains! And where does the miracle start? WITH ME! So now let me ask YOU: what kind of miracles do you want to see in your life and in the world around you?!

Stop waiting for the miracle, and <u>BE</u> THE MIRACLE!

When you fully believe—mind, body, soul and spirit—you allow what you believe to happen. For those of you who are spiritual, you will understand that the brain itself is a body part, but the mind is tied to a person's soul (the soul is said to be the mind, will and emotions). Finally, the spirit is the heart of man and is where one's inner dreams and callings come from, as the spirit knows no limits. The **spirit** says, *"I can fly. I can conquer any mountain!"* The **soul** says, *"Let me think things through and determine how I feel about it."* And the **body** says, *"I just want to survive and reproduce."* It is ultimately <u>the mind that ties the body, spirit and soul together</u>…this is why your thoughts are so powerful.

When your mind—spirit, soul and body—comes into agreement, there is NOTHING you cannot do!

Miracles happen when faith causes you to step out as you fully believe and EXPECT that you will obtain your desired results. It may not happen overnight, but it will happen in time if you do not lose HOPE. Faith and hope are tied together as faith is birthed out of hope. That which you hope for (envision as yours because you trust in God's promises/the laws of the Universe) produces faith that then compels you to step out in action toward what you desire. FAITH is the EVIDENCE of what is HOPED FOR—<u>your persistent steps of faith are the evidence</u>. In time, that faith will materialize IF YOU DO NOT LOSE HOPE. Faith and hope must work together.

Hope theory[xlii] reveals how visualization exercises, goal setting, agency thinking (positive self-talk) and pathways thinking (breaking goals down into smaller "chunks" and creating multiple "pathways" to achieve goals) are all critical in creating HOPE. Hope theory proves that hope is essential and foundational to creating SUCCESS. Without hope, there is no faith. Without faith, there is no action. Without action, there is no achievement and success.

Do you clearly know what you are hoping for? If not, then make the vision crystal clear. Now think about your faith level? Is it high or low? Unfortunately, most people waiver in their faith. Few believe 100%. Therefore, most give up or lose hope before the miracle has had time to manifest in its physical form. However, if you study the highly successful 1% of the population, what do they have in common?

When you believe 100% in your dream, nothing can take it from you. You will persist until it is yours!

UNWAIVERING FAITH!

They believed 100% in their dream. Failure, rejection, miscalculations, criticisms, persecutions did not stop them. Take a look at Thomas Edison, Albert Einstein, Abraham Lincoln, Vincent Van Gogh, the Wright Brothers, Walt Disney, Stephen Spielberg, Dr. Seuss, Elvis Presley, Oprah Winfrey, Charles Schulz, Colonel Sanders (Kentucky Fried Chicken)…the list could go on for miles; you will see how each one faced seemingly unending rejection and failure. However, they PERSISTED until they obtained their desired results. WHY? Because they believed 100% in their dream. They EXPECTED it to happen! Their dream (hope, vision) was so crystal clear and REAL to them that they would not stop STEPPING OUT in FAITH (persistence) until it materialized. The creator of the LEGO® toy had his factory/barn burn down not once, not twice, but THREE times! What would have made him keep going after so many huge setbacks? He BELIEVED in his dream, and LEGO® is now the BIGGEST toy company in the world!

Do you believe 100% in your dream? Or do you continually waiver in your beliefs? Indecision produces no decisive answer or physical manifestation. How do you get the doubt out? You must create unwavering belief by constructing a crystal clear vision of your finalized goal and seeing it as **DONE**! Then mediate (focus) on this vision day and night. Why? <u>Because you will move toward what you **EXPECT** to happen</u>! Therefore, clearly see yourself in full possession of what you desire. Otherwise, without clarity, there is confusion and thus no conviction.

Daily, you are bombarded with the world's negativity (which can pull you down, distract you and destroy your dream). Therefore, you must DAILY bombard your mind with BELIEF! Your spirit longs for you to bring your body and soul in alignment with its limitless potential. A crystal clear vision does this because vision breeds hope. Hope breeds faith. Faith (believing 100% that your dream will manifest) breeds action. Action breeds persistence. Persistence breeds success.

VISION=HOPE=FAITH=ACTION=PERSISTENCE=SUCCESS

If you truly believe and see yourself as ALREADY accomplishing your goal, you will naturally find ways and solutions to accomplish it. You will, in essence, attract this goal to you in its manifested form. Even as a seed is genetically programmed to attract the nutrients needed to grow into a plant, so also you must create your seed in the imagination of your mind. You must choose to continually nurture this seed. A starved seed will only remain as a seed. You must allow your seed (dream) to attract the needed nutrients so that it might grow and manifest in fullness—as what it is intended to be. You cannot plant a tomato seed and expect a watermelon to grow. Neither can you plant a seed of doubt and double-minded thinking and expect success to grow from it.

> **"Faith is 'PICTURE IT DONE.'"**
>
> ~Josiah Cullen, (Age 7, Autistic)

Believe and You Shall Receive!

When you finally stop doubt, worry and negativity, the miraculous will happen. And choose to believe for the miraculous in ALL areas of your life! Choose to live a truly abundant life. Think about this fact: your body is designed to want to heal itself—that's a miracle in and of itself! When you remove the obstacles, your body will heal itself and even become its proper body weight. Therefore, let's take a few minutes to look at some obstacles to your health because *good health is foundational to living an abundant life.*

Creating Abundant Health

Our health is an essential and yet often overlooked subject. We can have all the fame, glory, money and power the world could ever offer, but if we don't have our health, the rest doesn't matter much. It's hard to enjoy life when you don't feel well. Since the body is naturally designed to move toward health, let's look at how to remove the obstacles in our lives to good health.

Often obstacles to our health are lack of exercise, water intake and sleep. A big culprit is poor diet as processed foods/drinks and refined sugar can cause major inflammation in the body, which is a forerunner for disease. These obstacles can all be fixed. (I highly recommend the book *Eat Right 4 Your Type* by Dr. D'Adamo, which is based on how foods chemically react with each blood type, and also *Your Body's Many Cries for Water* by Dr. Batmanghelidj).

Another big obstacle is the stress of our lives. Stress is a byproduct of the fight-or-flight response (a fear response to protect our survival) and was only meant to be used for emergencies, not on a daily basis. Day after day, we subject ourselves to these fear responses and destructive hormones that continually break down our immune system and our cell health. The body cannot properly heal itself when it is in a fight-or-flight/stress state as healing is part of the "rest and digest" response. Further, stress blocks our rational brain from working properly!

What is stress from? We alone allow stress into our lives either by how we view what is going on or by what we allow to come into our lives. Ultimately, stress can be managed by stopping the FEAR response. If fear is not protecting you from a real, imminent danger, it is only in your mind as **F**alse **E**vidence **A**ppearing **R**eal. Research reveals that by simply taking a few deep belly breaths (breathing through the nose), we can help reset our parasympathetic nervous system to get out of this debilitating fear/stress response.

However, taking back control is a CHOICE. By simply choosing to stop and take a few deep breaths, we can begin to regain control of our lives. By choosing to do simple things like evaluating our busyness, making time for ourselves to rest and regroup, and by keeping a positive outlook, we can do wonders to allow our bodies to get out of its fight-and-flight mode.

But again, it is a CHOICE. When we make the CHOICE to walk in faith and positivity, stress is easily removed. When we make the CHOICE to take control of our lives and responses, when we choose to become proactive instead of reactive, when we believe that everything we need is always there and that there is always a solution, and when we know that somehow everything is working out for our good, then we finally begin to walk in PEACE. At this point, we finally CHOOSE to let worries and cares just slide off our backs knowing that we will find the solution, take appropriate action and that things will somehow work out.

Sometimes, you have to realize that things do happen for a reason. Maybe that "slow poke" driving in front of you is actually protecting you from a car accident or speeding ticket. Maybe that store clerk who was rude to you is having a really bad day and needs your positive thoughts or prayers instead of your angry frustration. Maybe that kid who keeps picking on your kid is actually suicidal, and your kind words could change the course of his or her life. Choose to walk

Insight

Do you ever feel overwhelmed?

We all do. Sometimes we get so focused on what's right in front of us that we forget to take a bird's eye view. When you begin to feel overwhelmed, take a step back, take a deep breath, and try to see the big picture. What is happening at that moment in time is not the end of the world. However, it can easily become a joy-killer and bring our spirits and health down…if we let it. Remember, we cannot always control what is happening around us, but we can control our actions and reactions. We can decide to take a step back, look at the big picture, re-evaluate, make adjustments and proceed in a new direction. A simple mental adjustment is much better than a nervous breakdown. Even just taking a five minute breather can make a big difference in gaining perspective and seeing new solutions.

So, the next time you feel overwhelmed, step back, take a deep breath, and take a bird's eye view! Remember, you're not a worm any more. You were born to FLY!

in positivity, and your perspective will change.

Sometimes, you just have to take a step back, take a deep breath and remind yourself that everything is going to be OKAY. Other times, you must let go of things that are truly out of your control as you can neither control the world nor carry everyone else's burdens. <u>You are not God nor are you a donkey</u>!

DAILY, choose to pause, regroup and **LET GO**. Take a deep breath, and see the cares of life falling off of you. See yourself falling into the hands of your Higher Power who has everything under control. When stress, anxiety, worry, fear, frustration, irritation and the like come at you, release them. TELL them to leave you—to go out of you. Further, choose to forgive yourself…your mistakes, your procrastinations, your allowing fear to control you. Let go of every hindrance. Then invite and envision love, joy, peace, hope and faith being poured into you from above (from God, the Universe…).

Otherwise, it is those worries and cares that will <u>eat you alive</u>.

Another obstacle to health is related to memories of your past that are bringing tremendous hurt and pain into your life. These memories cause internal stress and promote the beliefs that you do not deserve a better life. You must decide to release these hurts from your memories. You must choose to forgive and let go. You must see the bad feelings of each memory being erased and replaced with peace and wisdom as these past experiences become beautiful stepping stones for growth. Your life then becomes a beautiful story that can touch others…especially those facing similar experiences.

Further, toxic emotions affect us at a cellular level and are a breeding ground for illness. It's *OKAY* to feel sad, mad, upset, frustrated or disappointed. Our emotions allow us to process situations. When tragedy strikes, you *need* to allow these negative emotions to come forth instead of holding them inside of you to fester. Cry, scream, talk it out with others, write in your journal, etc. so that you can process these feelings. Seek professional help from a counselor or pastor if needed. Give yourself TIME to heal. Just be careful not to let these negative emotions hang around for so terribly long that they begin to RUN YOUR LIFE. Healthily deal with them, then let them go. Look for the good in the situation and *focus* on it. Shake yourself from the dust of the earth. You're not a worm anymore. You were born to fly! Say, "*NEXT, I'm moving on!*"

Finally, you must continue to kick out those subconscious beliefs that tell you that you're not worthy or good enough. Think about that for a moment. What is the response of your cells (which are made of energy and respond to your words, thoughts, and beliefs) when you continually tell them that they're not good enough? Remember Dr. Emoto's water crystal video (Day 16) and the impact of words and thoughts? Your body is 60-80% water!

Stop the lies, and believe that you are worthy of fantastic health! Visualize healing coming to your body. See your body healed. Envision yourself doing things you couldn't do before, and your body WILL begin to respond! Maybe not at first, but with time, as your thoughts and beliefs become stronger, your body *has to obey*! Your subconscious mind controls your vital bodily functions. It regulates your nervous system, lymphatic system and blood pressure. It controls your immune response, regenerates your skin, grows your hair, heals your wounds and so on.

Your brain is simply an electrical switch board
sending messages that tell your cells what to do.

Think of the "Placebo Effect;" this is where a sugar pill (unbeknownst to the patient) replaces a real medication. Studies show that people taking the sugar pill report similar effects as those taking the real medication. Why? Because healing begins in the MIND. You are as healthy as you WANT to be! You are as young or old as you *THINK* you are! (Plus, when you see yourself as truly healthy, your actions/choices will follow suit.)

Therefore, start telling your cells to be healthy! Start SEEING your cells as healthy. Start believing that you are in incredible health! Choose to no longer be a victim of your environment and your heredity. You can certainly choose not to believe what I have shared here. I am not a doctor, and I am not promising that you will have perfect health. However, what do you have to lose by trying this?

Maybe you've heard stories of those who have overcome terrible illnesses through positivity. In fact, science has proven that a happy heart is like medicine to the body! (Remember all the health facts we discussed concerning positive thoughts, words and emotions?) Therefore, put on some happy, upbeat music. Watch funny movies. Read inspirational books. Listen to uplifting messages. Keep good vibes coming your way *every day*. The goal must be to bombard yourself with so much positivity that your subconscious mind no longer listens to all the outside world's negativity and lies.

Also, decide to stay thankful. Rejoice in seeing yourself in wonderful health. Rejoice that you are finding those who can help you achieve better health. Rejoice that you have all you need (resources, finances) to create the healthy life you deserve! Let joy overflow and be your strength! The choice is yours. Decide to give yourself the gift of health. You DESERVE to be healthy! It's time for you to program your mind and body for abundant health! Now I dare you to repeat the following statement <u>five</u> times. I double-dog dare you!

"I am Happy, HEALTHY and Wise!"

Insight

Ways to keep your brain healthy:

1. Hydrate your brain which is around 75% water. Daily water intake below 50% of your body weight in ounces will cause dehydration, and your brain must have water to function properly. For example: a 100 lb. person would need to drink 50 oz. of water each day. A 200 lb. person would need 100 oz. a day. Also, it's better to drink water separately from food to not dilute digestive enzymes. Start slowly, and build up your water intake. Ideally, you should drink 75% of your body weight in water a day for optimal hydration and removal of toxins. (Please note that too much water intake, especially all at once, can be dangerous. Water intake over 100% your body weight in ounces should only be used for limited time periods for those in health crisis and/or under medical supervision.)

2. Get 8 to 9 hours of sleep a night. That may sound like a lot of ZZZs, but according to the latest research, your brain needs time to not only process the new information you took in that day but also to "synaptically prune" unused neural connections and clear accumulated toxins. "Brain fog" is a build-up of toxins in the brain. Plus, adequate sleep improves memory function and longevity (research telomeres).

3. Nourish your brain. You are what you think, and you are what you eat. Eat whole, natural foods (versus processed) as well as food-based vitamins (versus synthetic). Vitamins B, C, D, and E do wonders for brain health. Also, your brain is 60% fat, so eat healthy, all-natural fats such as olive oil, wild salmon, avocados, nuts, free-range eggs, coconut oil and grass-fed butter. Further, probiotics are essential to the proper functioning of the brain and immune system. (Check out Dr. David Perlmutter's book *Brain Maker: The Power of Gut Microbes to Heal and Protect Your Brain—for Life)*. There are also many great natural supplements to boost your brain health such as Ginkgo Biloba—just be sure your source is labeled as pure "USP Grade." Finally, consider limiting your caffeine intake as too much caffeine can trigger your fight-or-flight response, releasing hormones and causing your brain to be irrational instead of positive and empathetic.

4. Strengthen your brain by doing mental exercises like reading this book. Your brain is like a muscle. When you challenge it with new information, it gets stronger!

5. Get moving! Get up and move your body to get blood and oxygen flowing to your brain. If you have a desk job, get up, walk around, and stretch every hour. Even five minutes first thing in the morning of walking in place, stretching and deep belly breathing will do wonders for your thinking abilities, creativity, positivity and stress levels.

6. Pray, meditate, and/or spend time in nature to ground and center the mind, body and spirit (and turn off electronic devices which can have the opposite effect). Further, being "mindful"—choosing to be fully present in the moment—is powerful as it allows the brain to be in an optimal state of awareness and creativity. Take time to stop and "smell the roses."

The life you desire is waiting for you. Will you believe it? Will you take steps toward it? When you see your desired life (*every* area) so clear and vivid, your mind (body, soul and spirit) will accept it as real and will allow you to attract what is needed to bring it to fruition. You will finally see it, believe it, expect it and TAKE IT!

Think it. See it. Believe it. Expect it. TAKE IT!

So...what are your EXPECTATIONS?

What seeds are you planting in your imagination today?

Will you walk in faith or in fear and doubt?

Will you choose to use your faith to create abundance and miracles?

The world is counting on you...what will you do with your life?

Today is always a new day. It is NEVER too late to live your dreams.

The future starts now. No more excuses. Live life to its fullest.

Live a life of no regrets!

Remember, at the beginning of this program you signed the following statement:

I, _____ (name), commit to complete this 30-Day Boot Camp to train my brain for success and a life of happiness and abundance. No matter how much I want to quit, I will fight for my future. This day, I choose to live my life with purpose knowing that I have incredible potential within me. From this day forward, I choose to live my life without regrets. I choose to be free which means taking control of my life and my destiny. This day, I choose a life of happiness, abundance and success. I choose to live my dreams and be who I was created to be! This day, I CHOOSE TO SPREAD MY WINGS AND FLY!

When you signed this, did you really mean it? I challenge you to live the abundant life you deserve. I challenge you to be the success you are capable of...the *abundant* success. You will move toward what you **EXPECT** to happen! So expect only the **BEST**! Continue to dream BIG, set goals and daily work toward these dreams and goals. I know you can and will do it!

> "Every great dream begins with a dreamer. Always remember, you have within you the strength, the patience, and the passion to reach for the stars to change the world."
>
> ~Harriet Tubman

Assignment:

You are an incredible person full of fantastic potential. I can't wait to see what you will do with the life that is before you! Now please write down where you want to be one year, five years and 10 years from now. You must know where you want to go (career, relationships, health, spirituality, finances, etc.) if you are to get there. I encourage you to put these statements on your vision board.

I Choose to Design My Life!

In one year, I am/have…

Health

Relationships (friends/family/romance)

Finances

Career

New Skills, Knowledge, Mentors

Spirituality

Environment (home/office)

Leisure & Fun

Personal Attributes ("I am a person of Integrity, a Role Model…")

My Contribution to the World

In five years, I am/have…

Health

Relationships

Finances

Career

New Skills, Knowledge, Mentors

Spirituality

Environment

Leisure & Fun

Personal Attributes

My Contribution to the World

In 10 years, I am/have….

Health

Relationships

Finances

Career

New Skills, Knowledge, Mentors

Spirituality

Environment

Leisure & Fun

Personal Attributes

My Contribution to the World

"The me I see is the me I'll be."

How do you SEE yourself? What do you EXPECT for your life?

Next...

Write down what you are most proud of accomplishing over the past 30 days. Be sure to do something **EXTRA SPECIAL** for yourself too. You deserve it!

I am proud of myself for:

I will reward myself by:

And remember!

See it Sunday—What does your perfect future look like?

Motivated Monday—What are your goals and tasks for this week?

Thoughtful Tuesday—What are you thinking?

What and Why Wednesday—Are you living your core values?

Thankful Thursday—What are you thankful for?

Fearless Friday—How will you overcome your fears and obstacles?

Celebrate Saturday—How will you reward your victories and accomplishments?

Also, don't forget about your **FREE BONUSES!** I have included a **Toolbox** at the end of this book that is full of great "tools" to use as you continue on your journey to happiness, abundance and success! In the toolbox, you will find a cut out of the day name reminder in the **"Declaration Cut Out"** section. I encourage you to post this day name reminder where you will see it daily. Otherwise, keep these names of the days in your journal, mobile device, calendar, etc., and keep the program going! Also, when you complete a goal, cross it off, add a new goal and KEEP GOING because you have decided to be victorious in this life! You are a WINNER!

CONGRATULATIONS!

You ARE a winner! A steady pace wins the race, and you are WINNING! You are awesomely amazing! Success is YOURS! Now go inspire others! Go live your dreams! Go be who you were created to be! I am so incredibly proud of you! I knew you could do it! Now keep going!

A Final Word...

I would like to now share with you a very important law. It is the law of attraction and is in regards to abundance. I have purposely not shared this earlier, because read without the knowledge you have now received, you would only be able to understand the following at surface level. However, I now trust that you will begin to "see" and understand this law at a much deeper level so that you can <u>ACTIVATE</u> it in your life.

The Law of Attraction: Abundance

While this book is not about becoming rich, it is about creating the life you desire. In creating this desired life, you will be required to see yourself living in a state of ABUNDANCE: mentally, emotionally, physically, financially, relationally, spiritually...every area of your life. Abundance is a *result*, a state of mind, as abundance operates at a higher level of thinking and understanding. To truly comprehend and embrace abundance, you must learn to become "more." You must *"become more to have more."* But what does this really mean?

Becoming more is choosing to have a higher view of life and view of your purpose in this world. It's about creating a higher level of awareness. Isn't your perspective from an airplane much different from your perspective from the ground? When you choose to see things from a higher perspective, solutions and possibilities become more readily apparent. Remember the eagle and the worm? Are you going to have a worm's perspective (eating dirt and feeling small, insignificant and powerless) or will you choose to have an eagle's perspective (seeing the big picture, taking control/responsibility for your life, and being assertive in pursuing your dreams)? There is no limited view or lack mindset when you see things from a higher perspective.

Becoming more is also about becoming the best possible YOU. It's about continually developing your skills, abilities and knowledge (self-development). It's about becoming a person of excellence and integrity. Becoming more is about loving and forgiving others as well as yourself. It's about learning to laugh at your mistakes and moving on. It's about taking the high road and being faithful in the small things, even when no one else is looking. Becoming more is about going beyond your selfish desires and wanting to be a blessing by serving others. It's about *"getting over yourself"* and recognizing that the world (your loved ones, clients, the less fortunate....) is counting on you to be who you were created to be! So, it's not just about YOU, it's about THEM! It's about giving back! It's about your contribution to the world! Staying poor, broke, sick and depressed is not going to help anyone else!

Also, becoming more is about keeping yourself at a higher mental and emotional state (positive frequency) to attract that which you desire. It's about learning to be thankful in ALL things. It's about *deciding* to be so extremely thankful and joyful (by focusing on the good) that you can't help but attract amazing ABUNDANCE into your life! It's about keeping a mindset that says:

"I AM blessed! I AM Happy, Healthy, Wealthy and Wise!"

Finally, becoming more is seeing yourself WORTHY and capable of obtaining the life you desire. If you never feel worthy, you will either subconsciously block abundance from your life, or you will lose it shortly after you obtain it. To operate in the law of abundance, you *must* accept that abundance is YOUR BIRTHRIGHT in this universe. Abundance is available to *whomever* will receive it.

Becoming more is taking on the mindset of ABUNDANCE.

If you are to achieve your desired life—to live out your full potential—you need to take on an attitude of abundance. If you are to attract abundance, you must begin to see those things that you desire coming to you and in abundance. There is no end to the amount of love, joy, peace, happiness and success you can have in your life. You alone determine what you *allow* to come to you. Also, if you are to be honest with yourself, to live in abundance in this world requires money.

We all know that money does not bring happiness—sadly, it is too often the root of many destroyed lives and relationships. However, this does not mean that money is inherently evil. Money is only printed paper, how then can it be good or bad? Instead, money is simply a means to an end. Money is your tool or vehicle to obtain your greater purpose in this life. But you must see money as just that—an instrument. Money is not power. Money is not god. Money is not your answer. Money will not fulfill you or bring true happiness. However, money used properly can become a fountain of good things to not only help you in your endeavors but also to be a blessing to many others. Therefore, it's time to fully let go of your old subconscious views of money as being evil.

Next, let's get serious and start looking at what kind of money you would need to support the life you seek. This means creating a *budget* for the lifestyle you desire. It means beginning to see the specific numbers and figures required to support this desired future. What amount of money do you need to live and maintain your desired lifestyle?

Let's do the math:

Monthly Budget:

Mortgage(s): $ _____
Cars: $ _____
Food: $ _____
Electric: $_____
Cable: $_____
Phone: $_____
Household expenses: $ _____
Supplies: $_____
Clothing: $ _____
Vacations: $ _____
Memberships: $ _____

Savings: $_____
Paying Debt: $_____
Giving: $_____
Investments: $_____
Christmas/Gift fund: $_____
Other: $_____
Other: $_____
Other: $_____
Other: $_____
Other: $_____
Other: $_____

Total: $_____ monthly x 12 months = $ _____ annually

> **Achievement Priming:** *staring at a word repeatedly to imprint it on the subconscious mind.*

Write this total amount down where you will see it often.

In 1937 Napoleon Hill published his study of the top 500 successful people of his day in his book *Think and Grow Rich*. In his studies, Hill discovered the technique of writing down on a piece of paper (notecard or check), the dollar amount a person wanted to obtain. The person would then keep this written dollar amount in his/her pocket or wallet and would repeatedly touch and look at the piece of paper throughout the day. This is achievement priming at its finest, and it has worked in modern days for a few "slightly" successful people such as Jim Carrey and Barbara Streisand.

You must give your mind a **specific and clear** goal to work toward. Jim Carrey and Barbara Streisand didn't just put into their pocket a piece of paper with a number on it and then sit around wishing their dreams to reality. They took action. When you start moving forward, things will begin coming toward you. This is the law of attraction at work. Everything you need is there waiting for you to take it, but you must clearly define it. How can you move toward something if you don't know what it is?

You must also see yourself in possession of this desired money and begin to think and act as if you are already in possession of it NOW. What does this mean? This is NOT about reckless spending as you PRETEND to be something you are not. This is about "seeing" life from this new perspective until it becomes "real" in your mind (eagle perspective). This is about seeing that car, home, business, relationship, ministry or lifestyle you desire as truly being YOURS. For example, when that amazing car you desire drives by, instead of feeling jealous, you SEE YOURSELF driving the car. You breathe in wonderful positive emotions because you FULLY KNOW and BELIEVE that the car is **ALREADY** yours and will (in due time) manifest in your life. This is the definition of faith. Faith is thinking and acting as if you are ALREADY in possession of that which you desire—whether it is finances, health, career, relationships or personal success. Faith is when you know without a single doubt in your mind that your vision/desire will come to pass, and you walk with <u>PEACE</u> and <u>CONFIDENCE</u> in this fact.

Today begin to think BIGGER! Begin to see this amount of money coming to you quickly and easily. **Stop ALL thoughts of worry and doubt,** and see this income as destined to be a part of your life.

Start DOING!

Begin to think of viable ways to make this amount of income a reality. AND taking on five jobs and working 100 hours a week is not living a life of abundance. This is about following your passion, because when you do what you love, the money will follow. (Don't seek money because what you chase will run from you—*ALLOW* money to follow and chase you!) Put your focus on your passion and increase your skills and knowledge in this area so that people will WANT to pay you and pay you well. The highest paid people are experts in their field. Plus, doing what you love brings joy and fulfillment into your life as you use your talents and potential to *serve* others.

> "We make a living by what we get, but we make a life by what we give."
>
> ~Winston Churchill

Do you want to know a false belief that most of us entertain in the back of our minds? For some reason, we tend to hold a faulty belief that "living the dream" means that we must "retire" from using our gifts and abilities into a lifestyle of lying around all day on some beautiful island or traveling to exotic places around the world. While those pleasurable activities are absolutely fabulous, they <u>ALONE</u> will not fulfill you but will eventually leave you feeling empty and bored. Many retired people walk away from using their gifts and abilities to pursue a life of total "leisure" only to wind up feeling dead inside as their lives are now going nowhere and their brains are shriveling up from not being challenged. No matter your age or background or your beliefs about a perfect life, if you don't use the gifts inside you (your talents/abilities), you will not feel fulfilled.

Therefore, by investing in yourself to enhance your gifts, abilities and talents, you further release your God-given potential, a sense of happiness and fulfillment, and a greater income potential. No matter how young or old you are, keep yourself ACTIVE using your gifts and talents (in one form or another) to serve others. YOU are of great value. YOUR potential is ENDLESS. YOUR ability to influence others and to impact this world is LIMITLESS. Every day, find a way (no matter how small) to make this world a better place. There is no limit to the amount of happiness, success and abundance you can have *AND* give away. There is no limit to the amount of income you can obtain—and there are endless ways to create the income you want. If you don't now earn the income you desire, continue to brainstorm ways you can achieve this desired money.

Active and Passive Income

It is important to understand the difference between active and passive income. For example, my **active income** is my coaching practice as it requires my presence in coaching sessions. My active source of income keeps me fresh and growing in my skills. It forces to me to stay up-to-date on new information and techniques and to develop new relationships and connections. It challenges my brain to stay strong, healthy and vibrant. However, it is **limited by how many hours I can work in a week**.

In contrast, writing this book, creating online coaching programs and affiliate networks enable me to create **passive income** which has **no time or income restraints**. Passive income is when you create systems that generate money for you while you sleep…*or while you lie on the beach of some beautiful island or travel to exotic places around the world.*

Creating passive income often involves doing a lot of work at the beginning without a lot of money to show for it. But guess what? At the end, it could produce a lot of money with very little work. For example, researching, writing and testing this book has been *very* labor intensive for me for over two years. However, I trust in the long run, it will bring in good money while I do very little. Another example is when my husband worked in the insurance industry. He worked hard up front to get the sale, but then he worked very little to maintain the residual or passive income. Most home-based businesses and network marketing opportunities are based on this same concept.

> "The key to financial freedom and great wealth is a person's ability or skill to convert earned income into passive income and/or portfolio income."
>
> ~Robert Kiyosaki

We live in the greatest days *ever* for having opportunities to easily build wealth. (Three to five years is a very realistic time frame to become a six or seven-figure income earner with the *right* opportunity). Therefore, begin to keep your eyes open for opportunities that could—with time and effort—begin to generate greater income (both active and passive) such as starting (or expanding) your own business, consulting, network marketing, home-based businesses, real estate, investments, affiliate programs, inventions, educational and speaking opportunities, book writing, app development, online stores and marketing and so on. Just make sure that whatever you choose, you have done your *research* on it, and you truly "believe" in it.

For instance, if you join a network marketing company selling vitamins, weight loss or skin care products, be sure that you like the products and *believe* that they can help others. (Don't join a cause you don't like or feel excited about.) Then begin to use your natural talents and abilities while also developing effective marketing, communication and leadership skills by studying those in the company who are successful. Success breeds success. Keep an eye on the successful in your industry, copy what they do, and let them inspire you to push you forward.

By creating active and passive income, you create multiple streams of income that allow you to more easily create your dream life as you take on a mindset of ABUNDANCE. An abundance mindset sees that there is always a way—there is always a plentitude of available resources to tap into. Unfortunately, the average person walks in a LACK mindset as he/she sees limited resources and opportunities and typically survives by staying "just over broke"—living paycheck to paycheck with little in savings or investments and tons in credit card debt and loans. Does this sound familiar?

However, creating streams of active and passive income allows you to not only increase your income potential but to also have a "backup" in case an income stream dries up such as an industry collapsing or your company being bought out and laying off workers. This may come as a big surprise, but there is no perfect company, industry, ministry, boss, advisor, attorney or leadership team. Life can take many unexpected turns and twists. However, diversifying your income by having your "eggs" in multiple baskets allows you to stay in the driver's seat instead of going down with the ship. (And trust me…I've had to learn the hard way!) Diversifying also helps you to stay in the mindset of abundance.

Kick your Lack Mindset to the CURB!

Let me tell you how I began to kick my lack mindset to the curb. Did you know that in business, it often (but not always!) takes money to make money? This can be a big block to many people as they focus on the lack and never step out to make their dreams a reality. They wait for a silver platter loaded with money to be handed to them…which typically never happens. But what if they created an income stream—that may or may not be their "passion"—but would allow them to generate money to fund the business (or organization, ministry or lifestyle) that is their heart's desire? This is about changing one's view from *"I can't…"* to *"How can I…?"*

For example, my coaching business didn't magically appear out of nowhere with a line of clients wanting to pay me the big bucks. Businesses often take time and money to build (never mind the cost of my training and master's degree). While coaching is my passion, I was facing real obstacles (limited finances) and had to choose to find solutions. Therefore, I began to take on the mindset of abundance and opened myself up to other streams of income, such as my photography business. Later, I saw another amazing income opportunity and teamed up with some highly successful friends to begin to create both active and passive income. With just a few hours a week, these other opportunities not only fit seamlessly into my life but also added much joy as they pushed me to *become more.*

Plus, these new opportunities began to actually help my coaching business as I gained new contacts, connections and insights. No longer was I just a "bone on my own," but now I was meeting so many amazing people—many of whom sowed into my life and helped launch me to higher levels of success. (Remember, find a way to hang around the highly successful and then copy them!) In the end, I know I will go much farther in life than had someone just handed over a big check on a silver platter. My original "problem" was really just a way to move me on to bigger and better things and allowed multiple streams of income to begin to create greater abundance in my life.

The highly successful understand the importance of multiple streams of income. Remember, you want to stay in the mindset of things and opportunities *easily* falling into your lap, but you also must be OPEN to WHAT is falling into your lap!

However, don't get stressed out and think you have to go out tomorrow and start five businesses….*and PLEASE DON'T!*

Your *first priority* is to your "passion." Work at what you love, and it won't feel like work at all. Then begin to think of ways to create passive income from your passion. Brainstorm ways you can "package" and sell something you are really good or knowledgeable about that could solve others' problems. If you're not sure how to do this, don't worry; you will figure it out in time.

For the time being, begin to step out with what you have *now*, and new doors will open before you. You will soon become AWARE of the amazing opportunities that are available to you—and they are truly endless! With time, you will feel drawn to certain opportunities as they will "resonate" with something within you. Choose *wisely*. Choose what *excites* you. Choose what will help move your "passion" forward versus working against it. Choose what works for YOU. Add these income streams *slowly*, one by one over time. However, your other income streams should always work AROUND your passion versus hindering/distracting you from your passion.

My goal here is not to overwhelm you but to help you to think BIGGER, to see solutions instead of obstacles, and to learn to *work smart, not just hard*. This is about making money work for you, not you killing yourself to make an extra buck. Plus, trying to start five businesses all at once will only divide your time, focus and energy. Remember, there is only ONE YOU to go around. Therefore, decide where you want to put your FOCUS. Big success requires laser sharp focus. I want you to have multiple income streams (preferably passive income streams), but I want it to bring joy into your life and not conflict and overwhelm. Scattered focus brings confusion and can end up paralyzing you from moving forward as you feel like a rag doll tossed around with no control. Some of you may be in this situation now. Therefore, always be sure to designate specific *chunks* of time to give 100% focus to each business/income stream. Slow and steady is much more productive than fast and out of control. Take control, and decide your focus.

Visualization

Imagine for a moment how wonderful it would be to have multiple streams of income.

Imagine how fantastic it would be to have passive income flowing to you so that you have more CONTROL over how much time you must give your active income.

Imagine how AMAZING it would it be to not even need your active income and to simply do it because you absolutely **LOVE IT**!

Learn to *work smart, not just hard*. Sacrificing all your time for money will never bring happiness. Choose (or learn how) to make money serve you, instead of you serving money. Choose to create a life you LOVE!

Now it's your turn. Think of ways you can generate more income. Think BIG! However, working yourself into the ground, waiting around to win the lottery or inherit a massive fortune, or following some "get-rich-quick" scam should NOT be on your list.

Possible ways I can generate more income:

1.

2.

3.

4.

5.

So many times we see our pot of gold at the end of the rainbow and assume it means winning the lottery, winning a "dream house" from some television contest or receiving some huge inheritance from an unknown relative. We waste years—doing nothing—just waiting for our miracle to fall out of the sky or come in the mail. (I must admit this was my mindset for *many* years!) While it is possible that you could win the lottery, a dream house or inherit a ridiculous amount of money, the chances are pretty slim. In the meantime, how will you move your life forward? Years from now, those you know will still be waiting for their jackpot to fall out of the sky, while you will have made it happen by doing the small, daily things to get you ahead—this is the true secret to success. When you clearly see the life you want, you can then brainstorm ways to responsibly make it happen. You now have clarity on how to daily **STEP OUT**.

How will you STEP OUT?

How will you step out beyond your obstacles, fears and excuses and into the realms of success and abundance?

It is the small, consistent, daily steps forward that will give you the edge in life.

For me personally, I had to begin to kick my lack mindset to the curb (as I just shared with you) by seeing solutions instead of just focusing on all the obstacles. I also had to choose to step beyond my limitations and excuses and accept that for me to have more, I had to become more. And I knew that I wasn't going to charge the "big bucks" until I could truly offer high-class services. Therefore, I began by investing in increasing my skills, knowledge and expertise to thus increase my "marketplace value." This is my ***external money value*** or my value in how well I can help, serve and fix other people's problems. Remember, the highest paid people are experts in their fields.

Then I began to work on increasing my ***internal money value***. I did this by attacking my lack/poverty mindset that had held me back for way too long. Every day, I repeated the phrase, "*I love my life, I am so blessed, good things come to me.*" I even made it into a catchy little tune and made it pop up on my mobile devices throughout the day. I was surprised when I would catch myself feeling so happy and even saying under my breath how much I LOVED my life and that I was the most blessed person in the whole world. I also had the words come up on my mobile devices every morning saying, *"I attract abundance, abundance, exceeding abundance!"*

When the law of abundance finally "clicked" in my mind, it was an "aha moment" as I finally "got it." A SHIFT happened inside of me as I finally understood that abundance was truly my birthright, and it was WAITING for me to receive it. In that moment, I felt as if I could walk on water, I could fly to the highest mountain top, I could conquer the world! My faith was coming *alive*, and I began to see my thoughts as literal "things" that would create the world I desired.

My mind—spirit, soul and body—was finally coming into agreement!

And guess what? Small but *amazing* things began to happen. The first week I came home from the grocery store with a free steak in my bag. The next week I came home from shopping with three items I had not purchased. The next week I came home from shopping and noticed that I was not charged for a big ticket item. When I called the stores, they either told me to keep the items, or if I returned them, they would give me a store credit. The next week I was contacted by a company on the West Coast who had found information about me and was interested in contracting me for business.

I then began to attract items that I had been looking for, and many were even given to me for free. For example, once I decided that I wanted a white, antique table to use as my office desk, I soon found a gorgeous one at a yard sale for next to nothing. One day, I went to the store and saw a coffee mug I liked but decided not to buy it. When I got home, guess what was sitting on my kitchen counter? The mug! A client of my husband gave it to him as a gift. One day I said to myself how I wanted to get away to the Bahamas for a weekend, and guess who called me the *next* day? A promotion group offering me a free cruise to the BAHAMAS! Shortly after, my husband won through a work contest, a free five-day cruise to the Bahamas. Coincidence...? I don't think so. I began attracting things so quickly and often that it was, honestly, quite SHOCKING. This is the law of attracting abundance at work. (You may not have a light bulb moment as I did, but you will know when you have activated it because of the "results.")

My new internal mindset was transforming my life!

I then began directing my thoughts toward attracting specific things, dollar amounts and business contacts and contracts that I wanted, and as I *stepped out* (through an email, phone call or even just visualizing it clearly in my mind), they would come to me. My new internal beliefs were causing me to remove all negativity; and to clearly SEE, THINK, SPEAK and BELIEVE what I wanted. This belief then caused me to take STEPS of FAITH that *unlocked* new opportunities before me.

It was almost magical at times as what I desired seemed to literally "appear" before me (i.e. gifts, checks in the mail, new clients, influential people, speaking opportunities, new business avenues and so on). However, it had nothing to do with magic and had everything to do with my choosing to CREATE unwavering faith in my heart through establishing a crystal clear vision of the life that I desired. It was about my beliefs, my faith, causing me to take ACTION to plant good seeds so that I could reap a good harvest. *For every action, there is an equal and opposite reaction* (Newton). But I had to take that STEP (plant that good seed) to create a REACTION (the harvest I wanted). I had to *ASK* if I expected to be given something. I had to *SEEK* if I was to find. I had to *KNOCK* for the door to be opened. I had to DO something to GET something.

And when I finally stopped focusing on debt and instead took action by focusing on the abundance that could pay off that debt, I received a letter that $6,000 worth of debt had been cancelled in FULL! Even better, after years of struggling to find multiple sources of income, I was now finding so many new income opportunities opening before me that it was truly unbelievable...I actually had to turn many of them down!

When I **stepped out** and put my focus on something specific that I wanted (fully believing I had already obtained it), **I drew it toward me as I was finally ready to <u>RECEIVE</u> it.** You will have only that which you ALLOW to come into your life. When you ask, you must fully believe that it will be given to you. When you seek, you must fully believe that you will find it. When you knock, believe with all your heart that the door will be opened to you (and *keep* knocking until the right door does open!). BUT then you must walk through the door! You must believe <u>and</u> *RECEIVE*.

HOWEVER, if I ever felt undeserving, unworthy, embarrassed or guilty for attracting these amazing things, they would <u>STOP</u>. If I did not feel worthy, I could not *receive* these good things. I would then have to consistently remind myself that I am worthy of attracting amazing things into my life. We are always attracting things into our lives, whether good things or bad things. Therefore, choose to attract abundance. Take on the mindset of abundance, and just watch how your life is transformed!

WARNING: SPENDING and DEBT

Now I must add that living a prosperous, abundant life is about creating mindsets and habits that allow money to freely flow through you (to you and from you) in a "balanced" way. This means that you are neither hoarding money, nor are you recklessly spending money. Hoarding is based out of a fear/lack mindset, and recklessness creates feelings of guilt and unworthiness. Be forewarned that money can quickly activate the emotional brain to do irrational things and is why many millionaires have squandered their riches away in wild living and spending. Also, "acting" as though you are in possession of great wealth does not mean spending money you do not have. If you are not faithful with the little that you have *now*, how do you think you will be faithful with much?

It's pretty simple—you will never get (or stay) wealthy if you mindlessly spend and never know where your money is going. Also, massive credit card debt is not living in abundance. Plus, spending when you have mountains of debt (and little in savings) will only make you feel subconsciously guilty. And guess what? If you make $50,000 a year now and have a mountain of debt, you will have an even bigger mountain of debt when you make $500,000 a year.

Do you want to know what typically happens when people double their income? They simply double their spending (a more expensive house, cars, vacations, clothes, dining, TVs and so on). They usually double their debt too. Their self-created money habits keep them locked in perpetuating, repeating cycles—unless they make the choice to change their money behaviors and mindsets. Without a change of habits, they will not be able to change their money situation but will only repeat it over and over…no matter how much money they make.

Either you will be a slave to money, or you will make money a slave to you.

I want you to prosper. I want you to live an AMAZING life full of beautiful homes, cars, vacations and so on…but all within your means; only then will you feel peace and balance. Purposely pushing your budget to the absolute limit will only create fear and a lack mindset. Instead, make financial freedom your primary goal. **Financial freedom** <u>is when you are debt free (mortgage</u> <u>included) and have created passive income streams</u>. It would be far better for you to be financially free making $50,000 a year than to make millions but be up to your eye balls in stress, debt and financial burdens. (Plus, financial issues are the #1 cause of divorce in America!)

However, when you choose to take control of your finances, when you know where your money is going, and when you are financially responsible, you will begin to *see ways to attract more money to you as you will feel WORTHY of having more*. To hold on to wealth takes wisdom, responsibility and living a balanced life. Balance is key. When your spending is done in wisdom and lines up with your values, goals and determined budget (there cannot be GUILT in your spending or you will plug up the abundance flow!), you will begin to spend money easily toward your dreams and goals and will also find yourself not spending money on as many unnecessary or wasteful items. A carefully planned and followed budget will take the guilt out.

You must take "GUILT" out of your budget.

For example, if you want more money to spend on "guilt-free" shopping, then budget the amount you want to spend each month specifically for shopping (i.e. $100). This money is then only for the purpose of shopping, and there is no guilt in using it for this purpose. You choose to spend this money in utter enjoyment and bliss. If you currently do not have enough in your budget for your shopping desires, begin to visualize this new money (name the specific amount) coming to you (quickly and easily), and you will find ways to create this new "guilt-free shopping money."

For me, my natural tendency has been to hold onto money for dear life. I would feel *guilt* for spending money on anything "non-essential." However, when I truly began operating in the law of abundance, I began to spend money more wisely and without guilt. For example, one day my husband and I decided that our family was now at a good stage for us to pursue winter sports. When I realized the cost of equipment and clothing (thousands of dollars), I was surprised. In the past, I would have freaked out and felt guilt and fear for spending this money. However, instead, I weighed the decision and decided that this money was going toward promoting family unity (a core value), was something we had waited to do for years (not an impulsive decision), we had the money available (responsible), and now was the appropriate time (timing). I released that money with no guilt and no fear, and I saw the money being quickly replaced with more money (which it was). I had finally begun to see money flowing through me and to me in a balanced way. I was finally at peace with my spending, instead of feeling controlled by guilt and fear of lack. The same is true in relationships. Healthy relationships are created when two people give and take in a balanced way. BALANCE brings PEACE.

Create balance and peace through GIVING.

Speaking of "give and take," did you notice that "giving" was on your "ideal" budget? When you give to others, especially to those less fortunate, you are letting go of your grip on money and breaking its power and control over you. You should be in control of money, not money in control of you. As you release money in the *right directions*, allowing it to flow through your hands, you will begin to attract more money because now it can easily flow to you and through you—versus you plugging up the flow by holding tightly to what you have, all because of a subconscious fear of lack.

Break this fear of lack by giving to good causes, and do it happily, not begrudgingly. I used to dread the charities who would set up in front of stores. Maybe you've heard them ringing their bell or seen the giving buckets. Now instead of cringing, I get excited about giving. While I used to just throw in a few coins in the bucket out of guilt, now I excitedly put money in knowing that I am positively sowing into other people's lives. I also have my kids put in money to teach them to be givers. This is the law of sowing and reaping. If you plant good things, you will reap good things. Therefore, get excited at opportunities to give. Seek out opportunities to give. See giving as an opportunity to attract abundance to you. When you give, see abundance drawing closer to you with each act of kindness. Remember, *every action creates an equal and opposite reaction*. If you truly want to attract abundance, make sure GIVING is in your budget.

> *"Give, and it will be given to you. A good measure, pressed down, shaken together and running over, will be poured into your lap. For with the measure you use, it will be measured to you." ~Luke 6:38-40*

An attitude of abundance will compel you to GIVE!

When you live from an attitude of abundance, you can't help but give! You will not be able to hold it all for yourself. *If you cannot happily release money to help others, then money still has control of you.* Grudgingly giving is not living out of the law of abundance; instead it is having a lack mentality, and this "giving" will only make you resentful and bitter. (*Please note: this is about giving to good causes, <u>not</u> to those who are trying to manipulate you by their <u>victim mentality</u>*).

Now you may be wondering about all those selfishly-rich people out there and thinking to yourself, "*Don't they live in abundance?*" While, yes, they have attracted great riches to themselves, they are not living a truly abundant life as their own selfishness will eventually destroy them. When you live from an attitude of true abundance, you will want to make the world a better place. You will want to be a blessing. You will feel the life-giving energy that is created by joyfully giving to others, and it will become addictive! Anyone who walks in true abundance will tell you that an amazing secret to increasing wealth is through giving. Don't take my word for it, do your own research! Better yet, try it for yourself!

Stop and think for a moment. When you go out to eat, what kind of tip do you leave? Are you stingy or generous? I used to get upset at my husband for his very generous tipping. I was STINGY and operating out of a POVERTY MINDSET. However, when you are a giver, good things will come to you. For example, when you are known as a good tipper, the wait staff will WANT to serve you, and they will serve you well! (I know, I waitressed through college. You don't forget a good tipper, nor do you forget a stiffer!)

Let's take a look at your **CURRENT** income and think about creating a budget that will move you forward toward the life you desire. Ideally, you want to set your budget to save 10%, give 10% and use 10% to pay off your debts. This 30% comes off the top before you spend a dime on anything else. You then can live on the other 70%. Once your debts are paid off, you will then have 80% to live on—or better yet, put that extra 10% toward investments for retirement. (Half the U.S. population ends up broke at retirement. I encourage you to research compound interest and the Rule of 72 to see how money invested *over time* can make you very wealthy.)

CURRENT NET INCOME $_____

SAVE 10% $ _____

GIVE 10% $ _____

DEBT 10% $ _____

BUT you may say, "*I can barely get by as it is! There is no way I can currently give up 30% of my income!*" Well, what can you give up? Can you give up 1% toward savings, 1% toward giving and 1% toward debt elimination? What needless things do you buy that you could eliminate in order to put this 3% toward moving your life forward? Isn't your future worth 3%? Instead of being overwhelmed with the 30%, start where you can. Instead of waiting until the 30% seems easy (which typically never happens), just step out and do the 3% now!

Remember, you are throwing out the mindset of your great "break" coming by winning the lottery or inheriting a massive fortune. Expecting everything to be handed to you on a "silver platter" will never allow you to grow or become more. To have more, YOU must become more—you must see life from a higher perspective and recognize the personal responsibility and control you have over your own life and destiny. If you still think the world owes you something, then you have not become more, and you will not have more. No one owes you anything. Take charge of your own life which includes your financial future.

My husband's and my ultimate goal is to give 90% of our income to helping others and to live off the other 10%. There are many charities and organizations we want to fund and even create to help those in need in our community and around the world. We have mentally pictured this money and marked it as ours. We have sent our thoughts, words and energy to secure this money. We know that this great treasure has our name on it—it is OURS. We have claimed it and decided that nothing will take it from us.

However, it can often seem as if there is a huge gulf between us and our promised land of grand goals and dreams. Nevertheless, daily we take small steps of action toward this goal. With time, consistency and persistence, we will obtain that which we have claimed. You see, my husband and I truly believe that this abundance is ours, and we *will* someday obtain it as our God-given right. This abundance is awaiting us; it is being held for us until we can close the great divide between where we are now and where we want to be—a place of amazing abundance. Daily, we choose to take small steps forward (as well as an occasional leap of faith) causing the gulf between us and our treasure to become increasingly smaller.

Great dreams are not created overnight.

Unfortunately, if along the way we give up, this treasure is lost. So many times we can give up too soon and lose out on our reward. Great dreams are not birthed into reality overnight. Is a baby conceived, birthed and grown to manhood in a day? Of course not! Would you give a toddler the keys to the car? No way! There is much that must be accomplished before a child grows old enough, big enough, mature enough and wise enough to drive a vehicle. Or think about this: anyone can become a businessman or woman overnight. However, a "great" businessman or woman is built over time....years, even decades. Why? Because there is a learning curve; there is wisdom and experience that must be gained; there is a decisiveness, confidence, mindset and "belief" that must be established before he or she can truly exude greatness. He or she has to BECOME MORE, before he or she can truly HAVE MORE.

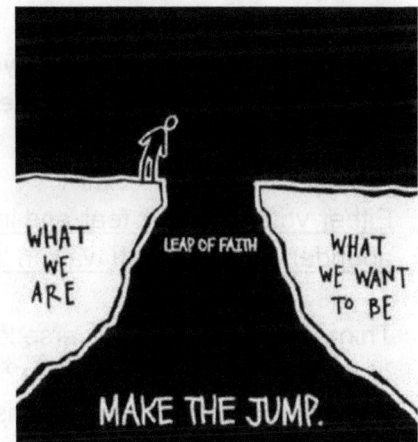

So too, as you consistently travel the path to success, you become wiser, stronger, more mature, more skilled, more knowledgeable, more creative, more decisive, more confident, more secure in who you are and in what you truly want.

**As you <u>daily</u> walk the path to success,
you become more of what and who you were created to be.**

You BECOME MORE and, therefore, you are able to HAVE MORE. Your potential is endless. However, you must choose to daily take those consistent steps along this path. A steady pace wins the race. So just keep going! Decide to put your name on your treasure. See yourself living the life you desire. See yourself debt free. See yourself giving and giving with excitement. Feel thankful that you have the opportunity to give. See yourself as an awesome tipper. See yourself having no lack in any area of your life. See yourself attracting new avenues of income that just *flow* to you. SEE what you WANT!

Choose Your Focus

AND refuse to allow lack to even enter you mind. Give lack NO ATTENTION and NO POWER. It does not EXIST in your life! Dismiss it from your mind. Also, do not focus on BILLS and DEBT. Focus on the abundance that is coming to you (that will quickly pay off the bills and debt). *What you focus on you give power to, and it will increase!*

Focus on what you want, not on what you don't want!

And yes, I know you must live in the "here and now" and can quickly become discouraged at "reality." However, even in looking at the "now," choose to walk by faith and not by what you "see" with your physical eyes. Begin to speak how your situation is changing. Speak what you want to happen. Declare that you accept ONLY ABUNDANCE in your life. Life and death are in the power of YOUR tongue. Tell doubt, fear and unbelief to leave you and allow faith, hope and love to fill you.

<u>Either you feed your fear and invite lack into your life, or you feed your faith and begin to walk in abundance. When you walk in true faith, there are no limits, and there is no lack.</u>

Think about this: the universe knows no lack. Look up in the sky. Is there any lack to the number of stars in our grand universe? When one star dies, another is born. Look at the shore. Is there any end to the number of grains of sand as the earth continually makes more beneath the ocean floor? Look in the sea and the seemingly limitless number and kinds of sea life. The universe is more expansive than our minds could ever conceive, and it knows no lack because it is made of energy and matter constantly changing forms.

Use your thoughts and words (ENERGY) to create the life you desire (MATTER).

Now see, think, speak, and believe that abundance is coming to you. Not just a little abundance, but overwhelming abundance. I challenge you to see so much abundance coming to you that your biggest issue will be figuring out how to spend it and who to give it to! What a great problem to have! And see not only money but also happiness, love, kindness, favor, peace, creativity, wisdom and success flowing easily and effortlessly to you and though you.

And don't forget: if you are truly living in abundance, then you are being the BEST YOU that you can possibly be. It also means that you will have a heart to help others become the best they can be. Sow into others' lives, and just watch what happens to your own life. If you want your business to grow, then encourage and help others to grow their businesses. Be a channel for abundance to flow to you and through you. Be a blessing to those around you and in the earth, and just watch how your life will positively change! Doesn't this excite you?! It should!

SELF IMAGE: What is your self-worth based on?

Always remember! Your self-image should not be defined by your physical abundance—your possessions. Your self-worth is not based on your house, car or bank account. If this was the case, then you would *never* have enough because you would always need more to feel worthy. This is a lie, and this is not the mindset of abundance. Always needing more to feel satisfied is really greed. Greed crosses all income levels and social classes—you don't have to be rich to be greedy. Greed is based out of a poverty mentality that tells you that you must keep spending in order to feel worthy. Greed can NEVER be satisfied and will leave you struggling and penniless.

Right now, think about whether there are physical possessions in your life that you love more than anything. Are there things that you own that you could NOT give away or let go of? That's a tough question, but it is very revealing about what you truly value and what you feel you need to spend money on. *Either you will own your possessions, or your possessions will own you.*

Currently, you are more than likely spending money on *autopilot*. Begin to think about where your money goes. How and on what you spend your money speaks volumes about your own sense of self and ultimately your self-worth. Exactly how many designer shoes, watches, purses, cars or vacation homes will it take to make you feel worthy? If you don't feel worthy *now*, then you will not feel worthy even if you gain all that the world has to offer (and you will end up subconsciously sabotaging your life in some form or another). Choose to feel worthy *now*. Worthiness and abundance go hand in hand. You attract what YOU ARE.

As your mindset, beliefs and inner worthiness grow,
so will your level of abundance.

Wealth is simply a manifestation of a person's mindset, inner beliefs and the personal responsibility they have taken for their own life. Money simply *amplifies* what is going on inside a person, for good or bad. Money reveals what is *already* in a person's heart.

You see, being rich and being wealthy are two totally different things. Anyone can be born into great riches. However, the rich serve money and allow their money and possessions to *define who* they are. In contrast, the wealthy are those who have learned how to make money serve them and work for their chosen purposes. A rich person could lose all they have and stay poor the rest of their life. However, a wealthy person could lose everything only to recreate it many times over because the *blueprint for wealth lies within them.*

What you ARE determines your level of abundance.
When you become more, you will be able to HAVE more...and KEEP more!

Choose to become a person of abundance as your self-worth is based on the fact that you are a precious and unique life created in the image of an infinite Creator who has put you on this planet to do something EXTRAORDINARY with your life. Abundance and wealth are simply your means to create the extraordinary—to make this world a better place.

So What Are You Waiting For?

For me, as a very spiritual person, I have in humility always "waited" for God to do things (you can substitute the Universe, Higher Power, Great Spirit, etc.). However, waiting has not produced much fruit in my life.

FINALLY, I woke up and realized that **God is waiting on ME**! God is eagerly waiting for ME to step out in faith and use the amazing talents and potential He has put in me (and as I use them, these gifts will increase!). He is waiting for **ME** to **CREATE** the amazing life that He wants me to have—that He created me to have! If I am made in God's image, then I have the same creative powers He does. What I create starts with an image or thought in my mind. My thoughts and words have creative powers, and I can use them for good or evil, to build or to destroy. The choice is always mine.

After 40 years on this earth, I finally feel like I am walking WITH God, as a **co-creator** of my life. Instead of trying to "earn" my worthiness, I know that I am worthy simply because I am His creation. Now I walk with God as a friend and heir of His inheritance, fulfilling my purpose and claiming and receiving what is rightfully mine as His child. It's a dream come true. How could I be so blind for all these years?!

Abundance was WAITING for ME to reach out and take it!

And finally, I AM taking it! I DAILY CHOOSE to focus not on the lack, debt or problem but on the abundance that WANTS to come to me! The abundance that's waiting to come to me! As soon as worry or doubt begins, I choose to stop it, and visualize everything working out and having all the resources, finances or whatever else I need. Daily, I choose to walk not according to what I see with my physical eyes but according to the vision and faith in my heart. Every day, I choose to close the door to fear (and its by-products of doubt, worry and hopelessness) and open the door to believing *and* receiving. ALL things are possible to those who believe! I finally believe!

Daily, I <u>choose</u> to walk in FAITH and not in FEAR,
in HOPE and not in FEAR,
in LOVE and not in FEAR.
What I walk in is MY choice!

Either I am controlled by fear, <u>or</u> I walk in faith, hope and love. Period. End of story! I never realized it was this simple. Either I allow fear to control and destroy my life, or I allow faith, hope and love to build the life I was created to have. Out of faith, hope and love comes peace, joy, contentment, confidence, creativity, wisdom, health, abundance and all good things. Faith, hope and love birth an abundant life. (Please refer to the Vibrational Frequency Scale on page 212.)

You see, *HOPE creates FAITH; FAITH creates action, and action done in LOVE creates a better world.* You were created to love and be loved because God IS LOVE. When you begin to walk in LOVE, you open yourself to freely walk in God's great abundance. Love always hopes and always perseveres. Love drives out fear. Love conquers all. Love never fails. Faith, hope and love make all things possible.

> *Love is patient, love is kind. It does not envy, it does not boast, it is not proud. It does not dishonor others, it is not self-seeking, it is not easily angered, it keeps no record of wrongs. Love does not delight in evil but rejoices with the truth. It always protects, always trusts, always hopes, always perseveres. Love never fails. ...And now these three remain: faith, hope & love. But the greatest of these is love.*
> *1 Corinthians 13: 4-8, 13*

Faith, Hope and Love create *MIRACLES*.

Either I align myself with the frequency of abundance (the frequency of God, heaven, love, faith, hope and miracles) or I align myself with fear, doubt, worry and destruction. The choice is always mine. And I can see what I have aligned myself to by the fruits in my life. I now realize that God responds to faith, hope and love...not doubt, not worry, not bitterness, not complaining (these are not His frequency). When I walk in faith, hope and love, I ALLOW God to work miraculously in and through me. Now when I find myself having a troubled mind, I stop and ask myself whether this is a fear <u>or</u> a faith, hope and love response. When I recognize that I either walk in one or the other, I realize that I can create my life to be *anything* I want.

What an amazing opportunity I have been given! I never knew the power I possessed over my own destiny. I never knew I could be so FREE. The truth has set me free! I have finally ALLOWED myself to be happy and to live in a mindset of abundance. I can finally see the great gift given to me from above: **the POWER of CHOICE**.

I daily CHOOSE to say goodbye to the disappointments of yesterday (and when they rear their ugly heads, I tell them they are now powerless over my life). I daily CHOOSE to let go of the stress and cares of my life. I daily CHOOSE to keep my eyes on the prize. I daily CHOOSE to take on the mindset and belief that ALL things are working out for my good as I walk in faith, hope and love and rest secure in the hands of my Creator.

This is the true secret to living an abundant life.

When you finally do this, a huge weight will be lifted from your shoulders. I pray you will draw upon your spirituality and find the true Source of all true faith, hope, love, happiness, success and abundance. You were made for more. You were made for greatness. You were made to live an EXTRAORDINARILY ABUNDANT LIFE!

> *It's time to stop begging, and it's time to start walking as a CO-CREATOR with your Maker to fulfill your purpose on this earth....an ABUNDANT LIFE.*

So I will ask you again....

What is YOUR vision for an ABUNDANT LIFE?

Define it now. Define it clearly. See it as REAL. Why?

Because your vision will define your purpose.

It is in purpose (passionate purpose) that you will persist until you have that which you envision. Vision breeds hope. Hope breeds faith. Faith breeds action. Action breeds achievement. Everything that has ever been created has come from a vision in the mind. Your thoughts operate at a spiritual level as they have the ability to create. Thoughts are not only creative, they know no limits. Your imagination is one of the most powerful forces in the universe.

What is in the imagination of your mind?

If you removed the limits of your current thinking and opened your mind to limitless potential, what would you see for yourself and your future? What is your vision for your better tomorrow? Not just a little better, but incredibly, *ABUNDANTLY* better.

What are your BIG dreams and ambitions? How will you live out your purpose on this earth? How will YOU make this world a better place? There is only ONE YOU, and only you can do what you were put on this earth to do! Only you can live out YOUR God-given potential! The choice is yours. It's time for you to go set this world on fire!

Stop Waiting and START DOING!

Rise up, spread your wings,

IT'S YOUR TIME TO SOAR!

FINAL THOUGHT:

What advice would you give your younger self if you knew what you know now?

_____

_____

Now go do it! Be all that you are capable of!

My Story: Overcoming Fear & Unworthiness

It is interesting to note that while Napoleon Hill wrote one of the best self-development books of all time, *Think and Grow Rich,* and followed the formulas of the most successful of his day, he could never keep the wealth that he gained. Over and over, he followed the formula and amassed great fortune only to lose it. In fact, he lost most of his close relationships as well. This always puzzled me until I looked at my own life.

After reading this book, can you now guess why Hill kept losing the very thing he wanted the most? My guess is that he didn't feel worthy of it. His *deep* internal beliefs were not in line with his thinking. This is very common. As people increase their income and success levels, they must also continually *increase* their belief of worthiness or they will sabotage their success.

Let me tell you my story of how I had to fight to overcome my fear of lack and my beliefs that I was not worthy of abundance. <u>You will only allow yourself to have and keep that which you feel worthy of having.</u> While I told you how my husband and I obtained our new home, I did not tell you the obstacles that we had to overcome to finally get there. Let me rewind a few years prior to that event. At this earlier time, my husband and I were making good money. We were big givers. We were living in an incredible home, and we were living "our dream." Therefore, our lives should have been perfect at this point? Right?

WRONG!

It didn't matter that we were earning the amount of money we had envisioned or that we were living in the kind of house we had pictured in our minds; I was still living with a poverty mentality and was a captive of the fear of not having enough.

<u>You see, obtaining the life you desire and keeping the life you desire are two different things.</u>

For much of our marriage, my husband and I have worked on 100% commission, meaning one month could have huge sales/contracts and the next month nothing. Instead of seeing unlimited potential and abundance because there was no cap as to what we could earn, I focused only on lack and thus on all the *"What Ifs?"* What if we didn't make enough? What if sales dried up? What if we couldn't pay our bills? This is where I allowed fear to come into my life.

You attract the very thing that you fear the most because you repeatedly think it and see it happening to you. You begin to "believe" it. Thousands of years ago, Job said, *"For the thing which I feared the most has come upon me, and that which I was afraid of is come unto me"* (Job 3:25). <u>What you fear, you give power to.</u>

For me, my biggest fear was this ongoing worry and dread of not having enough. Financially, we would have fantastic months followed by terrible months. We would pay off all our debt in the good months only to acquire tons of debt again in the bad months. We were caught in a vicious cycle. Therefore, I would hold tightly to money. I would give my 10% away but with mixed feelings deep down inside. I would be stingy in buying gifts for others. I would dread paying bills and wait until the last possible moment to pay them. I would complain about money all the time. I would even complain when my husband bought me flowers or little gifts because it was money for *"non-essential items."* On the outside, we appeared to be living a life of abundance, yet inside, I was living a life of constant fear of lack. I had an unconscious belief that the universe would run out of money—that there wasn't enough to go around.

When my thoughts became fearful or negative toward our income, our income would ALWAYS decline over the next few months. When my thoughts stayed positive, our income stayed growing and healthy. It was almost eerie at the very apparent relationship between thoughts and outcomes; however, it took me YEARS to recognize this!

Because of my fear of lack mentality, we lost our home not once, but twice. (Do you see the repeating cycle?). The first time was many years ago when our business collapsed. The second time was when we were renting the above mentioned "dream house" after moving across country to the Greater Boston area where my husband was newly hired. This dream home was stunningly beautiful; it was even better than what I had imagined. It had a guest house and the yard looked like a park. The home was up on a big beautiful private hill overlooking the mountains and the ocean was only minutes away. When we went to the open house to apply to rent the home, I literally said to myself, *"This house is too nice for us."* Amazingly, of all the people applying to rent, we were chosen. We had attracted this dream home to us; it truly was a dream come true.

However, when people would come to the house and say, *"Wow, this place is a mansion,"* I would feel embarrassed inside as I assumed they thought that we were really *"rich."* I would quickly tell them that it wasn't our house and that we were *"just renting."* You see, deep down inside I felt UNWORTHY to live in this kind of home and to be associated with this kind of lifestyle. While the home was a dream come true, all I could see was money slipping through our hands every month in order to live here. To make matters worse, the cost to heat the home was as much as an average mortgage payment. After the second long New England winter, I said to myself these exact words: *"If nothing changes, I don't want to go through another winter in this house."*

Guess what? We didn't! That summer the owners gave the house to their daughter, and because my husband (who was currently the main bread winner) had just been offered and accepted a new business opportunity, we were in a situation where we couldn't buy and had to rent AGAIN (another repeating cycle). However, there were no rentals in the highly-coveted town where we lived and where our children attended school.

So…where did we moved to? A hotel! Yes, instead of being in a huge, stunningly beautiful house for another winter, we were now a family living in a HOTEL ROOM! Instead of stepping up to the plate and becoming "*more*" so that we could properly hold on to the life style we desired, I gave in to my thoughts of fear of lack. Even though we had obtained our dream, I still had a poverty mindset. All I could see was LACK, and thus LACK kept coming to us! However, I had *no* idea that I HAD CREATED this dreaded reality.

Some months later an apartment in our town opened, and we moved there. Now being a person of faith in God, I repeatedly complained to God about this awful living situation. About how this was not what I wanted. About how this was not what I had believed for. Complain, complain, complain!

Then it finally occurred to me…

I had attracted all of this into my life. I had been "saying" one thing, but my true beliefs were totally different. You see, even though I did not like living in this apartment, it was what I had attracted to my life because I did not feel worthy of living in that big beautiful house. Even though we made good money (despite the ups and downs), I subconsciously felt that I did not deserve that kind of lifestyle. I finally came to realize that our current living situation was where *I did feel worthy*. I had to choose to recognize that I was living in the world that I had created, and I had to decide to change my thinking. I could blame God (or the Universe) for giving us a beautiful house only to take it away, or I could see where God was trying to help us to *become more* by putting us in a situation for us to grow and think BIGGER.

I accepted that I had failed that lesson and had also pulled my husband down with me. We finally took personal responsibility for our lives and began to enlarge our thinking to become more. You have to *become more to have more*. A poverty mentality will never get you more, but will take away even what you currently have.

So, what did we do? First, we had to learn to stop focusing on what we didn't want. We didn't want to live in this small place, we didn't want debt, we didn't want unhappiness, and we didn't want frustration. By focusing on all of this, we only became more unhappy, frustrated and UNGRATEFUL! Complaining was becoming a normal activity.

Therefore, we had to WAKE UP and make a CHOICE to focus on what we were THANKFUL for in our CURRENT situation. We still had so many things in our everyday lives to be grateful for. As we focused on what we were thankful for (such as having a roof over our heads and our beautiful family), joy and happiness began to fill our lives once again.

THEN, we started focusing on what we **DID WANT**. We focused on ABUNDANCE (as we were finally beginning to grasp it!). We focused on seeing money flowing easily to us and through us. We rooted out ALL thoughts of lack and fear…or stopped them dead in their tracks! We clearly saw ourselves in the kind of house that we wanted and with the specific income needed to support this lifestyle (not a guessed amount but one with a proper budget). We saw ourselves with the promotions and contracts we wanted, with the cars and vacations that we wanted, and with the joy and peace that we wanted to fill our lives. Then we began figuring out how to make this all happen. At first we had no clue, but with time, the plan became clearer and clearer.

No longer were we just hoping and waiting for things to magically work out. We were now *stepping out* to make it happen. Each step led us further along our path. New doors of opportunity began to open before us such as multiple income streams, bonuses and *amazing* connections with people who wanted to help us!

And most importantly, we DAILY reminded ourselves that we DESERVED this kind of lifestyle. We had to tell unworthiness to go from our lives because it had no right to us anymore. We finally got so fed up with the lies and faulty beliefs that we had been listening to that we developed a "dogged determination" to have more and to be *proud* to have more!

And you know what? Along the way, we began to BELIEVE. We began to feel worthy of this desired life. We began to be so incredibly thankful knowing that we were in *full possession* of that which we desired. We began to be determined that we were going to fight for our dream. No lies and no faulty beliefs would take it from us this time around. We were finally stepping up to the plate to make this dream life a reality. Finally, we believed that we deserved to have more and were determined we were going to have it. And guess what? We did!

Is this the end of our story? No. This is only the beginning for us as bigger and better is yet to come. The best is yet to come for you too, if you will *ALLOW* it.

BECOME MORE *so that you can* HAVE MORE.
I know you can and will do it!

PRAYER

Prayer to Allow Abundance to Flow Freely To and Through You

*Creator of the Universe, I ask You to help me fulfill my purpose on this earth.
I recognize and accept that You have created me for greatness. I recognize and accept that I am worthy of an abundant life because I am Your creation. I recognize and accept that I am created to be a co-creator with You to make this world a better place.*

I choose to stop waiting, and I choose to start thinking, speaking, believing and stepping out the way You desire me to so that I can release abundance—exceeding abundance—into every area of my life and into the world around me.

I am sorry for my fear and doubt. I am sorry I have been so ignorant and blind. I want to SEE. Help me to SEE. Open my eyes to the abundant life You have prepared for me. I want to see how YOU SEE. I want to be all that You created me to be. Thank you for showing me Your truth because the truth sets me free, so I can fully be who You created me to be. I choose now to walk the path to greatness and to be a blessing in this life that You have so generously given to me.

*Thank you for the abundance you have made available to ME.
I now BELIEVE and RECEIVE it as mine.*

AMEN and AMEN!

I highly encourage you to now go to www.trainyourbrainworkbook.com and listen to Earl Nightingales' *The Greatest Secret* (a 30 minute YouTube audio). You are now ready to truly understand what is being shared. You may just have an "aha" moment as I did.

Now What?

Thank you for taking the time to complete this book. This program took years of research and client application to refine and make it as effective as possible. I highly encourage you to repeat this program until it becomes a part of who you are.

REPETITION IS YOUR BEST FRIEND!

There are many "*levels*" to this book that you will discover only with repetition. Every time I repeat this program, I learn something new. As I continually gain a deeper understanding of the principles of this book, something will further "click" in my mind. It was around my fourth time through this program that I had a moment of enlightment concerning the greatest obstacle blocking me from my biggest dream. I had never even considered it, and it suddenly became crystal clear! So just keep going!

> Remember:
> The highly successful never stop LEARNING!!

Did You Know? It takes an average of being **exposed to something FIVE to SEVEN times** before your brain grasps the concept! The first time you read a book, you are simply reading it with your conscious mind; however, with repetition, the subconscious begins to understand. Therefore, it is better to read one book over and over than 20 books that you never internalize. It is not until you internalize the information that true transformation can occur. When something becomes boring to you, you have begun to master it. It takes time to move from the worm's perspective to the eagle's perspective. Therefore, my suggestion is that you do this program on an on-going basis for one full year. After that, repeat *at least* once a year but continue to *always* use the daily name prompts (See it Sunday, Motivated Monday…) to keep you moving forward. Put the daily name prompts on your calendar, mobile device (as daily alerts), and/or use my Weekly Goal Setting Template. I have also included a recommended reading list for future self-development (located in the **Toolbox**; turn the page). Take time to "digest" these books.

Decide to keep learning and growing, and you will rise to new levels of understanding and success. This is only the beginning for you. Keep up the good work! You are a winner!

Finally, A BIG THANK YOU to the fields of positive psychology, life coaching and neuroscience; to my educational intuitions; and to the amazing life coaches, mentors and authors that have dramatically impacted my life. I would also like to thank all my dear friends, family and clients who have supported my endeavors to make this book a reality. And most importantly, I would like to thank my Lord and Savior, Jesus Christ, for helping me to put this program together to help set people free from their limiting self-beliefs. My life purpose is to help others fulfill their purpose and destiny on this earth by being all that they were created to be. I hope that I have sparked something deep within you to be more and do more. I truly do believe in you! Now go set this world on fire!

Love & Blessings,

Coach Sharon

DON'T BE PUSHED BY YOUR PROBLEMS, BE LED BY YOUR DREAMS.

Ralph Waldo Emerson

"Not all readers are leaders, but all leaders are readers."

Harry S. Truman

"Our greatest weakness lies in giving up. The most certain way to succeed is always to try just one more time."

Thomas A. Edison

"Quality is not an act, it is a habit."

Aristotle

"It does not matter how slowly you go as long as you do not stop."

Confucius

"We suffer not from the events in our lives, but from our judgments about them!"

EPICTETUS

"Believe in yourself! Have faith in your abilities! Without a humble but reasonable confidence in your own powers, you cannot be successful or happy."

Norman Vincent Peale

"THAT WHICH DOES NOT KILL US MAKES US STRONGER."

FRIEDRICH NIETZSCHE

"THE PESSIMIST SEES DIFFICULTY IN EVERY OPPORTUNITY. THE OPTIMIST SEES THE OPPORTUNITY IN EVERY DIFFICULTY."

WINSTON CHURCHILL

"Comparison is the thief of joy."

Theodore Roosevelt

"All battles are first won or lost, in the mind."

Joan of Arc

"Knowing Is Not Enough; We Must Apply. Wishing Is Not Enough; We Must Do."

Johann Wolfgang Von Goethe

"Continuous effort – not strength or intelligence – is the key to unlocking our potential."

Winston Churchill

"IT IS NOT IN THE STARS TO HOLD OUR DESTINY BUT IN OURSELVES."

WILLIAM SHAKESPEARE

"Whatever the mind of man can conceive and believe, it can achieve."

Napoleon Hill

"You have power over your mind - not outside events. Realize this, and you will find strength."

Marcus Aurelius

IF THERE IS NO STRUGGLE, THERE IS NO PROGRESS.

FREDERICK DOUGLASS

"A journey of a thousand miles must begin with a single step."

Lao Tzu

The
Toolbox

Suggested Book List

The following books are a suggested starting point and are only a few of a multitude of incredible resources available to you. All the resources you could ever need await you!

MINDSET

Think and Grow Rich, Napoleon Hill

You Were Born Rich, Bob Proctor

First Steps to Wealth, Dani Johnson

The Slight Edge, Jeff Olson

HABITS

Million Dollar Habits, Brian Tracy

The 7 Habits of Highly Effective People, Stephen Covey

MONEY

Rich Dad, Poor Dad, Robert Kiyosaki

The Secret Language of Money, Dr. David Krueger

The Total Money Makeover, Dave Ramsey

INFLUENCE

How to Win Friends and Influence People, Dale Carnegie

Who Gets Promoted, Who Doesn't, and Why, Donald Asher

Emotional Intelligence, Daniel Goleman

Emotional Intelligence 2.0, Travis Bradberry and Jean Greaves

EMPOWERMENT

The One-Life Solution, Dr. Henry Cloud

Super Brain, Dr. Rudolph Tanzi and Deepak Chopra

Words Can Change Your Brain, Dr. Andrew Newberg and Dr. Robert Waldman

The Happiness Advantage, Shawn Achor

The Five Second Rule, Mel Robbins

RELATIONSHIPS

Why Don't We Listen Better?, Dr. James C. Petersen

The Five Love Languages, Gary Chapman

HEALTH

Eat Right 4 Your Type, Dr. Peter J. D'Adamo

Your Body's Many Cries for Water, Dr. Fereydoon Batmanghelidj

The Biology of Belief, Dr. Bruce Lipton

Brain Maker: The Power of Gut Microbes to Heal and Protect Your Brain, Dr. David Perlmutter

Younger, Dr. Sara Gottfried

Feelings Buried Alive Never Die, Karol K. Truman

SPIRITUAL / CHRISTIAN

Unlocking Your Legacy: 25 Keys For Success, Paul J. Meyer

The Purpose Driven Life, Rick Warren

The Battlefield of the Mind, Joyce Meyers

Josiah's Fire: Autism Stole His Words, God Gave Him a Voice, Tahni Cullen

Glory Invasion: Walking Under An Open Heaven, David Herzog

40 Days in Heaven, Rev. Elwood Scott

From Faith to Faith: A Daily Guide to Victory, Kenneth and Gloria Copeland

My Top Ten Rules to Live By

1. Always plan out your day or else your day will plan you. Choose to take control of your life and to live by design. By focusing on priorities, you will accomplish more and faster.

2. Always remember that the only person you can change or control is you. While you cannot always control what is happening around you, you can control how you respond. You alone are accountable for your words and actions. Never allow yourself to make excuses, but choose to take control of your own life—every day, every moment. Never allow others control over how you feel or see yourself.

3. Always know your boundaries—what you will and will not do—and live by them. Do not feel guilty for saying *"yes"* or saying *"no."* Choose to uphold your values and priorities.

4. Always own your own happiness. Choose to stay positive and solution-focused (versus problem-focused). Choose to see the good in every situation, to look for the opportunity in difficult times and struggle, and to truly believe that there is always an answer. Never allow anyone or any situation to steal your joy. Let all worry and fear leave you as you choose to walk in faith, hope and love. You are a victor!

5. Always take time to slow down and practice mindfulness. Make a conscious choice to *daily* slow down to "stop and smell the roses" as you begin to take joy and appreciation in life's simple pleasures. Also, pick one day a week to rest, relax and have fun. Studies show you are more productive if you take one day off a week to give your mind, body and spirit time to rest, recover and regroup so that you can regain clarity, vision and energy to pursue your big dreams. Decide the day of the week that will be your "Sabbath Day Rest."

6. Always be motivated by love, your core values, and your decision to a blessing to others. Daily, ask yourself what your true motives are. Choose to be a person of integrity, excellence, a role model and one who always takes the "high road." Continually look for ways to serve others and to be a blessing in this earth. Choose to help others succeed, and you too will succeed far beyond your dreams.

7. Always live out of a mindset of abundance. Abundance flows most freely in an attitude of gratitude. Be grateful for what you have *now* and also grateful for what it is yet coming to you. (Never allow envy to control or manipulate you as this negative energy will only act to destroy and hinder what you really want. "Keeping up with the Jones" will not allow you to live a life of abundance.) Daily pray, *"Thank you God (Universe) that I always have more than enough, all things are working out for my good, and all things are possible with You."* Abundance is waiting on you to take it…so take it!

8. Always remember that life is about the journey. Embrace and appreciate each day. Every day is a precious gift. Remember, life is about progress not perfection—so don't beat yourself up for missing the mark. Daily, forgive yourself and others, and choose to move on. Let go of yesterday's disappointments, enjoy the moments of today, while keeping a steadfast eye on tomorrow.

9. Always choose to see yourself at the finish line of victory. Refuse to allow setbacks to deter you in your journey to your goal. Keep your eyes on the PRIZE! You will get there if you don't give up.

10. Always determine who you are, what you are becoming, and where you are going. Own your own life. Never allow others to define you or your future. Choose to live out your potential and be all that you were created to be. Nothing is impossible! Go set this world on fire! I know you can and will do it!

BONUS!
Weekly Goal Setting Template

I Choose to LIVE MY DREAMS!

Week of _____ (date)

See It Sunday: Visualization, Vision Board, Weekly Goal Setting

Visualization Audio: www.trainyourbrainworkbook.com

This Week's Goal Focus:

Motivated Monday: Eat Your Frog, Chunking, 80/20 Rule, Reverse Engineering

Key Goal Task:

Secondary Goal Task:

General Tasks:

Thoughtful Tuesday: What Are You Thinking?

Key Goal Task:

Secondary Goal Task:

General Tasks:

What and Why Wednesday: Are You Living By Your Core Values?

Key Goal Task:

Secondary Goal Task:

General Tasks:

Thankful Thursday: What Are You Grateful For?

Key Goal Task:

Secondary Goal Task:

General Tasks:

Fearless Friday: What Fears and Obstacles Did You Face and Overcome?

Key Goal Task:

Secondary Goal Task:

General Tasks:

Celebrate Saturday: Go Celebrate Your Achievements!

Make-up day for tasks:

Sample Positive Affirmations

The following are sample positive affirmations. You must say these affirmations until you **BELIEVE** them in order for them to work. Choose the statements you want to focus on first and keep saying them over and over until they become a part of WHO YOU ARE. (These statements are in audio format at www.trainyourbrainworkbook.com.)

I love my life! I am so blessed! Good (amazing, incredible, extraordinary) things come to me!
I am happy, healthy and wise!
I am so grateful for everything in my life.
I love me! I am thankful for me! I want to be me!
I am the best me possible!
I am a beautiful human being. I radiate beauty and light from the inside out.
I love all my uniqueness and diversity.
I am incredibly talented, skilled, gifted and creative.
I have unlimited potential.
I am worthy of the amazing life I desire.
I am worthy. I am capable. I am strong. I am powerful.

I am fulfilling my dreams and goals. I am walking in my purpose.
I have everything I need to create success in my life.
Everything is working out great for me. Everything is working out in my favor.
I walk in faith, hope and love. I walk in peace and contentment.
I keep going despite setbacks because I am determined to obtain the life I desire.
I am overcoming my every fear and obstacle and achieving my dreams and goals.
I am a winner, a victor, an overcomer!
I am highly favored.
I am a successful _____ (business owner, writer, athlete, salesman, student...).
I am living my values of _____ every day.
I am achieving my goal of _____.

I attract abundance...exceeding abundance!
I am a magnet for incredible things!
I walk in an attitude of gratitude and abundance.
I ALWAYS have MORE than enough.
I attract ALL that I need.
All that I need comes quickly and easily to me.
I continually find and create new sources of revenue that easily flow to me.
I attract money and build wealth easily.
Money flows to me and through me easily and appropriately.
I have peace in my spending and savings.
I rule over money—I take control and ownership of my finances.
Money obeys me as it is my tool to create an extraordinary life and world around me.
I have total peace and freedom in my financial life.

I love people, and people love me!
I love helping others become the best they can be!
Amazing and influential people are drawn to me.
My relationships are wonderful.
I give and receive love freely.
I always see the best in people.

Daily, I am kind, thoughtful, considerate and forgiving.
My life is beautiful.
My life is in balance.
New and amazing opportunities are continually opening for me!
I see opportunities where others see closed doors.
I am solution focused.
I always find the answer—the solution—to whatever issue I am facing.
My organizational skills are amazing.
My time-management skills are fantastic.
I have all the time I need as time expands for me.
I am incredibly productive and have more than enough time for life's demands.
I gain new skills and abilities every day.

I love my body.
I am attractive and healthy.
Every cell in my body is healthy and strong.
I am my perfect body size and weight.
I am lean and trim.
I nourish my body with good things.
I desire only healthy foods and activities.
I drink all the water my body needs.
I respect my body and honor it with appropriate rest, nutrients and exercise.
I am more and more attractive with each new day.
I am so incredibly positive and energetic.
Positive, life-giving energy flows to me and through me continually.
I have all the energy I need to accomplish great things each and every day.

I take time for myself.
I am important.
I am a priority.
I listen to my body and rest when needed.
I daily take time to slow down, reflect and ground myself.
I take wonderful vacations that are refreshing and renewing.

My mind functions at an exceptional level.
I am BRILLIANT!
My mind is sharp.
My memory is fantastic.
My brain is exceptionally strong and healthy.
I am a marvelous problem-solver.
I am an incredible communicator.
I am a fantastic speaker and listener.

Every day, I feel more alive!
Every day, I love life more!
Every day, I am so thankful for my life!
Every day, I make a positive impact in others' lives!
Every day, I am fulfilling my purpose in this earth!
There is no one else I would rather be than AMAZING me!
I have the BEST LIFE EVER!
I AM EXTRAORDINARY!
I am doing EXTRAORDINARY things will my life!
I am the happiest I have ever been!
I LOVE MY LIFE!

Habits of the Highly Successful

(The truly highly successful are those who have learned to "become more.")

Highly Successful People:

1. ARE DREAMERS <u>AND</u> PLANNERS
   - Are always dreaming BIG.
   - See the big picture, the long-term.
   - Pursue a clearly defined purpose as they have created laser focus.
   - Create simple and realistic plans of action that they accomplish day by day.

2. CREATE BELIEF
   - Take on a mindset that they CAN DO what they set out to accomplish.
   - THINK, SEE and BELIEVE that they are in full possession of their greatest desire.
   - ASK, SEEK and KNOCK with unwavering faith and persistence.

3. TAKE ACTION
   - Are self-motivated to create change instead of waiting for change to happen on its own.
   - Have an internal locus of control as they own their actions, decisions, results and happiness.
   - Are proactive instead of reactive as they choose to design their lives.
   - Take immediate action toward goals/dreams versus procrastinating and excuse making.
   - Make decisions quickly, and change them slowly.
   - Have a no-excuse mindset.
   - Eat their FROG.
   - Have stopped the "Blame-Game."

4. ARE SOLUTION-FOCUSED
   - Love a challenge and are comfortable thinking "outside the box."
   - Choose to find creative solutions and therefore, do not fear problems or change.
   - Solve problems instead of waiting for someone else to solve the problem for them.
   - Embrace life instead of resisting it—see where change is needed and create solutions.
   - Recognize that to get different results, different choices must be made.
   - Know that they are paid according to how well they create solutions to fix others' problems or meet others' needs.

5. ARE SELF-DISCIPLINED
   - Make self-development a priority (are avid readers).
   - Limit what they tolerate as they are okay with saying *"NO."*
   - Understand the importance of delayed gratification, self-control and daily, disciplined action.
   - Healthily release dopamine and other positive hormones through activities such as daily exercise, meditation, gratitude, kindness, learning, exploring and setting/achieving goals.
   - Take financial responsibility for their lives by setting a healthy budget and paying themselves first through putting 1) money in savings and 2) money toward assets (businesses, investments and other passive income streams) versus only liabilities ("things" and "stuff").

6. TAKE A HIGHER VIEW OF LIFE
   - Work with excellence, diligence and integrity as they always go the extra mile.
   - Employ high levels of emotional intelligence.
   - Communicate clearly their ideas, intentions, expectations, values and boundaries.
   - Understand the importance of team work, accountability and wise counsel.
   - Surround themselves with like-minded people.
   - Find wise mentors who can guide them to greater levels of personal/professional success.
   - Are good students *and* teachers as they allow success to flow through them to others.
   - Become financially educated so they can make money work for them (such as learning to create passive income streams to have greater control over their time, energy and focus).
   - Do not compare themselves with others as they have learned to like themselves and to be gratefully content. (They do not need to run the "rat race" to "Keep up with the Joneses.")
   - Understand the importance of giving and the laws of sowing and reaping (cause and effect).
   - Have learned to become mindful, thankful and to truly enjoy life's simple pleasures.
   - Recognize that they must become more to have more—if they are to keep it!

7. ARE GRITTY
   - Are flexible as they realize that life is a marathon and not a sprint.
   - See failure not as a dead end but as a stepping stone.
   - Are diligent and persistent as they constantly work to move their lives forward.
   - Realize that results are not always immediate but take time to create/manifest.
   - Know that their ability to press through difficulties is what separates them from the rest.
   - Understand that success is not an overnight process but the accumulation of small, consistent efforts compounded over time.
   - Recognize that there is always a solution, always an answer, and always an abundance to those who do not give up, who endure to the end, and who can RECEIVE their prize!

Vibrational Frequency of Emotion Scale

Your emotions are energy vibrating at varying frequencies. Frequency is linked to light and sound. The higher your frequency, the brighter you shine and the more beautiful your sound or "song." Faith, hope and love are the door keepers to an abundant life.

1000+	**GOD CONSCIOUSNESS/God's Infinite Love and Glory** ("I am intimately known and loved by God. Nothing can separate me from the love of God. I radiate God's love, glory and light. I am a co-creator with God. Miracles manifest around me.")	**100% White Light**
900	**GRATITUDE, Freedom, Empowerment** ("Life is a gift. I am incredibly blessed in every way. I give thanks in all things. I live in abundance. I walk in freedom and purpose. I am an overcomer in this life.")	
700	**ENLIGHTENMENT, Inspiration** ("I seek truth. I can see from a higher perspective.")	**Intense Light**
600	**PEACE, Harmony, Serenity** ("Everything is as it should be. I rest secure in the hands of my Creator.")	
540	**JOY, Bliss, Enthusiasm, Happiness** ("Life is beautiful. I love my life. My life overflows with joy.")	
500	**LOVE, Purity of Motive, Reverence, Generosity, Kindness, Compassion** ("I love and respect myself and others. I am worthy to give and receive love. I love people, and people love me. I live to be a blessing/to serve others.")	
470	**HOPE, FAITH, Optimism, Belief** ("ALL things are working together for my good. ALL things are possible.")	**Moderate Light**
400	**UNDERSTANDING, Empathetic** ("What can I learn from this?")	
350	**ACCEPTANCE, Forgiveness, Grace** ("I accept what is. I forgive and move on.")	
310	**WILLINGNESS, Trust, Readiness, Surrender** ("I let go. We can do this.")	
200	**COURAGE, Boldness, Nervousness** ("I think I can do this. I can do this.")	
175	**PRIDE, Vanity, Scornful, Frustration, Irritation, Entitlement** ("I have all the answers. I know it all.")	
150	**HATRED, Anger, Rage, Revenge, Unforgiveness** ("I hate this. I will make others suffer. I will not forgive.")	**Dim Light**
125	**JEALOUSY, Greed, Selfishness, Disappointment** ("I have to have it. I have to have more to feel worthy.")	
100	**FEAR, Anxiety, Worry, Doubt, Withdrawal** ("I'm afraid that.... I worry that.... I'm not sure about....")	
75	**GRIEF, Sadness, Regret, Depression** ("I should have.... I wish I had.... It's too late.")	
50	**APATHY, Helplessness, Hopelessness** ("I can't. There is no solution. No one can help me. I can't ever get ahead.")	
30	**GUILT, Victim, Blame, Self-Loathing** ("It's all my fault. I deserve to be miserable. I don't deserve to be forgiven.")	
20	**SHAME, Worthlessness, Powerlessness, Despair, Humiliation** ("I'm not good enough. I'm not worthy. I am not enough.")	
0	**DEATH**	**Darkness**

Left margin (top to bottom): Eagle Perspective — Awakening — Worm Perspective

(The information on the above chart is not meant to provide exact emotional frequencies but is a simplified explanation based on a scale of 0 to 1000. To learn more, please visit the works of Dr. David R. Hawkins, MD, PhD.)

Most people average a scale value of 200 or below because of fears, negative subconscious beliefs and self-defeating thinking patterns. They live in a stressed (fight-or-flight) mindset that allows fear to control their lives. They thus keep themselves stuck in the dark with a worm's perspective. They also continue to attract others (relationships, clients, etc.) operating at those same frequencies. However, faith, hope and love open the door to attracting abundance and manifesting incredible things in one's life. Therefore, choose to FOCUS on GOOD things!

Brain Wave Frequencies

Fast Short Waves

GAMMA	Euphoria, Inspiration, Love, Higher Virtues, Enlightenment
BETA	Alertness, Focus, Complex Thought, Excitement, Anxiety
ALPHA	Relaxation, Visualization, Creativity, Mindfulness, Daydreaming, Bridge Between Conscious and Subconscious Mind
THETA	Light Sleep, Deep Meditation, Dream State, Deep Hypnosis State
DELTA	Deep Sleep, Time of Healing and Regeneration

Slow Long Waves

Primary Brain Waves by Age

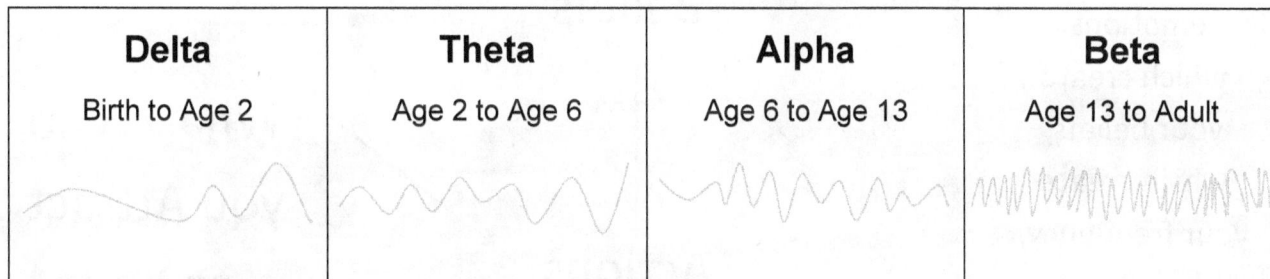

Delta	**Theta**	**Alpha**	**Beta**
Birth to Age 2	Age 2 to Age 6	Age 6 to Age 13	Age 13 to Adult

Subconscious Mind Overview

- ✓ Controls 95-99% of our lives.
- ✓ Instinctual, protective, primitive brain.
- ✓ Intuitive, emotional, contains creative genius.
- ✓ Never sleeps, never stops taking in information.
- ✓ Only understands present tense, very literal, acts as a massive memory data base.
- ✓ Controls automatic bodily functions, habit formation and motivation.
- ✓ Stores memories based on emotion and creates beliefs from those experiences.
- ✓ Cannot distinguish between what is real from what is imagined.
- ✓ Learns by repetition, creates "autopilot" programming.
- ✓ Simply reacts according to how it is programmed.
- ✓ Most easily influenced in an alpha or theta brain wave state when the "judgmental" conscious mind is not as active.

The Focus Funnel

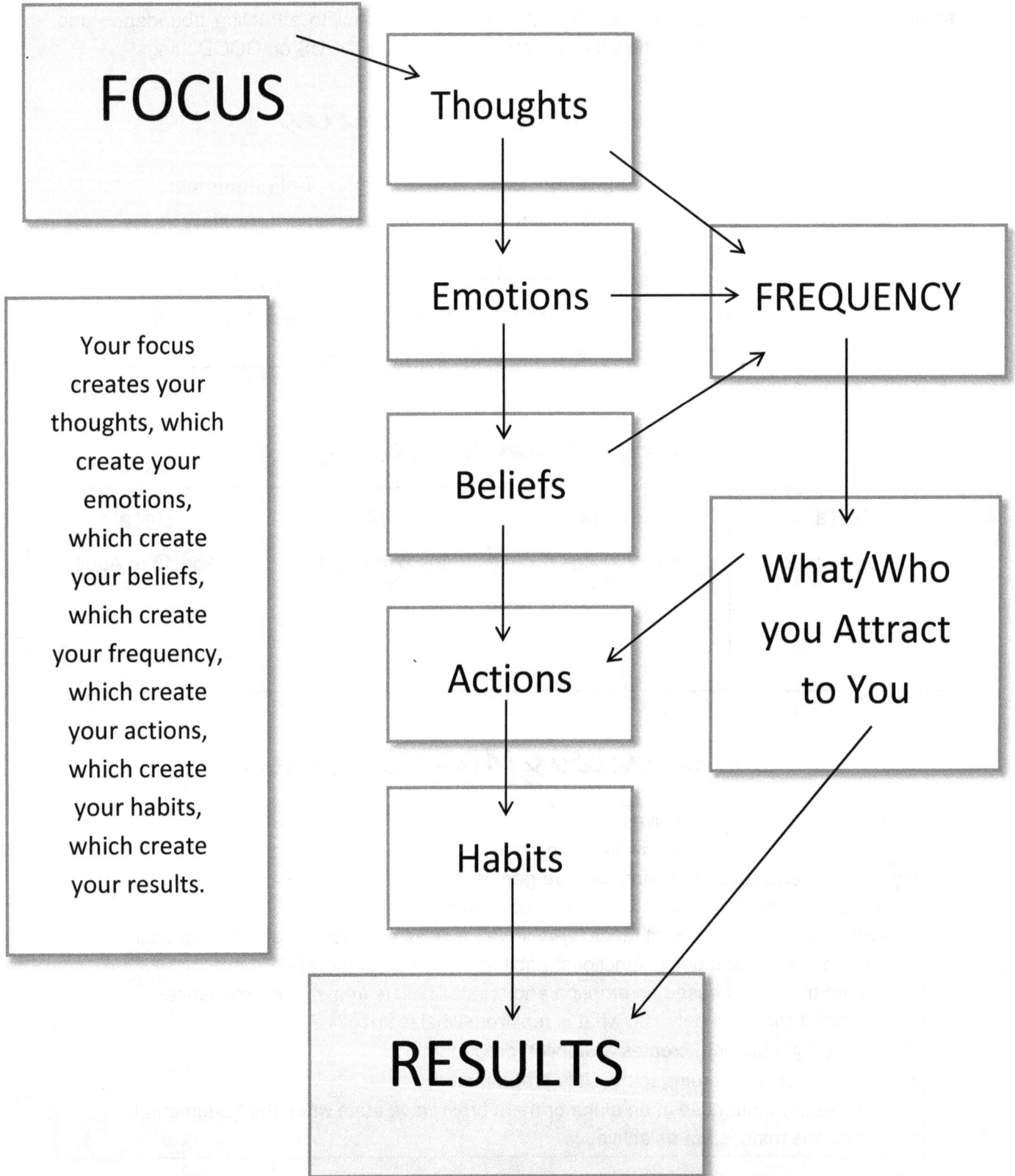

FOCUS

Thoughts

Emotions

Beliefs

Actions

Habits

FREQUENCY

What/Who you Attract to You

RESULTS

Your focus creates your thoughts, which create your emotions, which create your beliefs, which create your frequency, which create your actions, which create your habits, which create your results.

Declaration Cut Outs

Declaration of Commitment to Live My Dreams

I, _____ (name), commit to complete this 30-Day Boot Camp to train my brain for success and a life of happiness and abundance. No matter how much I want to quit, I will fight for my future. This day, I choose to live my life with purpose knowing that I have incredible potential within me. From this day forward, I choose to live my life without regrets. I choose to be free which means taking control of my life and my destiny. This day, I choose a life of happiness, abundance and success. I choose to live my dreams and be who I was created to be! This day, I CHOOSE TO SPREAD MY WINGS AND FLY!

Signature_____   Date_____

Witness Signature _____   Date_____

My Statements of Action

I overcome my fear of _____ by _____

_____.

I overcome my obstacle of _____ by _____

_____.

"I love myself deeply and completely. I acknowledge that I have allowed my fears and obstacles to hinder me, but I now choose to let go of the fear of _____ and the obstacle of _____. I release them from my life right now. (Breathe out a deep breath and see the fear/obstacle leaving you). I choose to forgive myself, to forgive others and to let go. (Breathe out another deep breath). I now invite joy, love, peace, faith, hope, happiness, confidence and success to fill this place in my mind, body, spirit and life. (Breathe in a deep breath as you receive these wonderful gifts). I allow abundance and freedom to flow through me. I now welcome new creative ideas for achieving my goals and overcoming my every fear and obstacle. I choose to live my mission, my purpose. I am powerful. I am worthy. I am lovable. I am capable. I am full of incredible potential. I am free to be who I was created to be. I welcome good things into my life from this day forward."

My New Money Mindset Statements

- ✓ I can have as much money as I want and allow into my life.
- ✓ I live in an abundant universe where there is no lack.
- ✓ I am a magnet for incredible things…including wealth!
- ✓ I walk in an attitude of gratitude and abundance.
- ✓ I am a lender and not a borrower. I am an amazing and generous GIVER!
- ✓ I ALWAYS have MORE than enough.
- ✓ I attract ALL that I need. All that I need comes quickly and easily to me.
- ✓ I attract abundance, exceeding abundance!
- ✓ I continually find and create new sources of revenue that easily flow to me.
- ✓ Money chases me. I attract money and build wealth easily.
- ✓ Money flows to me and through me easily and appropriately.
- ✓ I rule over money. I am a good steward of money. I take control and ownership of my finances.
- ✓ Money obeys me as it is my tool to create an extraordinary life and world around me.
- ✓ I have total peace and freedom in my financial life. I am financially FREE!
- ✓ Prayer: *Thank you God (Universe) that You are the source of all abundance and that through You, I always have more than enough. Thank you that You are blessing the works of my hands and daily guiding me into a life of abundance that I might be a BLESSING in this earth.*

Positive Affirmation Statements

Every day, my strengths are opening new doors of opportunity for me.

Every day, I turn my weaknesses into amazing stepping stones to a better life.

Every day, the weakness of _____ is improving and giving me the skills and knowledge needed to attain my dreams and goals.

Concerning my new habit of _____,

my plan of action is to_____

_____,

and I will find support and accountability by _____

_____.

Signature _____   **Date** _____

My "DOING" Core Values	Did I honor them?	
1.	Yes	No
2.	Yes	No
3.	Yes	No
4.	Yes	No
5.	Yes	No

My "BEING" Core Values	Did I honor them?	
1.	Yes	No
2.	Yes	No
3.	Yes	No
4.	Yes	No
5.	Yes	No

My Mission Statement

My Key Goal as a SMART Goal

My Legacy

My Personal Affirmations

I am a successful….

I am

I am

I am

I am

See it Sunday—What does your perfect future look like?

Motivated Monday—What are your goals and tasks for this week?

Thoughtful Tuesday—What are you thinking?

What and Why Wednesday—Are you living your core values?

Thankful Thursday—What are you thankful for?

Fearless Friday—How will you overcome your fears and obstacles?

Celebrate Saturday—How will you reward your victories and accomplishments?

I love my life. I am so blessed.
Good things come to me!

In one year, I am….

In five years, I am….

In ten years, I am…..

"But those who hope in the LORD
will renew their strength.
They will soar on wings
like eagles; they will run
and not grow weary,
they will walk and
not be faint."

Isaiah 40:31

"For I know the plans I have for
you," declares the LORD, "plans to
prosper you and not to harm you,
plans to give you hope and a
future."

Jeremiah 29:11

"The Spirit of the Lord is on me, because he has
anointed me to proclaim good news to the poor.
He has sent me to proclaim freedom for the prisoners
and recovery of sight for the blind,
to set the oppressed free,
to proclaim the year of the Lord's favor."

Luke 4:18, 19

Scriptural I AM Statements

I AM a child and friend of God. (John 1:12; John 15:15).

I AM loved and chosen by God. (1 Thessalonians 1:4; Ephesians 1:4).

As a child of God, I AM a fellow heir with Christ. (Romans 8:17, Galatians 4:7).

I AM accepted and complete in Christ. (Romans 15:7; Colossians 2:10).

I AM triumphant through Christ. (2 Corinthians 2:14).

I AM more than a conqueror in all things through Christ Jesus. (Romans 8:37)

I AM a new creation in Christ, the old is passed away. (2 Corinthians 5:17)

I AM light in the Lord and walk as a child of light. (Ephesians 5:8).

I AM guarded by the peace of God. (Philippians 4:7).

I AM joyful. I AM thankful in all things. (1 Thessalonians 5:16-18)

I AM fully provided for by God through His glorious riches in Christ Jesus. (Philippians 4:19).

I AM blessed with every spiritual blessing. (Ephesians 1:3).

I AM doing all things through Christ who strengthens me. (Philippians 4:13)

I AM God's workmanship created to produce good works. (Ephesians 2:10).

I AM a partaker of God's great promises. (Ephesians 3:6).

I AM justified, forgiven and redeemed through Christ. (Romans 3:24; Ephesians 1:7).

I AM set free in Christ. (Galatians 5:1) I AM healed by Christ's stripes. (1 Peter 2:24)

I AM redeemed from the hand of the enemy. (Psalm 107:2).

I AM walking with the mind of Christ. (1 Corinthians 2:16)

I AM taking every negative and lying thought captive. (2 Corinthians 10:5)

I AM ruling with Christ. I AM seated in the heavenly places with Christ Jesus. (Ephesians 2:6).

I AM walking in God's power and anointing to do greater things than Jesus did. (John 14:12)

I AM walking by faith and not by sight. (2 Corinthians 5:7)

I AM being conformed into the image of Christ. (Romans 8:29; 1 John 4:17)

I AM blessed in every way. Through God, I AM the head and not the tail, above and not beneath, a lender and not a borrower, a ruler and not oppressed. (Deuteronomy 28:16,15:6)

I AM soaring with eagle's wings. I AM renewed with God's strength and hope. (Isaiah 40:31)

I AM asking, I AM seeking, I AM knocking, and I AM RECEIVING. (Matthew 7:7)

I AM walking in God's perfect purposes for my life. (2 Timothy 1:9)

<u>You attract what you ARE. If God lives in you, then begin to say:</u>

I AM God's. I AM God's representation in this earth.

I AM a channel for God to freely flow to and through.

I AM God's hands and feet in this earth to perform His great purposes.

I AM God's love.

I AM God's light.

I AM God's joy.

I AM God's hope.

I AM God's prosperity

I AM God's abundance.

Prayer for New Life

If you do not know your Creator, I invite you to get to know Him personally.
He wants to bless you and help you to become all He created you to be.
If you desire, please say this prayer.

"Heavenly Father,

I come to You now and admit that I all my life I have felt unworthy of love and an abundant life. I recognize that You are the only true source of love because You are love and all good things come from You. I admit that I have allowed my sins to separate me from You and the life You want me to have. Thank You for sending Your son Jesus Christ to be a living sacrifice to die in my place so that His blood washes me clean of all my sins and brings me from death to eternal life. Jesus, I believe You rose from the dead, and I now ask you to come into my heart and be my Lord and Savior. Wash me clean of all my sins, and make me a new creation. Thank You for now living in me and empowering me to live the life You created me to live. I thank you that I can now do all things because You strengthen, help and guide me. I believe Your Word, the Holy Bible, that says nothing is impossible with You on my side. Thank you for showing me Your truth because Your truth sets me free to be all You created me to be. Thank you for giving Your life for me so I may have abundant life here on earth and eternal life with You forever in heaven. I love you Lord, in Jesus name, Amen."

Congratulations!
You have just been born into new LIFE—abundant and eternal life!

"Jesus said, 'I am come that they might have life, and that they might have it more ABUNDANTLY.'" John 10:10

"For God so loved the world that he gave his one and only Son, that whoever believes in him shall not perish but have eternal life." John 3:16

"And we know that all things work together for good to them that love God, to them who are called according to his purpose." Romans 8:28

"Jesus said to him, 'I am the way, the truth, and the life. No one comes to the Father, except through me.'" John 14:6

"Then you will know the truth, and the truth will set you free. He whom the Son sets free is free indeed." John 8:32,36

"I can do all things through Christ who strengthens me." Philippians 4:13

"Jesus said, 'All things are possible to him who believes.'" Mark 9:23

"In all these things we are more than conquerors through Him who loves us." Romans 8:37

"Ask and it will be given to you; seek and you will find; knock and the door will be opened to you." Matthew 7:7

"Now unto Him who is able to do exceeding abundantly above all that we could ask or think." Ephesians 3:20

References

i Illustration by Elen Abbas. Property of Sharon Minard. All rights reserved.

ii Illustration by Elen Abbas. Property of Sharon Minard. All rights reserved.

iii Curran, K., & Reivich, K. (2011). Goal setting and hope. National Association of School Psychologists. *Communique,* 39(7), 1, 44, 46.

iv Curran, K., & Reivich, K. (2011). Goal setting and hope. National Association of School Psychologists. *Communique,* 39(7), 1, 44, 46.

v Curran, K., & Reivich, K. (2011). Goal setting and hope. National Association of School Psychologists. *Communique,* 39(7), 1, 44, 46.

vi Curran, K., & Reivich, K. (2011). Goal setting and hope. National Association of School Psychologists. *Communique,* 39(7), 1, 44, 46.

vii Griffiths, B. (2009). The paradox of change: how to coach while dealing with fear and uncertainty. *Industrial and Commercial Training,* 41(2), 97-101.

viii Griffiths, B. (2009). The paradox of change: how to coach while dealing with fear and uncertainty. *Industrial and Commercial Training,* 41(2), 97-101.

ix Griffiths, B. (2009). The paradox of change: how to coach while dealing with fear and uncertainty. *Industrial and Commercial Training,* 41(2), 97-101.

x Koutsikou, S., Crook, J. J., Earl, E. V., Leith, J. L., Watson, T. C., Lumb, B. M. and Apps, R. (2014), Neural substrates underlying fear-evoked freezing: the periaqueductal grey–cerebellar link. *Journal of Physiology,* 592: 2197–2213. doi:10.1113/jphysiol.2013.268714

xi Griffiths, B. (2009). The paradox of change: how to coach while dealing with fear and uncertainty. *Industrial and Commercial Training,* 41(2), 97-101.

xii Curran, K., & Reivich, K. (2011). Goal setting and hope. National Association of School Psychologists. *Communique,* 39(7), 1, 44, 46.

xiii Saleem, A. (2014). Positive thinking and positive words: Why it's so important. I*ndian Journal of Positive Psychology,* 5(1), 86-89.

xiv Burke, A., Herlambang, C., & Shanahan, E. (2014) An exploratory study comparing goal- oriented mental imagery with daily to-do lists: Supporting college student success. *Current Psychology,* 33, 20–34.

xv Burke, A., Herlambang, C., & Shanahan, E. (2014) An exploratory study comparing goal-oriented mental imagery with daily to-do lists: Supporting college student success. *Current Psychology,* 33, 20–34.

xvi Burke, A., Herlambang, C., & Shanahan, E. (2014) An exploratory study comparing goal-oriented mental imagery with daily to-do lists: Supporting college student success. *Current Psychology,* 33, 20–34.

xvii Hill, N. (Author) & Pell, A. R. (Contributor) (2005). *Think and Grow Rich: The landmark Bestseller - Now revised and updated for the 21st century.* New York, NY: Penguin Group. www.naphill.org. Permission to reference granted by the Napoleon Hill Foundation.

xviii Curran, K., & Reivich, K. (2011). Goal setting and hope. National Association of School Psychologists. *Communique,* 39(7), 1, 44, 46.

xix Permission to quote granted by Ziglar Inc.

xx Korb, A. (2012). The grateful brain: The neuroscience of giving thanks. *Psychology Today.* Retrieved from https://www.psychologytoday.com/blog/prefrontal-nudity/201211/the-grateful-brain

xxi Korb, A. (2012). The grateful brain: The neuroscience of giving thanks. *Psychology Today.* Retreived from https://www.psychologytoday.com/blog/prefrontal-nudity/201211/the-grateful-brain

xxii Korb, A. (2012). The grateful brain: The neuroscience of giving thanks. *Psychology Today*. Retreived from https://www.psychologytoday.com/blog/prefrontal-nudity/201211/the-grateful-brain

xxiii Saleem, A. (2014). Positive thinking and positive words: Why it's so important. *Indian Journal of Positive Psychology,* 5(1), 86-89.

xxiv *The One-Life Solution: Reclaim Your Personal Life While Achieving Greater Professional Success.* Copyright (c) 2008 by Dr. Henry Cloud. Courtesy of HarperCollins Publishers.

xxv Cohn, M. A., Fredrickson, B. L., Brown, S. L., Mikels, J. A., & Conway, A. M. (2009). Happiness unpacked: Positive emotions increase life satisfaction by building resilience. *Emotion,* 9(3), 361–368.

xxvi Cohn, M. A., Fredrickson, B. L., Brown, S. L., Mikels, J. A., & Conway, A. M. (2009). Happiness unpacked: Positive emotions increase life satisfaction by building resilience. *Emotion,* 9(3), 361–368.

xxvii Cohn, M. A., Fredrickson, B. L., Brown, S. L., Mikels, J. A., & Conway, A. M. (2009). Happiness unpacked: Positive emotions increase life satisfaction by building resilience. *Emotion,* 9(3), 361–368.

xxviii Cohn, M. A., Fredrickson, B. L., Brown, S. L., Mikels, J. A., & Conway, A. M. (2009). Happiness unpacked: Positive emotions increase life satisfaction by building resilience. *Emotion,* 9(3), 361–368.

xxix Cohn, M. A., Fredrickson, B. L., Brown, S. L., Mikels, J. A., & Conway, A. M. (2009). Happiness unpacked: Positive emotions increase life satisfaction by building resilience. *Emotion,* 9(3), 361–368.

xxx Cohn, M. A., Fredrickson, B. L., Brown, S. L., Mikels, J. A., & Conway, A. M. (2009). Happiness unpacked: Positive emotions increase life satisfaction by building resilience. *Emotion,* 9(3), 361–368.

xxxi Cohn, M. A., Fredrickson, B. L., Brown, S. L., Mikels, J. A., & Conway, A. M. (2009). Happiness unpacked: Positive emotions increase life satisfaction by building resilience. *Emotion,* 9(3), 361–368.

xxxii Cohn, M. A., Fredrickson, B. L., Brown, S. L., Mikels, J. A., & Conway, A. M. (2009). Happiness unpacked: Positive emotions increase life satisfaction by building resilience. *Emotion,* 9(3), 361–368.

xxxiii White, J .B., Langer, E. J., Yariv, L., Welch, J. C. (2006). Frequent social comparisons and destructive emotions and behaviors: The dark side of social comparisons. *Journal of Adult Development,* 13(1), 36-44.

xxxiv Hill, N. (Author) & Pell, A. R. (Contributor) (2005). Think and grow rich: The landmark bestseller - Now revised and updated for the 21st century. New York, NY: Penguin Group. www.naphill.org. Permission to reference granted by the Napoleon Hill Foundation.

xxxv Dennis, A.R., Bhagwatwar, A., and Minas, R.K. (2013). Play for performance: Using computer games to improve test-taking performance. *Journal of Information Systems Education,* 24(3), 223-233.

xxxvi Dennis, A.R., Bhagwatwar, A., and Minas, R.K. (2013). Play for performance: Using computer games to improve test-taking performance. *Journal of Information Systems Education,* 24(3), 223-233.

xxxvii Newberg, A. B., and Waldman, M. R. (2012). *Words Can Change Your Brain: 12 Conversation Strategies to Build Trust, Resolve Conflict, and Increase Intimacy.* Hudson Street Press,

xxxviii Goleman, D., Boyatzis, R., McKee, A. (2004). *Primal Leadership: Learning to Lead with Emotional Intelligence.* Harvard Business Review Press.

xxxix Duckworth, A. L, Peterson, C., Matthews, M. D., & Kelly, D. R. (2007). Grit: Perseverance and passion for long-term goals. *Journal of Personality and Social Psychology,* 92(6,) 1087-1101.

xl Permission to quote granted by The Meyer Resource Group,® Inc.

xli Curran, K., & Reivich, K. (2011). Goal setting and hope. National Association of School Psychologists. *Communique,* 39(7), 1, 44, 46.

xlii Curran, K., & Reivich, K. (2011). Goal setting and hope. National Association of School Psychologists. *Communique,* 39(7), 1, 44, 46.

xliii Koutsikou, S., Crook, J. J., Earl, E. V., Leith, J. L., Watson, T. C., Lumb, B. M. and Apps, R. (2014), Neural substrates underlying fear-evoked freezing: the periaqueductal grey–cerebellar link. *Journal of Physiology,* 592: 2197–2213. doi:10.1113/jphysiol.2013.268714

If this program has helped you in anyway,
I would LOVE to hear your story!

Please email me at
coachsharon@acceleratecoachingusa.com

My prayer is that I have sparked something deep
within you to be more and do more so you can have more.

Also, please help others to transform their lives
by recommending this workbook to them.
Spread happiness, abundance and success
to the world around you!

You are AMAZING!
I truly do believe in you!
Now go set this world on fire!

Blessings,
Coach Sharon

ACCELERATE
COACHING

www.ingramcontent.com/pod-product-compliance
Lightning Source LLC
Chambersburg PA
CBHW080700110426
42739CB00034B/3341